AF505825

Karin J. MacHardy
WAR, RELIGION AND COURT PATRONAGE IN HABSBURG AUSTRIA
The Social and Cultural Dimensions of Political Interaction, 1521–1622

James Mackintosh
VINDICIÆ GALLICÆ
Defence of the French Revolution: A Critical Edition

Robert J. Mayhew
LANDSCAPE, LITERATURE AND ENGLISH RELIGIOUS CULTURE, 1660–1800
Samuel Johnson and Languages of Natural Description

Jeremy C. Mitchell
THE ORGANIZATION OF OPINION
Open Voting in England 1832–68

Marjorie Morgan
NATIONAL IDENTITIES AND TRAVEL IN VICTORIAN BRITAIN

James Muldoon
EMPIRE AND ORDER
The Concept of Empire, 800–1800

Julia Rudolph
WHIG POLITICAL THOUGHT AND THE GLORIOUS REVOLUTION
James Tyrrell and the Theory of Resistance

Lisa Steffen
TREASON AND NATIONAL IDENTITY
Defining a British State, 1608–1820

Lynne Taylor
BETWEEN RESISTANCE AND COLLABORATION
Popular Protest in Northern France, 1940–45

Anthony Waterman
POLITICAL ECONOMY AND CHRISTIAN THEOLOGY SINCE THE
ENLIGHTENMENT
Essays in Intellectual History

Doron Zimmerman
THE JACOBITE MOVEMENT IN SCOTLAND AND IN EXILE, 1746–1759

Studies in Modern History
Series Standing Order ISBN 978-0-333-79328-2 (hardback)
Series Standing Order ISBN 978-0-333-80346-2 (paperback)
(*outside North America only*)

You can receive future titles in this series as they are published by placing a standing order. Please contact your bookseller or, in case of difficulty, write to us at the address below with your name and address, the title of the series and the ISBN quoted above.

Customer Services Department, Macmillan Distribution Ltd, Houndmills, Basingstoke, Hampshire RG21 6XS, England

---

The Organization of Opinion

Open Voting in England 1832–68

Jeremy C. Mitchell
Lecturer in Government, The Open University

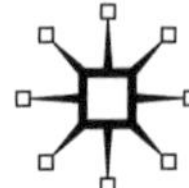

First published 2008 by
PALGRAVE MACMILLAN

Palgrave Macmillan in the UK is an imprint of Macmillan Publishers Limited, registered in England, company number 785998, of Houndmills, Basingstoke, Hampshire RG21 6XS.

Palgrave Macmillan in the US is a division of St Martin's Press LLC, 175 Fifth Avenue, New York, NY 10010.

Palgrave Macmillan is the global academic imprint of the above companies and has companies and representatives throughout the world.

Palgrave® and Macmillan® are registered trademarks in the United States, the United Kingdom, Europe and other countries.

ISBN-13: 978–0–230–21965–6 hardback
ISBN-10: 0–230–21965–9 hardback

This book is printed on paper suitable for recycling and made from fully managed and sustained forest sources. Logging, pulping and manufacturing processes are expected to conform to the environmental regulations of the country of origin.

A catalogue record for this book is available from the British Library.

Library of Congress Cataloging-in-Publication Data

Mitchell, Jeremy, 1943–
     The organization of opinion : open voting in England 1832–68 / Jeremy C. Mitchell.
        p. cm.
     Includes bibliographical references and index.
     ISBN 978–0–230–21965–6 (alk. paper)
     1. Voting – Great Britain – History – 19th century. 2. Elections – Great Britain – History – 19th century. 3. Great Britain – Politics and government – 19th century. I. Title.

JN955.M543 2008
324.941'081—dc22   2008029962

10 9 8 7 6 5 4 3 2 1
17 16 15 14 13 12 11 10 09 08

Printed and bound in Great Britain by
CPI Antony Rowe, Chippenham and Eastbourne

For Polly

Contents

List of Figures

List of Tables

Acknowledgements

The author and publishers wish to thank the Open University for permission to reproduce copyright material: Figure 7.3, and Appendix 3 Figure 1, from Michael Drake and Jeremy Mitchell, Introduction to Historical Psephology, D301 Second Series, Units 6–8 (1982).

Preface

It was Stein Rokkan who first suggested that 'there might be something worth looking into' in parliamentary poll books for the period between the First and Second Reform Bills. Indeed there was, and the subsequent research on electoral change and the development of the party system in England between 1832 and 1868 resulted in a Yale doctoral dissertation that Professor Rokkan supervised; some of that dissertation forms the basis of chapters, or parts of chapters, in this book.

Stein would have been as surprised as I am that it has taken so long for the final version of this book to appear. But, while the delay may not have been wholly of my own making, it has allowed me to draw on two related projects carried out jointly with others: research with James Cornford on politics in Cambridge between 1832 and 1868, financed by a grant from the (then) Social Science Research Council, and research with Jørgen Elklit, at the University of Aarhus, into open voting in Denmark, financed by a grant from the Research Committee at the Open University.

This work on nineteenth century voting was interrupted several times by other research. Whenever I returned to open voting, I assumed that the book would soon be finished, but it took several attempts to reach a satisfactory conclusion. Over this, by now, somewhat lengthy period, I have accumulated a number of institutional debts. First, in Oxford, to St. Antony's College where I spent a period as a Junior Associate Member, and Jesus College, where I was a Junior Research Fellow. I remain grateful to both institutions for the time spent there that allowed me to complete the research for my Yale dissertation. Second, at the Open University, I enjoyed the encouragement and support of Michael Drake and other members of the, now dissolved, Applied Historical Studies Research Group in the Faculty of Social Science. Also at the Open University, I owe many thanks to Fran Ford in the department of Politics and International Studies who skilfully typed more than one version of the manuscript, and to John Hunt who was extremely helpful with the graphics.

I also owe a debt to several libraries that allowed me to consult their collections of poll books, particularly the Bodleian Library in Oxford, the Guildhall Library and the British Library, both in London. I should also mention the contribution made by members of the antiquarian book trade in England who provided me with historical documents and poll books, particularly the manuscript material on the activities of 'Mr Jackson' that is essential to the analysis of electoral politics in Lancaster during the middle of the 1840s.

Several individuals have played an important role in encouraging me to continue or return to this book. In Oslo, Bernt Hagtvet and, in Washington D.C., Stephen Merrill both provided much needed encouragement and support; sections of the book also benefited from discussions with John Phillips.

However my major intellectual debts are to two colleagues, collaborators and friends, James Cornford and Jørgen Elklit. Not only did they work with me on the research projects mentioned earlier, and have allowed me to draw on that research in this book, both of them also read the complete manuscript at least twice, making helpful comments and suggestions. Many of these have made their way into this final version, immeasurably improving both the style and the analysis of the finished product. They will not necessarily agree with everything I say, nor are they responsible for any remaining errors of fact or interpretation, for these I take full responsibility; I do however owe them both the most heartfelt thanks, this book would simply not have appeared without their help and encouragement.

My other debts are closer to home. To Anno, Ben and Millie, I can only say that I am sorry for the grumpiness and air of pre-occupation that often accompanied work on this book over a very prolonged period, but I owe them much for the welcome distractions that they provided; my thanks also to Jude who helped with an early version. My greatest debt is acknowledged in the dedication; once again I am sorry it took so long!

1
Introduction – Explaining Open Voting in England 1832–68

Electoral politics in mid-nineteenth century England took place in a constituency social context. Interpretations of voting in Britain today suggest that it may be influenced by factors such as social class or house ownership. Different accounts put different weight on the separate or joint importance of the level of education of the individual elector, the type of community in which they vote or other social variables. But most analyses of British electoral behaviour in the first 30 years of mass suffrage after 1948 stress the importance of social class for partisan choice and would agree with Pulzer that 'class is the basis of British party politics, all else is embellishment and detail' (Pulzer, 1967, p. 98). Recent conceptualizations of class are multidimensional, and suggest that 'the relation of class to party … is not a static one' (Butler and Stokes, 1969, p. 94),[1] but given the continuities that exist in British political culture and institutions, if class is significant under mass suffrage, then it may also have been important under the previously more restricted franchise and under open voting between 1832 and 1868.

So some accounts of voting in the mid-nineteenth century see class as a major influence on electoral behaviour: 'voting patterns can be satisfactorily interpreted in terms of class and class conflict…' (Vincent, 1967, p. 28), with class referring to group characteristics, a shared identity that encompasses social attitudes, assumptions, experiences and beliefs. This type of explanation implies that a collectivity like a 'class' may have interests that are distinct and separate from those of its individual members and that politics can be conceptualized as at least partially autonomous and independent from other social attributes, perhaps even a private rather than a public concern.

Others see attitudes as a more important influence on open voting. Individual interests in mid-nineteenth century elections could be expressed through support for political principles and voting for a party. Given the public nature of electoral choice, the consequences, as Phillips and Wetherell succinctly suggest, are very similar to those for the contemporary idea of partisan identification: 'once a voter…cast his lot with a party…he remained loyal to that party permanently' (Phillips and Wetherell, 1991, p. 646).[2] However like a class-based explanation this interpretation also assumes at least a partial autonomy of the political, electoral behaviour need not be completely dependent on other aspects of social life or the social context.

Alternative accounts disagree and assert that 'political action was joint action' (Moore, 1961, p. 16). Voting was a public act, politics could not be considered part of an autonomous private sphere and instead was closely linked to the immediate social context of the individual elector. Finally, as in the fictionalized accounts of elections found in the novels of Dickens and Trollope, others emphasize the bribery and corruption surrounding elections. They accept that there was a connection between the elector and his social environment and see this not in group terms but as an individual, quasi-economic link that is defined by the market value of the vote through an economy of corruption and venality, 'voting as essentially a financial transaction' (Nossiter, 1975, p. 5).

These two distinctions – that voting is either an individual or a group activity, and that politics is separate from, or linked to, the social context – define four broad interpretations of voting between 1832 and 1868. Most accounts use these distinctions, emphasizing particular aspects of electoral behaviour and its social context. The

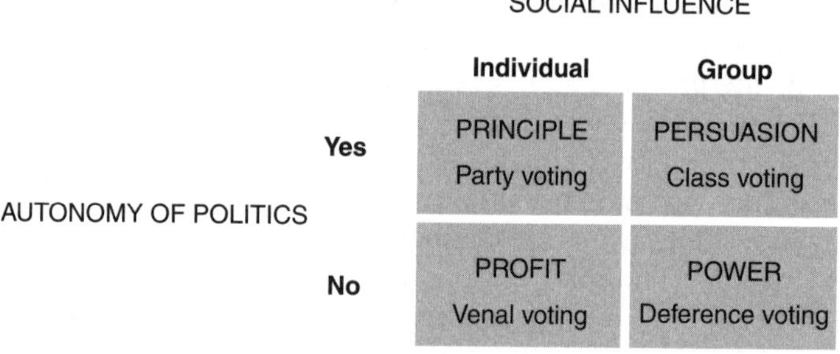

Figure 1.1   Explanations of open voting

four interpretations are mapped in Figure 1.1 that identifies the major emphases of each.

In his account of Buckinghamshire politics, Davis stresses the importance of both individual and political factors in voting. He argues for the role of *principles* and explains electoral behaviour in terms of party voting.[3] Foster too accepts the importance of political principles but suggests that the relevant interests in Oldham after 1832 are those of the group to which the individual belonged. He emphasizes the role of class and sees voting as an extension of class solidarity and cohesion, an expression of joint interests brought about by *persuasion*.[4]

Moore and Olney also stress social solidarity and cohesion in their studies of voting in county constituencies; they accept the primacy of the group in influencing electoral behaviour. However, for them, voting is not a distinct political act; it is an extension of those general hierarchical relationships that structure the interactions of social superiors and their dependants. These relationships define deference communities in which individuals have social rather than political ties in common, a link to a common social superior that is the main influence on their voting behaviour. So voting is primarily an expression of social *power*.[5] The electoral consequences of deference are usually outlined for rural constituencies but Joyce has put forward a similar explanation in an urban setting with the factory replacing the landed estate as the nexus of social relations between social/political leaders and the wider constituency electorate.[6]

Finally voting is also seen as linked to the social context but as part of a wider set of market transactions. Bribery, treating or the purchase of political support, reflect a market in votes. Voting is part of an economy of corruption and patronage, one that is explicable in terms of market rationality and individual *profit*.[7]

The schematic simplification of Figure 1.1 shows the underlying differences between these four general explanations and suggests some areas of overlap between them. It provides a framework within which descriptions of voting between 1832 and 1868 can be discussed and analysed. Note, however, that these explanations are not necessarily mutually exclusive and that some accounts employ more than one of them in accounting for elections and electoral behaviour under open voting between the First and Second Reform Bills.

I

Moore has advanced one of the most detailed explanations of open voting in his account of county politics after 1832. He analyses 'the politics of deference' and emphasizes a particular connection between social context and electoral behaviour. This explanation forms part of a more general account of politics in the period between the First and Second Reform Bills and is an analysis of three interconnected problems.

First, the 'causes' of the 1832 Reform Act and, in particular, whether the politicians who supported reform were genuinely committed to the idea, or were conducting a skilful defence of their own interests and of the existing 'natural' society of which they were the social and political leaders. This he links to a second theme: the nature of that society and of the social relations within it. He distinguishes between ideas and practice, between the ways that people thought about the existence and functioning of society and how it actually existed and functioned, particularly in its political aspects. It is here that he gives his most detailed explanation of electoral activity as an illustration of how society 'works'. But, third, he is concerned with the general effects of social change on the context of electoral activity, on the 'natural society' in which such behaviour took place, and with the perception that political leaders had of the effects of change – which returns him to his account of the motivation of the leading actors over Reform. The argument is complex but Moore sees the actions of political leaders as, in part, a response to the threats that they perceived to the existing hierarchical social order. This leads to a discussion of the effects of the 1832 Reform Act on electoral politics, and with it the subsequent emergence of a different social context for electoral behaviour from the mid-nineteenth century onwards.[8]

As the elements of his argument are linked, this separation of themes is slightly arbitrary. Moore's views on the nature of early nineteenth century society, and the effect of social change upon that society before 1832, underpin much of his argument on the genesis of the Reform Act. They form the basis of what he calls the 'concession' theory of reform – namely that in the early nineteenth century 'the support of the masses had specific electoral effectiveness,' (Moore, 1961, p. 9), in particular the election of MPs who supported the Reform Bill. For Moore there is a link between popular pressure and constitutional change.[9]

His analysis depends upon the consequences of the electoral arrangements based on open voting: 'until 1872 ... voting in England was a public act', (Moore, 1961, p. 10). Voting took place in a hierarchical social context in which social superiors could influence the political behaviour of their dependants. Both sides in this transaction accepted the legitimacy of this exercise of influence, and the interaction of deference and hierarchy created 'natural' communities: 'for a large proportion of county electors – probably a majority – political action was joint action, held together by the electors' common allegiance to an immediate social or economic superior' (Moore, 1961, p. 16).

Moore suggests that the 1832 Act had two consequences for this 'natural' society of hierarchical deference communities. First, it curtailed the power of the ministry of the day by eliminating many of the corrupt nomination or close boroughs. More importantly, it also limited the contaminating influence of the expanding boroughs in some rural constituencies, and so attempted to contain the social and political threats that such urban milieux posed to the traditional order.

Disenfranchisement made seats available to give representation to previously unrepresented boroughs – and this in turn legitimized the claims of some of the expanding middle class for political representation. This is very much the traditional interpretation of the Bill in which it is seen as part of the gradual extension of the franchise and the growth of democracy. However, as Moore points out, seats were also made available for increased county representation in which the older 'natural' society predominated. This increased county representation was concentrated in England, see Table 1.1.

This second aspect of the Bill is often overlooked in discussions of the changes brought about in 1832 but is a key part of Moore's argument. His interpretation depends upon the nature of politics in the counties, and its separation from a different type of politics in the boroughs. (In drawing this distinction Moore is implicitly suggesting that his analysis may not apply to many constituencies, particularly borough seats.) The separation was important because political leaders at the time assumed that social change was eroding the traditional hierarchical nature of society, and by so doing was undermining aristocratic rule. The Act attempted to preserve the representation of rural communities, and to contain the erosion of traditional authority, by redrawing constituency

Table 1.1 County representation (MPs) before and after the 1832 Reform Bill

	1830	1832	Increase
England	82	144	62
Scotland	30	30	0
Wales	12	15	3
Ireland	64	64	0
Total	188	253	65

Source: Smith (1844–50).

boundaries and by restricting the rights of borough electors to vote in the counties within which their constituency was situated.[10]

For Moore other consequences follow. Separation of urban and rural constituencies may have contained the seeds of future urban/rural conflict but it restored rural social leaders to unquestioned predominance in county seats, a result fully intended by the framers of the act. Finally, most counties were divided into two divisions. This reinforced the localism of politics in the counties, as they were now removed from contaminating borough influence. So: 'it was safe to extend the franchise to those men who were their own personal and ideological dependants – particularly if...they could assure themselves that these dependants behaved more or less as they should' (Moore, 1966, p. 58).[11]

To summarize, Moore sees electoral behaviour, particularly in county constituencies, as based on two factors: open voting interacting with the social structure, and the social relationships, that existed in traditional communities. In these circumstances men voted as members of a group and: 'poll books not only reveal the effective group in English society,...in many cases they also reveal the nexus of these groups' (Moore, 1969, p. 21). So his account of voting behaviour stresses the importance of the group nature of such behaviour and its essentially non-political content, or more generally the non-autonomous nature of politics.

The deference community as the 'effective social group' is central to Moore's analysis. It is defined as a face to face community of those who lived in close contact with each other, who had the same occupation, and who could be dependent on the same 'interest'. They may have had the same social or economic leaders too. They are easily identifiable in geographic terms where parish boundaries coincide with estate ownership. Most county poll books listed electors by parish and this simplifies the identification of patterns of behaviour amongst geographically grouped voters: 'examples of local electoral unanimity...(or)...near unanimity [can be] found in every county poll book' (Moore, 1967, p. 33). The unanimity in question derives from several mutually reinforcing factors – the influence of social superiors, usually landed families, transmitted through estates to their dependants, and from ties of financial or economic dependence, together with the communally shared social life and experience of electors.

Moore discusses deference communities in Northants, Cambridgeshire and Huntingdonshire in the 1820s and 1830s.[12] Olney found other examples in an analysis of the South Lincolnshire poll book for 1841; 44 parishes were owned by a single proprietor and of these 32 voted with absolute conformity in 1841. More strikingly there were 11 parishes whose voting records over the three elections of 1841, 1857 and 1868 were absolutely regular (see Olney, 1973, pp. 32–3).

But how common were deference communities and how important are they for understanding county constituency elections in this period? A glance at a county poll book will show many parishes in which voting was evenly balanced, or if not balanced was still not 'nearly unanimous'. Olney may have identified some parishes as deference communities but there were many places in Lincolnshire where competing influences were at work, and as Mills has remarked, villages there owned by a single proprietor were the exception rather than the rule, although the presence of several proprietors was not by itself a guarantee of conflicting interests.[13]

However deference communities, whether common or not, were also subject to general demographic change as voters left the electorate and new ones were added to the register. If the model is that of the great landed estate then seemingly, by extension, the electorate has acquired static and unchanging characteristics too – at least in terms of their electoral behaviour. Moore's analysis fails to distinguish between changes in the political preferences of individuals and the physical replacement of individual electors, between partisan change and electoral turnover. A unanimous vote for a party or candidate at two different elections does not necessarily mean that electors voted consistently at both elections, there will have been some turnover in the electorate and possibly some abstention too.

Evidence of change in deference communities can be found in West Kent between 1835 and 1865.[14] Using Moore's criteria, Mitchell identified four 'deference communities' there in 1835 and followed the behaviour of the electors over the series of polls up to 1865. Three of the communities were Liberal in 1835 – Benenden, Westerham and Woodchurch; a fourth, West Wickham, was Tory. By 1865 both Westerham and Benenden had Tory majorities, see Table 1.2.[15]

In all cases some electors left after each election and new ones can be identified at the next poll. The problem is not the stable behaviour of those electors who continue from one election to the next, but the behaviour of the new voters. Did they come from outside the community or were they previously resident non-electors? If previous residents, they could already have been subject to the same community or social pressures that influenced existing electors, but if they were outsiders how were they absorbed into the community and the existing pattern of partisanship? Was overt political pressure used – such as

Table 1.2 Four deference communities in West Kent 1835–65

	1835			1865			
Parish	L_1	L_2	T	L_1	L_2	T_1	T_2
Benenden	52	49	4	10	10	21	21
Westerham	43	43	18	12	12	36	36
West Wickham	4	3	16	2	2	18	18
Woodchurch	31	31	6	30	29	5	5

Source: West Kent Poll books 1835 and 1865.

political clauses in tenancy agreements – or was political conformity largely the result of more informal social factors?[16] Only in Benenden was there a permanent change in the electoral behaviour of a significant number of voters. But the causes are not obvious; it could result from the changing politics of a proprietor, from particular local issues, or from a change in the relationship of politics to social context at the individual level with the development of some political independence and individual autonomy.

As we do not have information on a change of proprietor, what other inferences can be drawn from the turnover of electors in the four parish communities? In Woodchurch the deference community was maintained by the recruitment of electors on a partisan basis. But there are at least two reasons why this may not always have been the case. Some landlords were unwilling or unable to apply political criteria to agreements such as tenancies, their first priority was to secure the best tenant and, in these cases, the vote may reveal the real political inclinations of new electors. Alternatively the pattern of proprietorship may not have been as monolithic as has been assumed from the initial poll book evidence. The political inclinations of local proprietors may not have all been the same, many parishes had several landlords rather than just one, and estates could be broken up over time.

So deference may be a misnomer. The modern conception of deference lacks the elements of reciprocity and implied sanctions that are often present in the mid-nineteenth century relationship between an elector and a local political leader.[17] Deference communities were a reflection of the hierarchical nature of authority within the immediate local community, but although deference might be a major factor in such relationships it was not the only one. As both Davis and Olney show, the pattern of influence between landlord and dependent was often a two-way process, 'political obedience was a return for services rendered, the provision of a shield against bad times' (Davis, 1972, p. 178). Olney is even more explicit: 'if deference was the normal attitude among rural voters, it was partly because deference paid' (Olney, 1973, p. 48) to the extent of a remittance of rent in years with a bad harvest or investment in farm improvement.

Of course sanctions existed but the use of them varied. Hanham concludes that the ultimate weapon, political eviction, was rarely employed.[18] One of these 'rare' cases is reported by Davis – 'Lord Carrington maintained a degree of political obedience...with eviction' (Davis, 1972, p. 174). But at the other extreme some landlords tried *not* to influence their tenants or asked for only one of their two votes, leaving the disposition of the second vote to the elector. In some cases too there was a degree of social solidarity and community reciprocity involved – 'tenants...voted with their neighbours as much as for their landlord' (Olney, 1973, p. 44).

The extent of influence may have been related to the social position of the individual concerned, so the changing politics of a large landowner could result in all his tenants being subtracted from one county electoral coalition and added to an opposing one. A change in the landlord's politics had obvious effects at the level of the individual voter. As Davis remarks of a change of proprietor in Buckinghamshire: 'the greater part of his tenantry [Lord Rothschild's] mostly former tenants of the Duke of Buckingham, undoubtedly changed their political allegiance with the landlord' (Davis, 1972, p. 177). But not all of them did. How are we to explain such behaviour – deference, influence, coercion? Or merely 'the irreducible tendency for genuine political preferences to be shaped by the situation in which people find themselves, and especially by the more important people within their daily horizon', (Vincent, 1967, p. 10). Shaped but not necessarily wholly determined; there were limits to social power and political influence. Indeed Salmon, after examining electoral behaviour in the English county constituencies in the decade following the passage of the First Reform Bill, concludes that landed influence was limited – 'only between 10 and 15 per cent of the electors appear to have exhibited behaviour consistent with the existence of local landed interest', (Salmon, 2002, p. 145). So social power and deference alone may not explain all of electoral behaviour even in county constituencies.

II

The format of many county poll books reveals the local electoral consequences of deference within parishes, and the relations of dependence that existed between landlord and tenant, the political consequence of inequalities of power and status. The communities analysed by Davis, Olney and Moore are rural phenomena. Did such structural relationships, or similar communities, exist in the urban, borough constituencies? Could the employer/employee relationship have the same political consequences as the rural landlord/tenant relationship? Did urban landlords have a similar influence on their dependent electors?

Some borough landlords certainly tried to influence electoral politics. In Grimsby proprietors bought up properties to build a political base in the constituency, although such urban property holdings were probably more dispersed than the tenancies of a rural estate community. In Cambridge the letting of college properties to enfranchised college servants was often linked to electoral conformity – voting 'the wrong way' could lead to the loss of employment or accommodation, or both.[19] In general we do not know the extent or effectiveness of such a strategy, but it seems unlikely that urban and rural authority structures were exactly the same, or that the two-way flow of influence found in some rural areas would function similarly in an urban environment. The process of urbanization may well have eroded the 'vertical' relationships of the rural social hierarchy, but there is little direct evidence on this process and borough poll books give no additional information that would enable us to isolate, much less to analyse, the relevant nexus.

While some studies of urban voting accept the role of the social group in influencing political behaviour, others suggest that politics became more autonomous in borough constituencies. In either case the model underlying the analysis of electoral behaviour is often one of class voting that combines group and political influences. However, from a survey of a large number of occupational poll books, Vincent concluded that 'the correlation between class membership and party preference, though positive, was too slight to be of any predictive value' and observed that, 'there is an apparent classlessness in voting at the top of the borough electorate' (Vincent, 1967, pp. 20, 24). This he sees as a paradox since this lack of a class basis to voting, as defined by occupational categories, does not accord with:

> the presence of an acute class sense in mid-Victorian political consciousness (i.e., la vision dichotomique of social structure was practically a matter of folk culture in areas that had never heard a loom creak), co-existing with relatively or even entirely 'classless'

patterns of voting even in quite free and pure elections. (Vincent, 1967, p. 29)

So, according to Vincent, as the enfranchised political society was pre-industrial, the marketization of social relations had not occurred, and the basis of conflict lay outside the economic order, 'by elimination... [it]...lay in the political order'. This leaves the way open for him to redefine class as a political category: 'class is a homogenous totality of those whose main aim is structural change in the political society' (Vincent, 1967, pp. 25, 31).

This is an interesting suggestion and one that avoids two major problems – the pre-industrial nature of large segments of British society, particularly many constituency electorates, and the contradiction between the well documented sense of class conflict and the lack of objective evidence of such conflict, at least as revealed in poll books. A more recent analysis by Phillips is in broad agreement: 'neither occupation nor relative economic status was generally and systematically related to the political preference of the enfranchised either before or after Reform. Socio-economically related voting patterns occurred spasmodically, but consistent patterns emerged neither over time nor across constituencies' (Phillips, 1992, p. 240).

But Vincent's suggestion raises as many difficulties as it solves. For, as Neale amongst others has pointed out, Vincent confuses occupational categories, which are strata, with classes, and he imputes a homogeneity to such categories which is notoriously lacking.[20] A man whose occupation is listed in a poll book as a carpenter may be a self employed master craftsman owning his own shop and employing others, or he may be a craftsman employed by a master, or again he may be a semi-skilled workman who at the time of the poll happened to be employed as a carpenter. At one end of the continuum of possibilities the carpenter could be a builder or employer, at the other an unskilled labourer. 'Carpenters' as a group may contain individuals in all of these situations, and can lack any collective or group identity, so any socio-structural inferences based on occupation alone must be questionable.

His definition of class brings it close to the conventional definition of a political party although Vincent differentiates them as follows:

class is a homogenous totality of those whose main aim is structural change in the political society; party is a heterogeneous alliance of people concerned to effect their own aims through the party. Party

> might in fact be made up of a core of 'class' and a fringe of 'interest group'…it might conceivably….be coterminous with class. But in fact the dissonance between party and class was much greater than one of fringes, for considerable sections in each party, entirely sound from a party point of view, were opposed to, or had no interest in, those ideas of political structure which animated the class conscious sections within each party. (Vincent, 1967, p. 31)

So for the minority of activists class and party were, by definition, completely congruent, and for the majority party and class were neither congruent nor non-congruent but disjoint. This 'core/fringe' model may be a useful one in understanding party organization, such as the Victorian Liberal party, before the emergence of modern mass parties, but apart from stressing the autonomous nature of politics it makes the class nature of party one of definition rather than evidence and leaves the non-activist elector déclassé by definition too.

It is also difficult to accommodate other political actors, such as the unenfranchised, within this analysis. Non-electors were formally excluded from the political community, but, as both Vincent himself and Foster have shown, they could be significant actors in political conflict and electoral activity. They agree too in stressing the class nature of political activism, although class, for Foster, is defined in terms of consciousness – the working class were those members of the labour force, definable both in occupational terms and in relation to capital, whose 'labour consciousness was heightened into class consciousness' (Foster, 1974, p. 131).

Foster's concern is with the development and expression of such class-consciousness in the industrial labour force of three towns, and its subsequent erosion during the liberalization of capitalism after 1850. In Oldham the working class had no direct role as electors in the parliamentary constituency but he shows that between 1832 and 1847 organized labour secured the election of 'its' candidates through the mass use of exclusive dealing:

> the techniques used were carried over from the traditional methods of labour bargaining; boycott, picketing and reliance on mass discipline. But while the unions used these methods inside a trade, their political application on behalf of labour as a whole put their operation in the hands of the essentially revolutionary nucleus of radical leaders. (Foster, 1974, p. 56)

Like Vincent he stresses the role of activists but he also pays attention to those formally outside the electoral process and Foster examines the possibilities of mobilizing influence from below, as well as the processes that occur within such groups. His analysis of Oldham is concerned with class pressures and collective interests, the social solidarity of individuals in a common subordinate relationship to those exercising industrial ownership and control.[21]

Similar assumptions about group pressures have also been used to account for the influence of religion on nineteenth century electoral politics. For the later period, from 1885 to 1910, Wald asserts that 'class…was secondary to religion in its capacity to structure the vote' (Wald, 1983, p. 161). However, for the period between the First and Second Reform Bills – from 1832 to 1868 – others are sceptical about suggestions that politics, and voting, are explicable primarily in terms of religious group conflict.

Religion was linked to electoral politics. There was a connection between non-conformity and Liberalism, and between the Tory party and the established church, both at the elite level and in a more diffuse popular sense.[22] While Phillips notes the preference of dissenting electors for Whig or Radical candidates in Lewes, Colchester and Great Yarmouth, the available poll book data cannot be used to establish a direct connection between voting behaviour and membership of a particular religious group.[23] Contemporary comment did suggest such a link, but in general we do not know how the parties related to the religious interests and opinions of voters.[24] In a very small number of cases, poll books do provide systematic information on the denominational affiliation of electors – at the 1868 Newry election it was easy to see that there was a strong connection between denomination and vote. But this was a result of the particular politics of Ulster rather than a general indication of the link between religion and politics.[25]

It is hardly surprising to find the pattern of sectarian politics so strongly expressed in Ireland although Hoppen suggests that there 'political parties are conceived as agencies that seek for reasons of sympathy and expediency to advance the interests of particular religious groups through the political process'. However he concludes that: 'as a shaper and indicator of electoral choice, religion often…melted into considerations of status and occupation' (Hoppen, 1984, p. 39).

All that this may mean is that for some electors, on some occasions, there was a significant co-variation between religion and class in influencing electoral choice. What is needed is a reformulated analysis that can take account of religion, class and other bases of social differentiation and group cohesion. This could avoid one further problem with Vincent's analysis – it is unhelpful in accounting for the transition from class-based politics in his sense to class-based voting behaviour in the modern sense. In part this is because his analysis, like that of Moore, suffers from a major methodological defect – it is largely based on cross sectional analysis and, as Davis suggests in his longitudinal study of voting behaviour in Buckinghamshire 'the methods of studying poll books that have been used thus far ignore individuals. Professor Moore studies the voting habits of parishes. Professor Vincent studies the voting habits of occupations. But it was electors who cast votes, and to ignore this obvious fact can be dangerous' (Davis, 1972, p. 100).

III

Disaggregating the electorate into cohorts and individuals avoids this problem and distinguishes change in individual behaviour from turnover and recruitment in the wider constituency electorate. But Davis does more than stress the important contribution of turnover in the electorate to electoral change. His account moves away from emphasizing the influence of the social group on voting behaviour and, while he agrees with Vincent and Foster that political principles were important, he differs from them in stressing the primacy of the individual, and provides an explanation of open voting that is based upon the assumption that electors have a basic, stable partisan loyalty that determines their voting behaviour over time.[26]

He is largely concerned with county politics in Buckinghamshire and the ruralized borough of Aylesbury.[27] He rejects Moore's analysis of electoral politics, which he sees as under-emphasizing the role of party and principle, and as distorting the nature of influence in rural communities: 'I do…believe that the importance of landed influence has been vastly over-rated, more especially, if… "influence" and "control" [are] used interchangeably' (Davis, 1972, p. 98).[28] This is the core of his difference with Moore and he goes on to suggest that in most situations other factors must have been at work. One he sees as 'party'; others include leadership and issues.

Davis analyses political leadership in Buckinghamshire and establishes, perhaps unsurprisingly, that between 1780 and 1885 it was drawn almost exclusively from the landed classes. 'But leadership is different from control. Effective leadership requires influence that flows upwards as well as downward', (Davis, 1972, p. 98), leadership is adaptive rather than being merely directive. In addition, issues such as Catholic Emancipation, the Corn Laws, and Reform itself, were important in bringing together different and diverse coalitions of activists and leaders. The positions of politicians on such issues provided cues by which voters could decide in the absence of, or in addition to, party ones: '...I shall argue that such lack of party loyalty as existed among electors in the early and mid-Victorian periods can probably be explained in large part by countervailing principles and interest' (Davis, 1972, p. 98).

This is similar to the contemporary use of the concept of partisan identification: voters have a basic party orientation but sometimes vote for another party, or abstain, because of short-term pressures or issue preferences. Davis defines party as follows: 'it is sufficient if men think of themselves as belonging to a party (which usually means giving themselves a label), and, more important, act as if they did – which means acting together' (Davis, 1972, p. 242).

His main evidence for the importance of party for electoral behaviour comes from a longitudinal analysis of 570 Aylesbury voters who were on the electoral register throughout the period from 1847 to 1859. Empirically party loyalty is simply defined: 'in general, I required that an elector always vote for the candidate of his party. I did not, however, require plumpers when only one candidate of that party stood; and I also allowed strategic splitting in cases where there was a division within parties' (Davis, 1972, p. 185).[29]

His findings for Aylesbury are summarized in Table 1.3 and, given his definition, party loyalty is impressive – either 66.1 per cent (rows 1 and 2) or 82.3 per cent (rows 1 to 7). Party and influence are connected. For Davis the explanation of electoral behaviour can be summarized as 'influence plus principle gives rise to party loyalty'. So the absence of party loyalty does not necessarily imply a lack of consistent influence. It may come from a lack of principle – something that is much more difficult to establish. And, as Hanham reminds us, party loyalty could be one element of a wider set of social relationships: 'the concept of influence and control...is fraught with difficulties. Party loyalty is one form of it: voting to please a neighbour or landlord another.... Voters hope to get something out of parties or neighbours...' (Hanham, 1978, p. xx).

In other words there may have been little difference between 'principle' and 'power' in determining an elector's vote. But in either case Davis's conception of influence weakens the link to social conformity suggested by Moore. For Davis such influence is not social control and, as a result, he implies some autonomy for politics and the political. This view is echoed by Cox who accepts that open voting exposed the elector

Table 1.3   Aylesbury voters 1847–59

	Number of voters	% of total	Vote characteristics
1	210	36.8	Conservative voters
2	167	29.3	Liberal voters
3	36	6.3	C→L 1848–50; change of influence on Grenville estate
4	10	1.8	C→L after 1851; attachment to C on protection only
5	14	2.5	Influence of Humphrey Bull
6	7	1.2	Voted only once or twice
7	25	4.4	Gave one eccentric vote or changed after 1852[a]
8	101	17.7	'Floaters'

Note: (a.) – 'usually because of influence'.

Source: extracted from Davis (1972) pp. 178–82.

to bribery and influence: 'one can divide the Victorian electorate conceptually into three classes based on their susceptibility to such pressures' – the independent, the dependent and the cross-pressured elector. His conclusion on the growing importance of 'party' echoes Davis: 'voting for the party rather than the man appears to be the dominant factor of English electoral behaviour after 1868' (Cox, 1987, pp. 117, 136). However he bases his conclusions primarily on the consequences of the decline of the private member in parliament, rather than any change in the social situation of the elector, and his conclusions apply to a lesser extent before the passing of the Second Reform Bill.

IV

Additional evidence for the role of 'party' is provided by Nossiter.[30] Where Davis was concerned with a rural area, and one primarily dependent upon farming, Nossiter analysed a more industrialized area in which the organized working class subsequently made an early breakthrough to parliamentary representation. Unlike Davis he downgrades the importance of party as an explanatory factor in individual voting behaviour: 'party was still a weakly held allegiance in the counties, mediated through...a primary loyalty to...or fear of...a particular landlord or employer', and his view of rural politics is very close to that of Moore: 'voting in rural society was far more a question of personal service than an expression of individual opinion' (Nossiter, 1975, pp. 91, 47).

For Nossiter the same kind of explanation can be applied in some urban settings, with the employer taking the place of the rural landlord. So as late as 1868 in Darlington 'no effect was, generally, made to separate the management's authorative role in the work situation from a legitimate influence in politics' (Nossiter, 1975, p. 140).

Drawing on an analysis of politics in this company town, which was enfranchised by the Second Reform Bill, Nossiter challenges Moore's interpretation of the consequences of urbanization and social change: 'the urban freeholder was often no more independent than the rural voter' (Nossiter, 1975, p. 61). He suggests too that there was a striking parallel with the idea-type setting for influence politics, the large country estate: 'ultimately [Darlington was]...a stratified community of leaders and led, indulging in the politics of influence' (Nossiter, 1975, ibid.).

Nevertheless, even if the urban voter was not free from influence then at least it could be a two-way process: '...the shopkeeper, publican and landlord were part of a more egalitarian and interdependent community than the agricultural or industrial estate and one in which influence was decidedly two-way' (Nossiter, 1975, p. 158).

However, industrialization and subsequent social change had no necessary, simple relationship with the decline of influence politics: 'the sheer fact of industrialisation was not enough to generate the new forms of politics...it was the development of a competitive and differentiated society which was to provide the necessary pre-conditions for the emergence of the politics of individual opinion and interest' (Nossiter, 1975, p. 107). He sees the processes of urbanization and industrialization as eroding the vertical authority of the rural hierarchy and fostering new 'horizontal' ties of community and class; new patterns of voting behaviour follow the emergence of this new social context.

In a study of factory politics in Lancashire, Joyce too stresses the community element in urban voting behaviour. Here it emerges at a level similar to one suggested by Moore but with the estate or landowner replaced by dependency on the factory or employer: 'the larger mills were the main islands of political influence in the town' (Joyce, 1975, p. 526).[31] Joyce also notes that the two-way nature of such influence was based on dependency and not coercion – the factory was a community of shared experience and in cotton towns the workforce tended to live close to their place of work. Taken together these factors produced distinctive neighbourhood voting patterns: 'in the large majority of cases for both towns [Bury and Blackburn] the line between home and work was a clear one, and the unambiguous political domination of industry over cohesive areas was clearly expressed in street voting patterns' (Joyce, 1975, p. 534).

But were such patterns expressions of common social interests, class interests as Foster would suggest? Or were they merely the result of the close proximity of a group of individuals, perhaps with diverse backgrounds and interests, who shared common experiences and common social conditions – a community rather than a class? Do we need to look for an alternative social explanation for what they have in common, and its link to political behaviour? Perhaps, but it may also suggest that the individual basis of the politics of principle, that is party voting, was not easily separable from class or group influences, and that such voting could also be produced in other ways – even perhaps by the use of financial incentives or through corrupt practices.

V

The explanations discussed so far have attempted to account for open voting in terms of a variety of social or political factors – influence and deference, class and party, leadership and issues. One other factor has been suggested as a key to understanding electoral behaviour in this period – corruption.[32] Accounts emphasizing corruption stress the economic, non-political basis of the vote transaction, the existence of a market in votes that is characterized by the willingness of electors to exchange their political support for monetary or other equivalent benefits. Here too 'politics' is viewed as closely linked to the social and economic context within which it takes place, and voting is seen as equivalent to other types of social behaviour and not as a distinct activity in its own right. The description of the election at Eatanswill is a fairly typical account of the role that corruption is sometimes held to have played:

> a small body of electors remained unpolled on the very last day. They
> were calculating and reflecting persons, who had not yet been

convinced by the arguments of either party, although they had had frequent conferences with each. One hour before the close of the poll, Mr. Parker solicited the honour of a private interview with these intelligent, these noble, these patriotic men. It was granted. His arguments were brief but satisfactory. They went in a body to the poll, and when they returned, the Honourable Samuel Slumkey, of Slumkey Hall was returned also.[33]

Dickens had been a reporter in Ipswich and his description of Eatanswill is probably based upon contemporary elections in Sudbury, a notoriously corrupt borough that was disfranchised in 1844.[34]

The existence of bribery, corruption and treating at elections before 1868 is hardly surprising. For, until the Ballot Act of 1872 introduced secrecy and so made it impossible to prove that a promise had been honoured, a vote was a commodity like any other that could be bought and sold, or exchanged. It was in demand by politicians seeking office, and by the party organizers who worked for them. Their activities created or maintained a market in votes. With the existence of such a market, and a relatively fixed supply of votes in any constituency, the attempt by electors to maximize the price of their votes – as did some electors at Eatanswill – is hardly surprising.[35]

The proportion of the electorate who traded their votes varied between constituencies. Some seats such as Sudbury or Beverley were notoriously corrupt. In large boroughs the sheer number of electors made the use of 'market forces' prohibitively expensive and elections could be much purer. While overall it may be difficult to gauge the importance of corruption, Vincent concludes that 'in the period of political balance corruption probably decided the day very often. But it did not touch the core of political behaviour' (Vincent, 1967, p. 11).

In terms of his conception of political behaviour this could well be true. The core of party may have been motivated by principle and so was likely to be more or less immune to corruption in its more extreme monetary forms. But it does leave unasked such questions as 'who bribed whom, when, how and with what effect'. Until such questions are answered, however tentatively, and more is known of the structure and dynamics of bribery, no inferences about its relationship to other forms of political activity can be drawn. Indeed if voting was a market-oriented activity then corruption could well be part of the 'core of political behaviour'.

There are several difficulties here and it is by no means clear what evidence would be needed to reconstruct the vote market in terms of its constituent transactions. Where evidence of voter payment is given in reports of parliamentary commissions or other official sources, it might be possible to link payment to changes in electoral behaviour. But, for obvious reasons, systematic contemporary records are almost non-existent. The assertion of extensive bribery and treating by the other side during an election was often a convenient excuse for the shortcomings of your own campaign. Many election petitions reflected this, and were withdrawn before proceedings had gone very far.[36] Although the difference between legitimate and illegitimate influence was recognized, the line between them was a fine one, and the distinction was frequently unclear. To induce voter A to vote for candidate X through the use of £N in cash was bribery and illegal. But to include A – or a group of A's – to vote for the same candidate through the use of non-monetary resources, or a promise of future payment, was not necessarily bribery and indeed was common practice.

Corruption often went beyond the simple money for votes transaction that Nossiter considers the least common form of corruption. Downright 'venality' – the straightforward buying and selling of votes – was probably a good deal less common than the three major variants of market politics; 'colourable employment, politically motivated orders for goods and the post-hoc acknowledgement of services rendered' (Nossiter, 1975, p. 196). Both colourable employment – the specific employment of individuals at election times for minor purposes – and the politically motivated order for goods, are in effect varying forms of direct cash payment. The post-hoc acknowledgement of services shades over into the regular payment of political supporters, other diffuse exercises of influence, and the general exercise of social patronage.

Such regular payments were not unusual, especially if they were in the form of monies given to institutions and charities, the 'regular blackmail' referred to by Ostrogorski.[37] The dividing line between this and corruption as part of the continuing exercise of influence was not always easy to define, as the evidence at the parliamentary inquiry for the Peterborough by-election of 1852 shows. The report also illustrates some of the other methods of influence available to landlords.[38]

Peterborough was a small two-member borough. In 1847 it had an electorate of 416. According to Dod, influence in the constituency was 'wholly in the hands of the Earl Fitzwilliam'.[39] This seems to have been an exaggeration as the Fitzwilliam influence was not strong enough to secure both seats without a contest, although contested elections may have been partially a mechanism for the transfer of financial resources.

The general election of July 1852 had been a three cornered fight and one of the successful candidates died soon afterwards. An anti-Fitzwilliam candidate stood at the subsequent by-election in December 1852, was elected and then unseated. A parliamentary inquiry brought out some striking facts about the exercise of influence and the use of post-hoc payments in the constituency.

At the July election of 1852 some 262 out of the 437 electors were Fitzwilliam tenants. It emerged that money was distributed to some voters at Candlemass. This was clearly a post-hoc payment and the evidence to the enquiry shows the discriminatory nature of this financial distribution:

> a practice seems to have grown up (after 1837) of discriminating between electors who gave their votes in the Milton interest [i.e., to the Fitzwilliam candidates] and those who either split their votes with the opposite party, or abstained from voting altogether; and thence forward the general, though not uniform, practice seems to have been to distribute two crowns to such Scot and Lot voters who demanded it, after giving both their votes in the Milton interest, and one crown when the vote was split. (Parliamentary Papers, 1852–3, XVII, p. v)

It is not clear whether payment as such, or the discriminatory nature of the payment, was the issue here. What does emerge is that it was one of a range of incentives and disincentives used for electoral purposes: 'one or two instances in which voters who have supplied goods in their trade to the family or establishment at Milton, complain of having been partially or totally deprived of that custom since voting against the Milton interest' (Parliamentary Papers, 1852–3, XVII, p. vi).

Or again there were the eight tenants who received a notice to quit after giving a vote against the Milton interest, presumably as an example to the 63 other tenants who voted in the same way but were not served with notice. Eventually, perhaps because of the parliamentary enquiry, these notices were allowed to lapse.

This use of bribery shows that there was a degree of rational behaviour behind the actions of politicians and voters in Peterborough, and that the dividing line between bribery, coercion and influence was not a clear one. The differences were often of degree rather than of kind, but it is doubtful whether corruption alone can provide a systematic or general explanation of voting behaviour between 1832 and 1868.

VI

Many of the factors used to 'explain' electoral behaviour varied across regions and constituencies. Social class was not just of changing importance over time, the nature of class itself varied regionally and locally. It was only late in the century that a 'national' class structure developed, and even then there were probably still substantial differences between constituencies and regions. Similar variation occurred in the other social factors that may have influenced electoral behaviour in this period too. As a result the effect and importance of the different factors in Figure 1.1 varied as well. The form of 'profit' or electoral corruption, and the operation of the vote market, reflected local circumstances. If the role of 'party' increased between the First and Second Reform Bills, then this too was not a uniform process with the importance of 'party' varying not just over time but across constituencies as well.

So whether they emphasize power, persuasion, principle or profit, none of these accounts of open voting provide an inclusive and general explanation of electoral behaviour in the period between the First and Second Reform Bills. Indeed different 'explanations' may appear more or less applicable in different types of constituency. Perhaps this is not surprising since, as Hanham puts it, 'general elections were not general' (Hanham, 1959, p. 191) during this period. So if elections were primarily local then they would essentially differ in each constituency, and the nature and 'causes' of voting, its explanation, could differ too. If we are to find a more 'general' explanation of electoral behaviour, it will have to be at a different level of analysis.

Many of the accounts of open voting stress the two-way nature of the dependency between an elector and those seeking his political support. As Hanham notes 'there is to some degree a reciprocal relationship' between them (Hanham, 1978, p. x).[40] However despite variations in the importance of social and political factors, in the structure of electoral communities, and in the extent of market politics, there was one constant in electoral behaviour. Until 1872 voting was open, and as Bourke and DeBats note:

> the principal insight afforded by these studies of the mid-Victorian electorate...is that the establishment of politics as an autonomous sphere of life would require the severing of electoral performance from visible social networks...it is clear that the whole electoral process would ultimately be transformed once the voter began to conceive of his political actions as distinct from the demands of the

immediate social roles that he was obliged to play. (Bourke and DeBats, 1978, p. 268)

So a more general explanation of electoral behaviour between 1832 and 1868 requires some re-examination of the consequences of open voting and its social context. It also requires an analysis of such 'visible social networks', and, in particular, of the role of politics within them. Incorporating the consequences of partial enfranchisement, and the reciprocal relationship that existed between electors and politicians, may then provide a more inclusive explanation of voting. But first we need to explore the institutional context that defined such behaviour, and the nature of the evidence about open voting, before examining the pattern of electoral contestation and the dynamics of electoral activity between the First and Second Reform Bills.

2
Elections and Party Organization in Victorian England

'Party is organized opinion'. (Disraeli, 1864)

Political parties play a central role in British politics and the main modern parties can trace their roots to the nineteenth century. Disraeli's comment implies that parties have at least two characteristics – they are organizations, and they are based on the opinions of their supporters. Today they are also agencies of mobilization and politicization through which individuals and groups channel their political and policy preferences to collective ends. They are multi-level structures with three major elements – electors who vote for or support a particular party (the 'party-in-the-electorate', the organized opinion), the leadership of a party who form an administration when in government (the 'party-in-government') and the machinery that links these two elements (the 'party organization', the organizers of opinion).[1] Voters identify with the national party, and vote for party candidates at general elections and the parties themselves are defined by differences on major issues. In 1832 electors voted for local candidates, locally selected, on predominantly local issues and the national or parliamentary parties were coalitions of MP's that shifted from issue to issue. In the first case governments are defined by voters, in the second by MP's.

In Britain these three elements of the party system developed separately and their origins can be identified in the period between 1832 and 1868. It is then that parties came to exist more continuously as organized groups in parliament, as organized supporters within constituencies and later as organizations or structures linking electors, constituency MP's and the party in parliament. If in 1832 electors in the constituencies voted as a result of their attitude to 'reform' or for some local and particular reasons, rather than from a generalized attitude to a 'party' and its policies, this was less the case later in the nineteenth century. After 1832 'party' developed as a differentiating factor behind support for particular candidates both within and across constituencies, and increasingly came to refer to those who supported the same policies in parliament too.[2]

Several political 'tendencies' can be identified among MP's in the period following the Reform Bill of 1832 – Whig, Liberal, Radical, Peelite, Conservative, Protectionist. All at some time had support in the electorate but, during the period between the First and Second Reform Bills, there was the gradual development of an essentially two-party system.[3] Over this same period political competition and participation were increasingly structured by and through the two emerging coalitions of Conservative and Liberal interests. By 1885 the opinions of the electorate were more consistently organized behind these two political identities, and W.S. Gilbert could suggest:

> That every boy and every gal,
> That's born into the world alive,
> Is either a little Liberal,
> Or else a little Conservative[4]

However these party coalitions were neither stable nor permanent and the period after 1885 was one of change, so by 1906 there were five recognizable 'parties' in the House of Commons.

There is some dispute about the early stages of the process of party formation. Political competition in parliament and in the constituencies certainly existed before 1832, as did some of the structural and organizational elements of the later nineteenth century party system, and some modes of electioneering originated during the pre-Reform period too. The general election of 1832 saw an increase in constituency party activity to organize the registration of the newly enfranchised electors and to mobilize candidate support in the now wider electorate. In some borough constituencies the passing of the Municipal Reform Act in 1835 introduced annual local elections for the reformed corporations. This gave further impetus to the development of local organization, and the annual registration of electors for both parliamentary and municipal elections provided another opportunity for agents and managers to recruit and organize political support. In many of these constituencies there was regular competition for votes at the two levels and this helped to produce a specific context for voting and electoral behaviour.[5]

Table 2.1   The structure of representation 1830–85

Date	Number of constituencies	Number of constituencies returning				
		1 member	2 members	3 members	4 members	Total
1830	373	106	270	0	3	658
1832	401	153	240	7	1	658
1868	420	196	211	12	1	658
1885	643	616	27	0	0	670

Sources: The figures for 1830 and 1832 are from Brock (1973), pp. 19–20 and 310–313; the other figures are from McCalmont (1971) and Hanham (1959).

Between 1832 and 1868 the parliamentary electoral system had four distinctive features – most constituencies elected more than one MP; electors in these multi-member seats had more than one vote; there was only partial enfranchisement with relatively few adult males qualifying for the vote; and voting was open rather than secret.

In 1832, 248 out of 401 constituencies elected two or more members, see Table 2.1. In all seats the elector had as many votes as there were members – one vote in a single member constituency, two votes in a two member seat, three in a three member seat and so on. The only restriction was that the elector could not give more than one vote to any one candidate in a multi-member seat. This structure of multi-member seats and the multiple vote created strategic opportunities for local parties and for electors – how many candidates to put forward, and how to use the multiple vote.[6]

The majority of the constituencies returned two members and in such seats there were frequent 'triangular' contests in which two candidates campaigning together faced one opponent. The single candidate would try to persuade electors either to give just a single vote to him or, if they were going to support his opponents, he would suggest that they split their vote and give one vote to him and only one vote to the opposition. The two candidates running together would stress the importance of an elector giving them both votes. The elector's decision became more complex when four candidates were standing in a two-member seat, usually two from each 'party'. In either case the elector could use his votes to express differing degrees of support for the two candidates of the same party. He could vote for only one of them or, by splitting his two votes and giving one to an opposing candidate, he could express personal or policy preferences.[7] These strategic possibilities were not available in single member seats, but it was only after 1885 that such seats became the main element of the electoral system.

Enfranchisement was partial and relatively few adult males had the vote. Reform enlarged the electoral community after 1832 and further increases followed in 1867, 1884/85 and 1918 as the system moved towards full adult suffrage, see Table 2.2. In the early stages of democratization Butler and Cornford estimate that 1 in 5 adult males had the right to vote between 1832 and 1867, 1 in 3 after 1868, and 2 out of 3 after 1886.[8] Women were given the right to vote in 1918, and enfranchised on the same basis as men in 1928, but between 1832 and 1867 the 'non-electorate' was larger than the electorate.[9]

With full adult suffrage the proportion of the population with the vote is effectively constant across the constituencies, under partial enfranchisement it varied. There was growth in the electorate of some constituencies between the First and Second Reform Bills but overall the relative size of the enfranchised stratum in England remained roughly constant at about one in twenty of the population.

The Reform Bill in 1832 was a first step towards full manhood suffrage. It increased the number of electors but retained considerable barriers to membership of the electoral community. Formally, in borough constituencies of England and Wales between 1832 and 1867, these included the requirement for an elector to occupy a house of at least £10 a year in rateable value and to pay the rates. This was qualified by several technical factors and infringements could lead to

Table 2.2   The electorate and the population in England 1832–1918[10]

	Electorate (000's)	Population (000's)	Ratio Electorate:Population
1831	344	13,994	1:48
1832	653	14,165	1:22
1846	817	16,256	1:20
1860	965	19,902	1:21
1868	1,997	21,949	1:11
1886	4,377	27,522	1:6
1910 (Dec)	7,710	35,792	1:5
1918	21,392	34,024	1:1.6

disqualification at the annual revision and the removal of the elector's name from the register.[11]

During this same period the social context of electoral behaviour changed substantially. The population of England and Wales grew by 55 per cent and the distribution of the population between town and country was altered through migration to the towns and the growth of urban centres. In the course of a few decades England became a predominantly urban and industrial society, and the social structure was transformed with the emergence of a mature class society, one 'characterized by class feeling, that is, by the existence of vertical antagonism between a small number of horizontal groups, each based on a common source of income' (Perkin, 1969, p. 176). It was the growing industrialization that generated more general economic conflicts, solidarity within groups being helped by growing urbanization and the growth of new industrial communities. Over time such new class relationships displaced older ones of patronage and dependence replacing the underlying status inequalities with more extensive class antagonisms. By the end of the century the system of transport and communication contributed to the nationalization of news and political issues, and indirectly helped to bring about a growing uniformity of electoral response.[12] These changes were important in establishing the social context of mass politics, but they had a less direct influence during the mid-Victorian period of restricted suffrage and partial enfranchisement, in the transitional period before the full development of the new structure of class relationships.[13]

Finally, voting was open and electoral behaviour was public knowledge, so the elector was exposed to a range of social and economic pressures. This meant, as Elklit has noted, 'individual voters were constrained by their roles in the subordinate systems of the locality, the neighbourhood...and so on when voting' (Elklit, 2000, p. 193).[14] The promise of political support could be compared with actual behaviour and electoral choice could be linked to other relationships. A change in political partisanship was public knowledge and might have social or economic consequences. Once established, stable partisan loyalty helped the elector to avoid such costs. If this was the case then, over time, a constituency organization could build up increasingly accurate knowledge of its support from canvassing and elections, both in terms of the overall level of electoral support for a party or a candidate, and of the stability and loyalty of individual electors. The accuracy of this knowledge increased with its verification at regular or frequent elections. Under secrecy the promise of support and the actual vote cannot be linked, which introduces uncertainty for parties and candidates, and dissociates the voter from the context of voting, from other electors, and from the immediate consequences of his action. So secret voting is qualitatively distinct from open voting, and under open voting there could be a different relationship between the social context and electoral behaviour.

The evolving social structure forms one part of the background to this study which examines the nature of open voting and the links between electoral behaviour and party organization at the constituency level between 1832 and 1868. During this period the results of elections were influenced by the partisanship of the voters, the activity of local party organizations, and by change and turnover in the electorate, amongst other factors. Local constituency organizations tried to maintain the partisanship of existing voters, and attempted to identify and recruit additional political support. They used connections between new and existing electors to influence and predict votes, and assumed too that electoral behaviour was linked to the underlying social context in a regular and identifiable way.

So how are we to explain electoral behaviour and the nature of this link? Any general explanation of open voting needs to acknowledge the constraints derived from the structure of the electoral community and the relationship between electors and their social context. The next three chapters re-examine the context and consequences of partisan competition under open voting, the pattern of electoral behaviour that evolved in many constituencies after 1832, and the structure and dynamics of open voting between the First and Second Reform Bills.

Without secrecy there was a link between the social situation of the individual and his electoral behaviour. After voting, electoral preference was public knowledge and it could be counted as partisan support by a constituency party organization. It was assumed that those able to do so would try to influence the voting behaviour of their social or economic dependants. So, for example, a landlord would try to influence the vote(s) of his tenants. As a result these votes – and voters – were seen as resources that could be counted upon in an election campaign. A Reform League report for the East Retford election of 1868 illustrates both this assumption and its consequences:

the recognised agents of the two parties never talk of votes, or the voters themselves. It is simply how this landlord will go, or that landlord will turn. If 'so and so' is on our side, that will be 50 votes or 100, as the case may be. If he goes against us, we shall lose them.[15]

It was assumed that this held true for other social or economic relationships and that 'influentials' could assemble a coalition of electoral support from their dependant voters.

Such 'organization' of the electorate was particularly important where there was some doubt about the balance of opinion in a constituency, or the result of a contested election. Not only was an election more likely if the outcome was uncertain and if both parties thought that they could win, but consistent patterns of behaviour would probably develop first where there were regular elections. So the systematic consequences of open voting should be more apparent in frequently contested seats. Chapter 3 analyses electoral contestation at the ten general elections between 1832 and 1868 and shows that competition was most common in the English borough constituencies, confirming the importance of the medium-sized towns suggested by both Hanham and Vincent.[16] Urban constituencies with larger electorates were more frequently contested, and this regular competition for votes helped to establish the organizational consequences of the First Reform Bill. The 1832 Act, and later legislation on electoral registration, created systematic, regularly revised and publicly contested records of those qualified to vote. Local organizers used the opportunities provided by the annual revision of the register to build political support. They recruited new voters for 'their' party and objected to the registration of electors who were known to support the opposition: they tried to organize opinion.[17]

The annually published electoral register enumerated the electorate and, over time, allowed the study of patterns of growth and change within a constituency.[18] But they reveal nothing of the underlying partisan division, and nothing about political participation or individual voting behaviour. Before the introduction of secrecy, information on electoral behaviour was available for some constituencies from the poll books published after an election. This is a body of evidence on individual voting behaviour 'for which the modern social scientist would give his eye-teeth'(Moore, 1967, p. 23).[19] Poll books were a locally published record of a particular constituency election and they enable us to go behind the aggregate election data. Like an electoral register, a poll book is a listing of the constituency electorate, but it also records the vote(s) that the elector gave at the election in question,[20] they are systematic nominal data referring to particular historical individuals.[21] As well as making voting behaviour public knowledge, the information was used by candidates and party organizations to develop and extend techniques of persuasion and control. They made it possible to compare actual and promised behaviour and 'provided a basis for canvassing and for exerting every possible form of political pressure on voters' (Plumb, 1967, p. 53).[22]

Many poll books contain additional information on the elector apart from his vote. Some give an address or other locational data, and in others there is an indication of the elector's occupation. There is disagreement about the meaning and use of such occupational data, and this study does not attempt to resolve any of the problems of analysis and interpretation.[23] Instead it uses occupation simply as one of several identifying criteria for the individual elector. As such it can be used, with the other personal data in a poll book, to identify electors at different times and so draw together information on individuals from different records. Such nominal record linkage is essentially 'the bringing together of information concerning a particular historical individual derived from independent sources'.[24] By this process we can create time series data on the electoral behaviour of individuals, transition tables for electoral behaviour at two successive elections, and panels of voters over three or more elections. Such time series data allows a detailed analysis of patterns of stability and change in voting behaviour, both individually and in the aggregate.[25]

The data generated by the nominal record linkage of poll books is central to this study of electoral change between 1832 and 1868. It is used to examine the nature of political support, to establish whether electors voted consistently in partisan terms, and the extent of stability in their behaviour over time. Chapter 4 maps the short-term changes between two elections in Lancaster in the 1840's. This outlines the underlying continuities in individual voting, the extent of electoral turnover and the replacement of the electorate between elections, as well as the pattern of recruitment amongst the new electors. Canvass books, and other records of local party activity, are used together with poll book data to reconstruct the local organization of the vote. This analysis shows how an individual, or a local party organization, systematically identified, recruited and maintained electoral support within a changing electoral community, and suggests some general conclusions about electoral 'organization' in this period, both for Lancaster and for other similarly contested borough constituencies.

The linkage of poll book data is central to the analysis of long-term electoral change too. Chapter 5 examines voting in Bedford over the ten general elections between 1832 and 1868, and Chapter 7 studies the constituency level effects of the Second Reform Bill, and voting at the subsequent general election in 1868.

The pattern of aggregate and individual electoral change in Bedford reinforces the conclusions reached in Lancaster about nature of electoral support and the functions of local political organization. For electoral success in any constituency, it was important to retain the support of those who had voted for you previously, and recruit new voters to replace those who had left the electorate through death, migration and disqualification. Regular elections, and the annual registration process, were the basis of the organizational effort that sustained partisan support. The dynamics of change in Bedford, both the physical turnover of the electorate and the changing pattern of individual voting, are examined in detail. The analysis suggests that parties could rely on a core of consistent support and that underlying electoral change there was a relatively high degree of short-term individual partisan stability. Most voters usually voted for the same party at successive elections although disagreements over policy, or over candidates, could lead to a breakdown in this pattern of support. The analysis reinforces the earlier conclusions about the effects of reform on the development and functioning of constituency party organization in Lancaster.[26]

But what lay behind these patterns of stability and change in voting behaviour? In both Lancaster and Bedford the election results were linked to demographic change, with turnover in the electorate providing an opportunity to recruit new voters and influence the shifting electoral fortunes of candidates and parties. The overall electoral environment was often stable and predictable within relatively narrow margins; a majority of the constituency electorate at any one election were electors at the next election too.[27] So the major problem for local party organizations – and for electoral campaigning – was that of maintaining electoral support, and the partisanship of existing electors.

Previous accounts have tried to explain voting through social or economic factors such as class or bribery. However if Colomer is correct in his suggestion that secrecy 'allowed new voters to express their political preferences more sincerely than before', then it follows that electoral choice under open voting may have been less 'sincere' and more dependant.[28] Voting at each election was not an independent action and, over time, electoral choice linked two separate decisions – first, the initial expression of partisan choice and, second, its maintenance. If open voting is a constrained choice then, for most voters, the latter may have been less problematic than the former. In other words, once established, partisanship was easy to maintain. For the individual elector it was only 'costly' if they wished to change their political allegiance and vote for a different candidate or party.[29]

The analysis of electoral behaviour in Bedford and Lancaster suggests an alternative account of behaviour under open voting, one that is outlined in more detail in Chapter 6. Briefly, voting and the maintenance of partisan support in the electorate, as well as the methods of electoral campaigning, were all linked to the structure and dynamics of constituency social networks. Such a link can provide a more inclusive explanation of open voting and help to account for the overall pattern of electoral behaviour in many borough constituencies between 1832 and 1868. It also helps to explain the transformation in electoral politics after the Second Reform Bill, with the expansion of the suffrage in 1867, and the further changes that followed the introduction of the secret ballot in 1872. Finally, it has implications for the growth of mass politics after 1885.

A social network is a very general concept that refers essentially to the set of structural linkages between individuals. These links can be based on kinship, friendship or other social relationships, but the key point is that 'the patterning of linkages can be used to account for some aspects of the behaviour of those involved'.[30] Since enfranchisement was partial and voting was a public act, an elector's behaviour was embedded in a wider network of relationships that could be manipulated for social and political purposes, and that helped to reinforce the pattern of political and electoral organization. So the electoral activities in Lancaster and Bedford are only particular examples of more widespread social and political processes, and the constituency organizational response was a general one.

Several consequences follow. Explanations of open voting in terms of class, religion or the other social factors examined in the previous chapter are neither mutually exclusive nor incompatible. Such explanations have all been examining just one aspect of the total social network of the individual elector, or examining one specific content such as religious observance and affiliation, from the many that existed in the links between individuals. So, whether they emphasize the economic transactions behind voting, or the influence of hierarchical relationships of social and political dependence, they can all be subsumed within a more general social network explanation.

Such a more inclusive explanation also highlights some of the differences between rural and urban parliamentary seats in this period. Borough constituencies were usually based on a single urban community of varying size; rural seats – the county constituencies – were a wider set of geographically contiguous small and very small communities with relatively few electors in each. In such small rural communities the voters were also members of a set of relatively undifferentiated, almost coincident partial networks that maintained patterns of social inequality and the exercise of hierarchical socio-political influence. In urban constituencies the existing partial social networks were more differentiated and overlapped to a lesser extent. So the dynamics of the system are less readily discernible, social relationships were more diffuse and the mobilization of political support had to use multiple criteria and several social channels. The potential hierarchical dominance of an electoral community by a single individual or node in the small communities of a county constituency had been replaced by a system with multiple centres of influence in urban constituencies. These changes can be linked to the overall processes of role differentiation that followed economic and social change and that, after the introduction of electoral secrecy, eventually lead to the separation of the political role from other social roles, and a separation of the public and private political spheres. Note too that in this context a social network was not only a channel for the exercise of social influence, it was also a means by which electors could be mobilized and, more speculatively, a potential distribution structure for bribery and the spoils of local political office and local power.

However the network structure of social relations in the electoral community existed independently of 'politics', although politics may have been an important defining element of many networks. Under partial enfranchisement the personal network of an elector would include many who were not themselves enfranchised, such as the elector's wife and other non-electors. Without a formal role in the electoral process, these individuals could still be significant political actors. They could be included in the process of mobilizing political support since 'electoral politics involved…. Not only a high proportion of voters, but many others also, attracted by connections of family, business, dependence, belief …' (Hoppen, 1984, p. 71). This inclusion of both electors and non-electors is important. Non-electors participated informally in political life within a highly politicized environment and, as a consequence, they could later be incorporated relatively easily into the enlarged electoral community. The extension of the franchise in 1867 did not alter the structure and nature of personal relations but it changed the constituency balance between electors and non-electors and modified the nature of the elector's personal network.

The smooth assimilation of the newly enfranchised contributed to continuities in electoral behaviour; it links political behaviour before and after the expansion of the suffrage by the Second Reform Act.

After 1867 – and after the Third Reform Act too – the new electors were not suddenly identified, absorbed into social networks, then politicised and finally mobilized to vote. They were already located within a web of personal relationships and were probably also politicized and partially mobilized. With enfranchisement, the new electors now had a channel of expression that they had lacked previously; they had become voters and full participants in the formal electoral process.

This explanation of the link between social life and electoral behaviour provides support for the interpretation of constituency electioneering suggested in Chapter 6 and outlines a more complex relationship between the voter and his social environment. It accounts too for the observed continuities in electoral behaviour, and suggests a new understanding of the effects of enfranchisement, and of the introduction of electoral secrecy in 1872.

The extension of the franchise in 1867 changed the relationship between an elector and the community, and Chapter 7 considers the implications of the growing inclusiveness that existed in borough constituencies after 1868, as well as the effect of enfranchisement on local party organization. Voting became a private act with the passing of the Ballot Act in 1872, and under secrecy the political behaviour of the elector could be separated from any interaction with his immediate social environment. As more of those within the constituency became electors, the potential 'vertical' influence of social superiors was diminished while 'horizontal' peer group pressure, such as that of 'community' or 'class', could become more important.

Secrecy allows the elector to insulate himself from some social influences, and the advent of mass politics reduced or eliminated the social costs of changing your vote. In the short term the local party organization provided an element of continuity but the emergence of mass politics was accompanied by the development of different, mass party organizations. The short final chapter considers the implications of the earlier organization of opinion for the overall growth of inclusiveness, and the development of democracy in England. It is possibly only after 1884/85, and more certainly after 1918, that mass democracy can be said to exist; before then the system was unrepresentative. But the continuities are such that institutions, organizations and modes of participation established in the period after the1832 Reform Act continue to influence later changes: 'the effects of the Second [Reform] Act were mitigated by the retention of the old constituency structure and by the growth of party organization; by controlling the process of electoral registration it proved possible to enlist the support of new voters for the two old parties' (Thomas, 1978, p. 72).

Registration and the recruitment of new supporters were important for winning elections. The more often a constituency was contested, the more important was electoral recruitment – and the more likely was there to be a constituency-based organizational response. However, given the local nature of elections in the mid-nineteenth century, if the growth of organization depended on electoral competition, we first need to examine the systemic pattern of competition and contestation in the constituencies between 1832 and 1868.

3
Some Electoral Consequences of the Great Reform Bill

Both contemporary and recent commentators agree that the passing of the First Reform Bill in 1832 was a landmark in the development of democracy in Britain. It initiated major changes in British politics, 'a complete and entire change of our whole political system'.[1] The Act enlarged the suffrage and marked the beginning of wider incorporation and greater participation within the political community, a process that ended with the achievement of full, equal adult suffrage after 1948. More recent interpretations of the Act have emphasized its conservative aims, or its organizational consequences. In either case the political changes that came after 1832 affected the electoral process, and were accompanied by long-term social changes that altered the context of voting too.[2]

But the immediate effects of the enfranchisement on greater incorporation, and subsequent participation, were uneven. There were significant regional variations in voting and political competition in the period between 1832 and further reform in 1867, with systematic differences between the more urban and the more rural constituencies. These are most apparent in England, and so a more detailed analysis of English constituencies may identify some of the major factors contributing to electoral change and voting behaviour in this period.

As well as changing the franchise, the 1832 Act eliminated some of the anomalies of the pre-Reform electoral system. Many of the constituencies with small and very small electorates were disfranchised, and the seats made available were redistributed both to the counties and to unrepresented boroughs. Reform struck at the basis of the 'old corruption' and, like the later controversies over the Corn Laws and the grant to the Catholic institution at Maynooth, it became an intense and widely discussed national political issue.[3]

These three issues had features in common. None were short-term and all were linked to very fundamental and divisive questions in British society and politics. Reform affected the structure of political power, the position of political elites and the nature of the political community. The Corn Law crisis sprang from the issue of free trade and was linked to the problems of agriculture and manufacturing industry. Maynooth raised questions about the religious settlement in the United Kingdom, the role of Protestantism and religious non-conformity, and the relationship between organized religion and the state. The debate on all three subjects involved many outside the existing electoral or political community – they became national issues rather than remaining sectional ones.

The partial resolution of the first issue by the Reform Act in 1832 did not mark a complete break with the past; there were substantial continuities with previous electoral forms and practices. Gash, in an influential study, noted the similarities between politics before and after Reform, and commented that 'the post-1832 period contained many old features that it inherited from the past. Between the two there is indeed a strong organic resemblance' (Gash, 1953, p. x).[4]

The workings of the un-reformed system have been re-examined and, from a detailed study of electoral politics before 1832, O'Gorman concludes that after Reform 'the electoral forms duly changed...but the substance of electoral life, already participatory, partisan and popular, continued' (O'Gorman, 1989, p. 393).[5] He does not suggest that the Reform Act made no difference to electoral politics, it obviously did, but points out that political practices in the constituencies changed little and that many of the important features of electoral life after 1832 can be identified in the un-reformed system.

Continuities existed at several levels. The parliament of 1833 was, like its predecessor, composed mainly of members of the aristocracy and the landed gentry. Even with the changes in the electorate, many MPs continued to sit for seats that had returned them before 1832. The existence of small proprietor or nomination boroughs had been one of the most corrupt features of the un-reformed system. These seats often had very small electorates and were easily influenced or venally corrupt. Notorious examples such as Old Sarum and Gatton were abolished but patron seats can still be identified after 1832 – Hanham lists 52 boroughs in which individual patrons may have controlled the return of a total of 73 MP's.[6]

The Reform Act enlarged the electorate but most electors in 1832 had first voted during the un-reformed period. Salmon estimates that there were 439,200 electors in 1831 and 656,258 in 1833 with 'new' electors making up about a third of the post-Reform electorate. So even after reform a majority of electors had been socialized into the politics and practices of the 'old corruption', and they remained an influential segment of the enlarged electorate in the period immediately after 1832.[7] Moreover, the effect of enfranchisement was not uniform. Some new constituencies were created to reflect the growth of urban and industrial centres but the relative increase in the number of voters varied across constituencies, and in a few constituencies the number of electors actually decreased.[8]

O'Gorman notes that extensive individual mobility existed in the period preceding reform and that migration contributed to a continuous process of change within the electorate. It also influenced the size and composition of constituency electorates after 1832. There was continuous electoral turnover as voters regularly left and newly qualified individuals were added to the register in all constituencies. In addition, the population of some parliamentary boroughs, and with it their electorates, grew more rapidly between 1832 and 1868.

The proportion of newly qualified electors was not everywhere the same, so the effect of enfranchisement varied at the constituency level. In some seats new electors were in the majority but, given the overall increase, this was not usually the case. The newly enfranchised 'Reform cohort' of electors was a varying fraction of constituency electorates in 1832, and a proportion that declined over time. As their numbers declined so did their influence – and the rate of decline varied across constituencies too.[9]

The continuities in the electorate helped to ensure that there was continuity in electoral practices and personnel, in the use of bribery and treating, in canvassing and the modes of electoral persuasion, in the relations between an elector and the community from which he was drawn and in the role of political activists, influentials and organizers within that community. In the short term, the social context of elections and politics did not change greatly and, as a result, there were continuities in the relationships that influenced political behaviour too. In some constituencies the context was a hierarchical one with the elector dependent upon a social superior or superiors for political cues; in only a very few seats could electors vote with a degree of independence from social constraints.

As the relative numbers of electors and non-electors changed with enfranchisement, so did the relationship between the two groups. This is obvious in numerical terms – after 1832 the possession of the

franchise became more common – but the social and political consequences of this change are less clear and the changes in the electorate
may have altered relationships within an elector's peer group as well
as with his social superiors.

Some contemporary commentators saw in Reform a sweeping away of
the old order and its replacement by 'democracy'. Others, less convinced
of the extent or effect of the change, recognized that the Act could not
be final and that there would be inevitable pressure for further reform.
Such pressure was both directly political, and more indirectly followed
from wider social and economic changes as industrialization and extensive internal migration transformed the structure of society. In 1832 the
programme of the radicals included annual parliaments, manhood
suffrage and the ballot. This agenda was not directly influential but
elements of it were assimilated gradually into the political mainstream
over the succeeding decades.

The local impact of change in 1832 depended upon differences in
social context as well as the change in the number of electors. Since social
structure varied across constituencies, the relationship between social
context and political behaviour varied as well. With a partially enfranchised population, the electorate grew rapidly in some seats; in others
change was more gradual. In Bradford the electorate grew from 1,139 in
1832 to 21,518 in 1868, an increase of almost 1,800 per cent. Boston, with
an electorate of about the same size in 1832, grew much more slowly
increasing from 1,257 to 2,537 electors over the same period. There were
differences between the counties too. Where there was substantial urban
penetration, as in South Lancashire, the electorate grew considerably. In
Herefordshire, which was not close to any large urban centre, the growth
was much smaller.[10] These differences underlay the diversity of political
opinion both within and between constituencies. Taken together they
suggest that from 1832 to 1868 there were substantial variations across
the constituencies in the nature of the electorate, and so differences too
in constituency pressures for a contested election.

Following Reform there was an increase in both inclusiveness and
participation – more individuals were electors, more electors voted and
they voted more often. But, as not all seats were contested at every election, for the individual elector the possibility of voting was not everywhere the same. The number of constituency contests varied at the ten
general elections between 1832 and 1868, see Table 3.1. This fluctuation
is well known, Gash was the first of several commentators to draw attention to the 'problem' of uncontested seats in this period, and later studies have discussed the variation between elections in some detail.[11]

Table 3.1   Uncontested seats at general elections 1832–1945

General election date	Number of uncontested seats	Per cent of all seats	General election date	Number of uncontested seats	Per cent of all seats
1832	189	28.7	1892	63	9.4
1835	271	41.2	1895	188	28.1
1837	234	35.6	1900	243	36.3
1841	336	51.1	1906	113	16.9
1847	368	56.1	1910 (Jan)	75	11.2
1852	257	39.3	1910 (Dec)	162	24.2
1857	330	50.5	1918	107	15.1
1859	379	58.0	1922	57	9.3
1865	301	45.7	1923	50	8.1
1868	210	31.9	1924	32	5.2
1874	187	28.7	1929	7	1.1
1880	108	16.6	1931	65	10.6
1885	44	6.6	1935	40	6.5
1886	224	33.4	1945	3	0.5

Sources: McCalmont (1971); Aydelotte (1971); Butler and Cornford (1969).

Some variation in the extent of contestation at general elections continued after 1868 and Table 3.1 shows an increase in the number of contests immediately after each extension of the suffrage. This may reflect the political activity at the time of each reform, and a subsequent increase in the mobilization of the electorate. It could also derive from uncertainty about the political behaviour of the newly enfranchised, and about the balance of political forces within constituencies. Except after the Fourth Reform Act of 1918, this increase in electoral activity was soon reversed but it is only after 1945 that the number of uncontested seats at a General Election becomes insignificant.[12]

Does the increase in the number of contests imply an increase in the mobilization and politicization of the electorate? Why did elections sometimes *not* take place? Before 1868 there could be several reasons for the lack of a contest. Within a constituency one interest, or a small cluster of interests, could control the process of nomination and election. This would have been relatively straightforward in small seats although the number of electors in the larger constituencies could pose problems of organization and social control. Alternatively local activists might not be able to find a candidate prepared to meet the substantial costs of an election campaign, or a canvass of the electorate might show that a majority of electors already intended to support one particular candidate. This would give any potential opponent a reason to withdraw before the poll, and so avoid a waste of time, money and organizational effort.

Party organization plays a key role in increasing mobilization and participation and after 1832 local organizations helped to finance and run election campaigns. Like the political clubs of the un-reformed system such groups 'furnished candidates with a steady supply of men, money and resources. They provided election workers, supporters and voters. They lent continuity and experience to local political causes' (O'Gorman, 1989, p. 33).[13]

Today political parties carry out most electoral activities and modern parties have four central organizational aims: (i) the selection and sponsoring of parliamentary candidates; (ii) the formulation of a common policy; (iii) financial provision and (iv) the mobilization and co-ordination of party activists and electoral support. While some of these activities take place locally, they are all directed to one central objective: the winning of a sufficient number of parliamentary seats for a party to form an administration and implement its policies. Today parties exist both as local and national organizations, but between 1832 and 1868 a multi-level structure linking parliamentary parties with local parties and constituency organizations did not exist. Constituency organizations can be found in some seats, but the other organizational elements of the modern party existed only in embryonic form, if they existed at all. Party organization in parliament developed after the Reform Act in 1832, and the Second Reform Act in 1867 opened the way for mass-based organizations linking politicians and supporters, but the integration of these separate elements into the modern party organization came later still.[14]

So the figures in Table 3.1 reflect the gradual evolution of national parties and national election campaigns. There was a growing nationalization of electoral response in the late nineteenth century and the completion of this process is shown by the virtual disappearance of uncontested seats after 1945. Only then do the major parties regularly contest seats that they know they cannot win, and only then is there a systematic structure of local and national organization with established channels of communication and control between them. This modern system depends upon support in the electorate that is both politicized and mobilized. Between 1832 and 1868 the population was only partially enfranchised, and the electorate was not fully mobilized.

Constituency organizations and national organizers can be identified but the crucial link between the centre and the local constituency was effected through individuals rather than through an organization, if it was effected at all.[15]

This again suggests that after 1832 much of the substance of electoral politics in the constituencies was local. There could be a convergence of national and local politics over the more important and divisive or critical issues such as Catholic emancipation, the repeal of the Corn Laws and Reform itself. Such issues had an impact that made national issues important at the constituency level. But this too was not completely new, before 1832 there was a 'growing centrality of national issues to electoral politics ...' (O'Gorman, 1989, p. 298). However the diffusion of such behaviour to other issues, across all elections and to all constituencies, was a gradual process and most constituency contests between 1832 and 1868 continued to revolve around relatively local issues.

As there were continuities among the individuals who voted and amongst those who staffed organizations, there is some continuity in political behaviour too. But Table 3.1 does not show the differences in contestation between the different types of constituency, between the more urban and the more rural constituencies, or between the separate parts of the United Kingdom. The social, economic and political processes that transformed British society had a varying impact as such changes were mediated through both differing social and economic structures and distinct local political cultures. We cannot assume that electoral politics, or even the impact of 'national' issues, was the same in England as in Scotland, Ireland or Wales, the same within the regions of England, or the same within county and borough constituencies.

The changes that mobilized and politicized the electorate after 1832 eroded traditional ties and gradually produced a relatively uniform political culture. Later this was helped by the creation of a national system of communication, the railways, and the development of mass circulation daily papers that nationalized political issues. But such developments only began to influence political culture and political behaviour towards the end of the period between the First and Second Reform Bills. Over this same period the electoral community continually changed as electors left through death, migration or disqualification. There were similar changes in the electorate following the Second Reform Bill in 1867 with the number of electors increasing by about 100 per cent, see Table 2.2. As in 1832, general demographic changes in the wider society influenced the impact of this enfranchisement and its effect was not uniform across the constituencies either.

The growth of a predominantly urban society, and the social changes that accompanied industrialization, changed the context of electoral behaviour and constituency politics. The important differences were those between urban, city and industrial constituencies on the one hand, and rural, agricultural, small town constituencies on the other. These were to some extent mirrored by the differences between county and borough seats between 1832 and 1868, and the data in Table 3.1 can be re-ordered to reflect distinct and systematic variations in the pattern of electoral contestation across the different parts of the United Kingdom.

There were ten general elections between 1832 and 1868 and each constituency could be contested up to a maximum of ten times. The more politicized or mobilized a constituency electorate, the more likely was there to be a contest at a general election; so the number of general election contests is one indicator of the level of political mobilization. A constituency with a low level of mobilization would not be contested at many of the general elections over this period, in extreme cases it might not be contested at all. The more mobilized constituencies would be contested more frequently, and a highly mobilized constituency would be contested at all ten general elections.

The small borough of Eye in Suffolk always returned a candidate unopposed and was not contested at any general election between 1832 and 1868 – so it has a contestation/mobilization score of zero. In contrast, Leeds, Cambridge and 20 other boroughs were contested at all the general elections in this period – they have a contestation/mobilization score of ten. Other constituencies fall between these extremes and Table 3.2 shows the number of contests between 1832 and 1868 by region – England, Scotland, Ireland or Wales – and by type of seat – county or borough.[16]

There are some intriguing systematic differences in Table 3.2. (The median number of contests in each category of constituency is shown in bold type.) In all regions, the boroughs were more frequently contested than the counties. The median borough constituency in England was contested seven times while in Ireland, Scotland and Wales they were contested only six, five and three times respectively. The median county constituency was contested four times in England, Scotland and Ireland, in Wales only twice. This suggests that the processes of change, and the political consequences that followed, were more advanced in some regions and in some types of constituency. Population growth and internal migration changed borough electorates as electors moved from county to town, or from one town to another. Migration disrupted pre-existing social ties and electors would have to establish new social

Table 3.2   The contestation of parliamentary constituencies 1832–68[a]

		Number of general election contests										
		0	**1**	**2**	**3**	**4**	**5**	**6**	**7**	**8**	**9**	**10**
England	Counties	2	8	8	15	12	11	4	4	1	3	0
	Boroughs	4	7	8	7	6	19	22	21	29	39	22
Scotland	Counties	2	3	3	4	9	7	2	0	0	0	0
	Boroughs	0	0	1	4	3	4	6	2	0	1	0
Wales	Counties	2	3	4	1	2	1	0	0	0	0	0
	Boroughs	2	1	2	3	2	1	3	1	0	0	0
Ireland	Counties	2	0	6	4	6	8	2	4	0	0	0
	Boroughs	0	1	2	5	3	5	3	5	4	3	2
Total	Counties	8	14	21	24	29	27	8	8	1	3	0
	Boroughs	6	9	13	19	14	29	34	29	33	43	24

[a] Table 3.2 does not include St. Albans or Sudbury that were disfranchised in 1852 and 1844 respectively.

Source: McCalmont (1971).

relationships within a different urban social and political context. The greater frequency of contests in borough seats is consistent with the suggestion that it is the urban political culture that facilitated political mobilization and weakened the social constraints that had traditionally been employed to control the nomination and election process, particularly in county seats. It is also in this same urban context that the 'new' class structure of the late nineteenth century first emerged.[18]

English boroughs formed the largest group of constituencies. In just under half of them – 90 out of 184 constituencies – there was an almost continuous pattern of contestation between 1832 and 1868 with a poll at 8 or more general elections (see Table 3.2). It is in these seats that new patterns of electoral behaviour first emerge. It is there too that the institutions and organizations associated with political mobilization developed most rapidly after 1832.[19] As the system changed, and the electorate became more fully mobilized, these new patterns of political activity spread and influenced the conduct of elections in all constituencies.

The table shows significant differences between the regions, and between borough and county seats within regions. Similar constituencies in the other regions were consistently less mobilized than those in England. So, for example, the proportion of borough seats contested eight times or more in Scotland was 20 per cent, in Wales 0 per cent and in Ireland 24 per cent. In all regions borough seats were contested more often than county ones. Only 29 per cent of English county constituencies were contested the eight times or more that is characteristic of the English boroughs, the median county seat was contested only four times. There is a similar difference in the other parts of the United Kingdom. Not only is the level of mobilization and contestation lower than in England, but within each region it is also lower in the county/rural seats than it is in the borough/urban ones.

This difference in the mobilization of regional peripheries compared to urban centres is similar to the pattern found in other European polities in the early stages of political development. It is usually attributed to the influence of urbanization upon political mobilization, combined with the lagged effect of social change in the more peripheral areas. This lag is linked to the developing pattern of communication, and the later cultural integration of regions further away from the more rapidly changing urban centres. In European polities it is the political culture of the dominant urban centres that influences the evolving national political culture.[20]

Not only was political mobilization highest in English borough seats, there was a high level of individual participation within the enfranchised stratum. One survey of the available data concludes that 'the evidence on turnout is fairly clear…under open voting [before 1872] turnout was almost uniformly and consistently high, over 80% and frequently over 90%' (Mitchell, 1976a, p. 116).

Although the Reform Act increased the number of electors, many constituencies still had small electorates in which it was relatively easy to manufacture electoral conformity and a high level of participation. As O'Gorman remarks of political activity before 1832, 'electoral relationships were all manifestations of a set of broad social relationships which were embedded in the theory and practice of both paternalism and deference' and he describes in detail the communal aspects of elections and electioneering as well as the mechanisms for influencing individual voters (O'Gorman, 1989, p. 215). Similar practices can be found in many constituencies after Reform.

Before the emergence of a modern-class society in the late nineteenth century, a change that brought with it a new set of relationships both within and between groups, the link between an individual elector and his community was of fundamental importance. Political loyalty was often part of a general set of social relationships. This has been extensively discussed in terms of social deference with many voters following the political cues of their patrons, proprietors and other political or social superiors.[21] But such relationships had other consequences that are important for understanding changes in electoral behaviour after 1832. The relationship between social superiors and dependants implies a direct link between the social situation of an elector and his political behaviour. Changes taking place within English society at the same time as Reform began to erode these hierarchical social relationships and, together with urbanization, fundamentally altered the structure of communities and the relationships between individuals within them. Partly as a result, political modernization and mobilization eventually differentiated politics from other social relationships. So, if there are differences in contestation between regions, and between urban and rural constituencies, are there also significant differences in contestation within the increasingly differentiated set of English borough seats?

There are several social and political processes involved here, but the existing data can be used to explore only one aspect of this change – the effect of community size on contestation in English borough seats. Under universal suffrage 'size' refers to the number of electors in a constituency. Under partial enfranchisement it has two separate and related dimensions: the number of electors in a constituency and the overall population of the seat. The 1832 Reform Bill represented communities, not individuals, so these two dimensions did not always coincide and the relationship between a constituency population and the size of its electorate was not necessarily a direct one.

We might expect relations of social dependence to become weaker in larger urban communities. An increase in the number of electors could result in more local political activity and more contested parliamentary elections. But, given the indirect relationship that exists between population and the size of a constituency electorate, we do not know whether this occurs as a result of a larger electorate or a larger constituency population. Is it the size of the enfranchised electoral stratum that is the relevant influence, or simply the size of the urban community as a whole?

But the electoral community was not distinct or separate from the wider community, it was embedded within it and voters interacted with non-voters. The social setting may become more complex for the individual voter within a larger population but the larger the electorate, the greater the possibility for social and political diversity, and the

Table 3.3 Electorate, population and contestation: English borough constituencies 1832–1868

	Number of electors:				
Population	0–360	361–690	691–1400	>1400	Total
<6,100	5.1	5.5	7.0	8.0	5.4
	(31)	(10)	(4)	(1)	46
6,101–10,150	3.6	6.9	7.6	8.0	6.2
	(13)	(17)	(14)	(2)	46
10,151–23,000	4.0	6.7	7.8	8.2	7.3
	(2)	(16)	(17)	(11)	46
>23,000	–	8.0	8.3	8.0	8.1
		(3)	(11)	(32)	46
Total	4.6	6.2	7.8	8.1	6.8
	46	46	46	46	184

Source: McCalmont (1971).

greater the potential costs of social/political control for social/political superiors.

In Table 3.3 the English borough constituencies are grouped by quartiles, in terms of the number of electors in 1832 and the constituency population in 1831. The upper figure in each cell of the table refers to the average number of contests for all seats in the cell, the lower figure to the number of constituencies. So, for example, a seat with an electorate of 350 and a population of 5,000 would be located in the top left-hand cell of Table 3.3; this cell includes 31 constituencies with a population less than 6,100 and with fewer than 360 qualified electors; these 31 seats were contested an average of 5.1 times between 1832 and 1868.[22]

The data in Table 3.3 does suggest a link between population and the size of the electorate in English borough seats. Large boroughs tended to have large electorates – Birmingham with a population of 146,986 in 1831 had an electorate of 7,309 in 1832; Bristol's population was 104,338 with an electorate of 10,939. Conversely small boroughs had small electorates; Petersfield population 4,922, electorate 234; Calne 4,973 inhabitants, 188 electors. However there were variations in the ratio of population to electorate and boroughs with similar populations could have very differently sized electorates. Aylesbury and Petersfield both had populations of about 4,900 in 1832 but the former had 1,654 electors, Petersfield only 234. Some large boroughs had small electorates: Halifax with a population over 31,000 had an electorate of only 531. Conversely, as in the case of Aylesbury, a relatively small town could have a relatively large electorate.[23] Subsequent changes in population after 1832 may have increased the inequalities of representation, as the growth in population was not uniformly distributed across the constituencies. As a result the relationship between population and the size of the electorate remained an indirect one.

However the data shows one relationship clearly: 'size' was related to contestation. Small constituencies, with a population of less than 6,100 and up to 360 electors – the top left-hand cell in the table – were contested only 5.1 times on average; constituencies with a population more than 23,000, the bottom row of the table, were contested at eight or more elections.

But the relationship between constituency size and contestation was not a simple one. If we hold the size of population constant, contestation increases as the number of electors increases (except in boroughs with a population over 23,000). So, in seats with a population between 10,151 and 23,000 the average number of times that a constituency was contested increases with the number of electors. In those with an electorate of less than 360 there were 4.0 contests on average; with an electorate between 361 and 690 there were 6.7; between 691 and 1,400 electors – 7.8, and where the electorate is larger than 1,400 the average is 8.2 contests. If we hold the size of the electorate constant there is some increase in contestation with population, but this is not as marked as the increase associated with a growth in the size of the electorate for constant population. In boroughs with between 691 and 1,400 electors, the number of contests increases from 7.0 to 8.3 as the population increases from less than 6,100 to more than 23,000, and similar changes can be found in the other ranges of constituency electoral size. This suggests that it is the size of the electorate that is the critical factor associated with increasing contestation, and not just a growth in the constituency population per se. But it is important to keep this analysis in perspective – in 1832 three-quarters of borough constituencies had fewer than 1,400 electors.[24]

We also know that county seats, often with large electorates, were less likely to have contests than urban seats (see Table 3.2). This may seem to contradict the conclusion about the relationship between 'size' and contestation but, unlike most borough constituencies, a county seat was not a single community. It was composed of a number of separate and distinct small and very small communities and often contained one or more urban centres.[25] In such small communities, relations of dependence could produce political conformity. Control of county constituencies was often in the hands of a coalition of landlords and proprietors, with the ability to secure the unopposed return of 'their' candidates.

With constant population, an increase in the number of electors is associated with an increase in contestation. Within very small communities it may have been easy to exercise political control, but as the electoral community increases in size the importance of hierarchy within it decreases and it becomes more expensive to use social pressure for electoral purposes. Political influences could be relatively independent of community size and may occur in large communities too. While the frequency of contestation may foster intense politicization, we can also find high rates of participation at elections in seats with very few contests.[26]

If general elections were not general in this period, then local issues would be at the centre of constituency campaigns. But increasingly between 1832 and 1868 candidates came to be identified in terms of their attitude to national issues, attitudes that differentiated the parliamentary parties too. Parties are coalitions of individuals with differing policy preferences, so party labels between the first two Reform Bills were often imprecise. However, over time, there was an increasing tendency for these labels to reflect the fact that there were more differences between those of different parties than there were between individuals who saw themselves as belonging to the same party. As attitudes and policy preferences became identified in party terms so, gradually, did MP's come to be identified by a party label at election time. While there might be differences between those who nominally belonged to the same party, identification with a party could serve as a reference point for local contests, and the organizational effort at the constituency level was increasingly linked to parties too. If Disraeli was right in suggesting that 'party is organised opinion' then it becomes important to know how opinion was organized at the constituency level, how local parties were formed and functioned.

The data on constituency size shows that middle-sized towns were both the main element of parliamentary representation and the site of most election contests between 1832 and 1868. It was probably in these seats that local organizations for registration and elections were first established and, through local records, we can analyse organization in one constituency, Lancaster, during the early 1840s. We can reconstruct the changing electoral environment facing local political activists, the pattern of partisanship within the electorate, and the process of organizing both voting and registration at the individual level. This sheds light on the relationship between social context, electoral registration and individual voting behaviour before the introduction of secrecy – the links between patterns of behaviour and the organization of opinion.

4
Organizing the Vote in Lancaster

After 1832, the register defined the electorate in a constituency. The official list was produced at an annual revision when there was an opportunity to add or object to new electors. The process was supervised by a revising barrister but 'the election agents of the parties soon learned to exploit the complexities of the Act. Despite the efforts of revising barristers, party machinations kept many bona fide electors off the register, and some dead men on it' (Brock, 1973, p. 326).[1]

The system was further reformed by the Registration Act of 1843, and in some boroughs the annual registration process became a surrogate election with intense partisan activity:

> The open voting system helped an election agent to identify claims to vote emanating from potential opponents of his party. It was his duty to object to these. A trifling objection was always worthwhile. The claim might not be defended. If it was, no costs could be awarded against the objector until the Registration Act of 1843. Even then they were limited to a pound and were seldom awarded. (Brock, 1973, p. 326)[2]

In Lancaster we can follow this process from surviving records, and outline the activities of a local party organizer in his attempts to add individuals to the register and organize the constituency vote.

I

Before Reform, Lancaster, the county town of Lancashire, was a two-member borough with an extensive franchise – 2,490 electors voted at the election in 1818. However by 1832 the registered electorate was reduced to 1,109, although by 1847 this had grown to 1,340.[3] In 1851 the population was 16,168, mostly 'engaged in the salmon fisheries, the coasting and foreign trade, in the making of cotton, cabinet goods, sail-cloth, rope, coaches, ships etc'. Politically in Lancaster the 'parties are so evenly divided that little personal power is centred on individuals' (Dod, 1853, p. 174). In making this assessment Dod did not add the phrase that he used for the more corrupt constituencies – 'influence wholly possessed by the plutocracy' – but there was a local culture of corruption and political malpractice that contributed to the unseating of candidates after elections in 1847 and 1852. Those in 1857 and 1859 passed off without an inquiry, but the 1865 election was also declared void, and a Royal Commission established. It reported:

> that corrupt practices very extensively prevailed at the election 1865, that 843 persons were guilty of bribery ... by receiving money or other valuable considerations for having given, or to induce them to give, their votes; that a further number of 139 were guilty of corrupt practices at the election, by corruptly giving or promising money or other valuable consideration to voters for purchase of their votes, or on account of their having voted or by corruptly advancing money for the purpose of bribery or treating, of which 139 – 89 were electors and 50 non-electors for the borough; that with rare exceptions, corrupt practices have for a long time extensively prevailed at contested elections for this borough. (Bean, 1890, pp. 286–7)[4]

After this report, Lancaster was disfranchised by the Second Reform Act in 1867.

Thomas Greene was one of the two MP's for most of period immediately after 1832.[5] Entering parliament unopposed as a Tory in 1824, he was re-elected in 1830 and continued to represent Lancaster until the 1850's. Immediately after Reform, in 1832 and 1835, the representation was shared with a Liberal, but by 1837 the Tories were able to win both seats. They did so again in 1841 with Greene, as in 1837, coming top of the poll, see Table 4.1.

The election results suggest that both 'parties' had a core of supporters in the electorate, both might be able to win at least one of the two seats, and so from 1837 to 1865 every general election in Lancaster was contested. Reform may have changed the composition of the electorate and the pattern of electoral politics but by using poll books and canvassing books we can go behind these aggregate figures and analyse the voting at the individual level. This identifies some of the processes that contributed

Table 4.1 Lancaster election results 1832–41

Year	Candidates	Party	Votes
1832 and	Greene	Conservative	Unopposed
1835	Stewart	Liberal	Unopposed
1837	Greene	Conservative	614
	Martin	Conservative	527
	Stewart	Liberal	453
	Gray	Liberal	347
1841	Greene	Conservative	699
	Martin	Conservative	594
	Armstrong	Liberal	572

Source: McCalmont (1971).

to electoral change, and links these changes to the underlying social context. It shows that the electorate in Lancaster changed in a regular and identifiable fashion, and that the requirements of electoral registration contributed to the development of local political party organization. So we can trace the origin of a particular pattern of local political activity from the records, and a set of campaign practices too.

The underlying electoral demography in Lancaster produced regular change as individual voters left the electorate and were replaced. Much systematic partisan activity was associated with this turnover, revolving around the annual registration. To become an elector an individual had to be included on the register. Potential new electors could be identified in the local community. The process of registration might be initiated by the individual himself, but the evidence shows that other political actors, local party activists or organizers, were involved in registering new electors, in maintaining the qualifications of those who moved within the constituency and in objecting to the registration of others who might support their political opponents.

Registration was a necessary first step towards voting and the annual revision produced an official and public record of the Lancaster electorate. At any given time the qualified electors could be divided into two groups – those who had voted before and those who had not. Those who had voted had an established political identity, one that was often publicly known and recorded in a published poll book.[6] New electors had no such established political identity, but they did have a social identity. Local activists used the links between new electors and the existing voters, as well as their links with the wider community, to establish a political identity. Connections of kinship, residence, employment, religion, and so on were used to recruit the support of the new elector for a particular candidate or party.

Surviving records can be used to outline this process, and assess the success achieved in building and maintaining electoral support. They show how it was possible to organize the vote in a small community, and how an individual or agent could – over time – recruit support for a candidate or party on a systematic basis. The records in Lancaster provide details of the local organization behind electoral competition during the mid-1840's.

II

Constituency politics in 1847 were very confused. The general election of that year took place after the split in the parliamentary Conservative party over the repeal of the Corn Laws had divided supporters of free trade and supporters of protection. Similar disagreement existed in the electorate and the divisions in parliament were reflected in the constituencies. In Cambridge, the Advertiser commented that 'there is considerable uncertainty as to the result – parties here, as elsewhere, having utterly lost sight of their ancient landmarks'.[7] During the general election candidates contested seats under a variety of political labels: Liberal, Conservative, Liberal-Conservative, Peelite and Protectionist. But while repeal of the Corn Laws was a major national issue, other non-economic issues were also prominent in local campaigns. During the previous parliament the Conservative majority had also been divided in 1845 over the grant to the Catholic institution at Maynooth that had raised questions about the position of Protestantism. To some this was the more important issue and indeed Gash suggests that the election 'was fought on the religious (issue)... in so far as it was fought on any general issues at all' (Gash, 1965, p. 98).[8]

But it was the division of opinion over the Corn Laws that produced unusual consequences. In some two-member seats the two Conservative candidates, or the sitting MPs, now found themselves on opposite sides of the free trade issue. Where they may previously have campaigned together and drawn upon a common body of electoral support, they might now conduct separate campaigns. Lancaster was one seat where this happened. Greene and Martin, two Conservatives, had been elected in 1841. After voting for repeal in 1846, Greene stood again in 1847. The other Conservative candidate, Edward Salisbury, stood as a Protectionist.[9] The *Lancaster Gazette* noted that Greene was running an independent campaign and quoted him as saying 'I neither ask a plumper for myself, nor would I presume to attempt, either directly or indirectly, to influence any man's second vote' (*Lancaster Gazette*, 24 July 1847, p. 1).[10]

Connacher has pointed out that there was a connection between a vote on the Corn Law issue and attitudes to the Maynooth grant.[11] This link was echoed in the constituencies and, after Greene had been re-elected, the *Lancaster Gazette* commented:

> It will be observed that the free trade question has been made the turning point in the enquiry…We need not inform the readers of the Gazette that this is not the question on which our politics is based…we believe we may assume that…the cause of Protestantism, and the cause of protection to native industry, are causes that go hand in hand, the first having the preference in men's hearts, and, therefore, it is not unreasonable to say that most of the avowed Protectionists returned are also steady Protestants. (*Lancaster Gazette*, 28 August 1847, p. 3)

The coincidence of two such deeply divisive issues, one economic and one religious, helped to produce a new pattern of political forces. In retrospect it can be seen as part of the lengthy process of change and political realignment, both in parliament and in the electorate, that later helped to form the Gladstonian liberal coalition from Peelites, Whigs, Liberals and others – and the Disraelian Conservative party as well.[12] However in 1847 it produced confusion in the constituencies over candidates and issues, over electoral support and voting behaviour.

The result of the election shows the changing aggregate support for candidates and parties. But the electorate changed too as voters left the electorate through death or migration, and new voters were added. If we are to understand electoral behaviour and party activity at the 1847 election in Lancaster, or constituency behaviour more generally between the First and Second Reform Bills, then we need to examine both individual voting and the physical change in the electorate.

III

There were two Conservative candidates at the 1847 Lancaster election, Greene, one of the sitting MP's, and Edward Dodson Salisbury, a local man who had been mayor in 1844. Salisbury stood as a Protectionist and, because of his disagreement with Greene over the Corn Laws, the two ran separate campaigns. Greene was again returned to parliament but, unlike the two previous elections, he was not top of the poll. Samuel Gregson, the single Liberal candidate, won the other seat and Salisbury was defeated. The Gazette commented that 'nothing but the greatest personal regard felt for Mr. Greene saved him from most decided defeat.' The full result is listed in Table 4.2:

Table 4.2   The Lancaster election of 1847

Gregson (Liberal)	724
Greene (Conservative)	721
Salisbury (Protectionist)	621

Source: McCalmont (1971).

Superficially this indicates a return to the political balance of 1832 and 1835 with representation again divided between the two parties. However, analysis of the pattern of individual votes shows a marked change from the preceding elections.

In many constituencies voting had become party based in the period after Reform with electors in two-member seats giving both of their votes to candidates of the same party, or using only one vote when there was no second candidate of the appropriate party standing. In 1837, 87 per cent, and in 1841, 85 per cent, of the votes at the Lancaster elections were given along party lines in this way. In 1847 this pattern was disrupted and only 63 per cent of votes were 'party' votes.[13] Participation was high with 95 per cent of registered electors voting in 1837, 88 per cent in 1841 and 94 per cent in 1847. An analysis of individual ballots in 1847 shows the decline in the number of double votes for the two Conservative candidates with many Tory supporters using only one of their two votes; see Table 4.3.

Table 4.3   Ballots at the Lancaster election, 1847[14]

	Gregson (Lib)	Greene (Con)	Salisbury (Prot)
Gregson	254	355	115
Greene		38	328
Salisbury			178

In 1847, 17 per cent of the electors voting gave a 'plumper' or single vote to one of the Conservative candidates – 38 for Greene and 178 for Salisbury; 37 per cent of votes were double ones given across party lines – 355 for Gregson and Greene, 115 for Gregson and Salisbury. There were more double votes of this type than there were double votes for the two Conservatives: only 328 electors, 26 per cent of those voting, supported both Greene and Salisbury. If the single votes for Greene and Salisbury are counted as party votes, as well as the double votes for these two candidates, plus the plumpers for Gregson, then some 63 per cent of all electors voted along party lines in 1847. If only the Gregson plumpers and the Greene–Salisbury double votes are used in this calculation then party voting falls to 46 per cent. If however the separate campaigns of Greene and Salisbury indicate the effective existence of three parties in the constituency, then party voting amongst the electors falls to 37 per cent. Under any of these assumptions there was a substantial decrease from the level of party voting at the previous election.[15]

One of the local papers was in no doubt about the cause of this result. In reporting the defeat of Salisbury, its favoured candidate, the *Lancaster Gazette* said little about free trade. Instead it stressed the importance of the religious interest and hinted at its role in electoral behaviour: 'Radical interest has triumphed. The Protestant candidate has been defeated.' This assertion was supported by an analysis of the votes of 'Romanists, Dissenters and Wesleyans' showing their support for the winning candidates, Table 4.4.

Increased abstention by Tory voters was another reason given for the drop in Conservative support. However, as turnout increased from 88 per cent in 1841 to 94 per cent in 1847, this can be discounted,

Table 4.4   Denomination and votes at the 1847 Lancaster election

	Salisbury	**Greene**	**Gregson**
Romanists	0	16	25
Socinians	0	1	3
Independents	1	17	27
Friends	2	22	23
Baptists	0	25	35
Wesleyans	12	25	35

Source: *Lancaster Gazette*[16]

although one local paper suggested that many Conservatives from the previous election had abstained in disgust since 'no true man came forward asking for their support' (*Lancaster Gazette*, 28 August 1847). After the election Salisbury petitioned against Gregson's return on the grounds of bribery. The House of Commons committee cross-examined witnesses and took submissions from interested parties before concluding that: 'it appeared from the evidence that treating was carried on to a great extent'. Despite the fact that Gregson's 'knowledge and consent' were 'not proved by the evidence', he was unseated and a by-election held seven months later, in early March 1848 (Powell, Rodwell and Dew, 1853, p. 44).

The annual registration took place between the two elections and, as was usual, new electors were put on the register and those found to be disqualified were struck off. A local paper detected an improvement in Conservative fortunes: 'A considerable number of claims and objections were made on both sides, and the result we are happy to say was, as nearly as could be ascertained, a majority of between forty and fifty in favour of the Conservative cause.' (*Lancaster Gazette*, 2 October 1848).

Neither Salisbury nor Gregson stood in 1848 and, despite the supposed increase in Conservative support; a Liberal candidate was again elected:

Armstrong (Liberal)   636
Stanley (Conservative)   620.

This close result was again much disputed. The Gazette claimed that 'the poll book has been examined, and the result is that Mr. Stanley has a clear majority of ten over his opponent'. When it became apparent that this was not the official result, the paper stressed the decline of the radical interest and the narrow majority it now commanded. Once again the defeated candidate lodged a petition but this time the committee allowed the result to stand although they struck off 33 electors as having no 'right to vote' (*Lancaster Gazette*, 22 May 1848).[17]

IV

What was happening at the election of 1847 and the subsequent by-election? Was there any pattern to the shifting balance of political forces in Lancaster? Did the annual registration, and the change in the composition of the electorate, favour one particular party or candidate? Can we link the behaviour of voters to wider social and political processes within the constituency? Answers to these questions will not only contribute to an analysis of the Lancaster elections of 1847 and 1848 but may also give further clues to the changing basis of electoral politics in many urban constituencies between the First and Second Reform Bills.

Evidence on electoral behaviour can be found in the poll books published after the two elections and in the breakdown of aggregate results into individual ballots (as in Table 4.3). This gives only a static picture. The support for a local party or candidate may have depended upon continuity in individual voting, but that was only one element behind electoral success. Candidates, local agents and organizations responded to two different types of electoral change. One was change, or possible change, in the behaviour of individual electors. Some voters always supported the same candidate or the same party, while others changed their vote between candidates and parties at successive elections. Still other electors might switch between voting and abstaining.

But the change in the composition of the electorate may be as important as change or stability in individual behaviour. The number voting in Lancaster increased from 990 in 1837 to 1,246 in 1848 while the electorate grew from 1,161 to 1,378. However the total change in the electorate was greater than is shown by the aggregate figures. The electorate was drawn from the wider population of the constituency and change was linked to the general demographic processes within that wider community – voters left the electorate through death, migration and disqualification, and new ones qualified.

The records of elections can be used to map these changes. The published poll books for 1847 and 1848 list the total electorate, both voters and non-voters. In addition to the vote they list other personal information such as occupation, place of residence for occupiers and address for freemen. Using this data, we can identify the electors from 1847 who were still qualified to vote seven months later.[18] After identifying the electors common to both elections we can define two other groups of electors: (a) those who were electors in 1847, but not in 1848, and (b) those who were electors in 1848, but not in 1847. The former are those who left the electorate after 1847, the latter the 'new' voters in 1848. Table 4.5 summarizes information on both of these two aspects of electoral change, the physical replacement of the electorate, and the behaviour of individual electors at both elections.

We know from the ballot totals that the pattern of voting along party lines changed in 1847; to help explain the result of the 1848 election we need to analyse how individual voting changed too. Table 4.5 shows the

Table 4.5 Voting at the Lancaster elections of 1847 and 1848[20]

		Vote in 1848				
		Stanley (Con)	Armstrong (Lib)	Non-voters	Exit	Total
Vote in 1847	Gregson (Lib)	9	199	21	21	250
	Greene (Con)	21	5	7	2	35
	Salisbury (Con)	157	4	7	14	182
	Gregson & Salisbury	57	34	9	9	109
	Greene & Salisbury	270	10	23	27	330
	Gregson and Greene	33	280	27	14	354
	Non-voters	19	10	24	27	80
	New voters	58	80	14	*	152
	Total	624	622	132	114	

Source: 1847 and 1848 Lancaster poll books.

behaviour of all voters over the two elections. Each cell in the table represents a particular pattern of voting in 1847 and 1848, with the row and column totals showing the number balloting for each possible combination of votes at the two elections. So, for example, 80 qualified electors did not vote in 1847; by 1848 some 27 of these had left the electorate, 19 then voted for the Tory candidate (Stanley), 10 for the Liberal (Armstrong) and 24 again did not vote. Similarly we can see that 21 electors voted for Greene (Conservative) in 1847 and Stanley (Conservative) in 1848; 4 voted for Salisbury (Protectionist/Conservative) in 1847 and Armstrong (Liberal) in 1848 and so on. Each row of the table corresponds to a different vote in 1847; the columns are the votes in 1848. The column headed 'Exit' consists of those voters who voted only in 1847 and the row of new voters those who voted only in 1848.[19]

There are some regularities in the overall pattern of change. Those who gave a plumper for either a Conservative or the Liberal candidate in 1847 tended to vote for the same party at the later election. Only 9 electors who supported Gregson (Liberal) in 1847 voted for the Conservative candidate in 1848. Against this 199 who 'plumped' for

Gregson in 1847 supported the Liberal, Armstrong, the following year. Similarly 178 of the 217 electors who gave a single Conservative vote in 1847 – 21 for Greene and 157 for Salisbury – supported Stanley (Conservative) in 1848; only 9 Tory plumpers switched to the Liberal. These figures confirm the existence of a substantial level of partisan loyalty even in the confusing circumstances of 1847–48. This is reinforced by an analysis of the double votes. Despite their policy differences and separate campaigns there were some electors who voted for both Greene and Salisbury in 1847. They almost all voted for the Tory in 1848: 270 supported Stanley, only 10 voted for Armstrong.

Electors who split their votes across party lines in 1847 favoured the Liberal candidate at the next election, by 314 votes to 90 in aggregate. However there was a difference between those who voted for Gregson and Greene (the Peelite) and those who supported Gregson and Salisbury (the Protectionist). When they had only one vote, the first group was more Liberal than the second. The first group favoured Armstrong in 1848 by more than 8:1, the second group Stanley (the Conservative) by 8:5. Perhaps we should regard the first group as Liberals who gave their second vote to the (liberal) Conservative candidate Greene in 1847, whereas the other group were Tories who would not, or could not, sup-port a free trade Conservative.[21]

Further analysis shows other systematic differences. Most electors were Freemen but about twenty-eight per cent of the electorate were householders, and the voting of the two groups differed.[22] The house-holders who split their votes in 1847 supported the Liberal candidate in 1848 to a greater extent than the Freemen electors who had voted the same way. The figures are 108:10 Liberal: Conservative amongst house-holders; 206:80 Liberal: Conservative amongst freemen. The difference between the two groups may be a reflection of differences in their political independence and social position, and their relationship to socially or politically significant others. The report of the committee of inquiry after the 1847 election confirmed the existence of corruption and commented that 'treating was principally confined to the freemen' (Powell, Rodwell and Dew, 1853, p. 44).

The differences are even more marked between the two groups of voters who divided their votes across party lines in 1847. Freemen who gave a vote split between Gregson and Greene went on to support the Liberal candidate (Armstrong) by a margin of about 6:1 (179 votes to 30) while support for the Liberals from householders who had also split their votes was even more overwhelming – 101 votes to 3. There is a clear difference too amongst freeman voters. Those who supported

Gregson and Greene tended to vote for the Liberal in 1848. The freemen who voted across party lines, for Gregson and Salisbury, behaved differently – they voted for the Conservative candidate in 1848 by a margin of 2:1 (50 to 27).

This analysis goes some way to supporting the comment in the Gazette that Greene owed his re-election to 'personal regard' as it shows that he picked up the second vote of both Liberal and Conservative voters. But, before looking at the linkage between individual political behaviour and the community, we can map another important factor in the change between the elections of 1847 and 1848 – the turnover in the electorate. Table 4.5 showed that some voters left the electorate between the two elections and that 152 new electors were registered.

The analysis has focussed on those electors who voted in both 1847 and 1848, but the constant turnover, change and growth in the electorate reflected other changes in the borough. The steady increase in the electorate after 1832 came from local population growth, and from the constituency activity of local party agents in registering potential electors. Underlying economic growth also meant that more individuals in the enlarged population reached the property qualification threshold for an elector.[23]

Electoral change was the result both of the change in the physical composition of the electorate and in the electoral behaviour of individual voters. The poll book data can be used to analyse both the physical change in the electorate and to map the net balance between partisan support lost and gained. This shifting electoral balance was a major factor in constituency campaigning during the mid-nineteenth century, and one of the primary concerns of a local party agent. Hanham suggests that turnover in the electorate encouraged local organizations to try and register new voters to ensure continuing party support for candidates. Such registration groups are one important aspect of constituency electoral organization after 1832, as is the growing role for local election agents.[24] The annual decisions of the revising barrister affected the local balance of political forces, and could decide election outcomes in marginal seats. Election results were also influenced by persuading voters to change their vote but the partisan recruitment of new voters was probably as, or more, important in seats where political opinion was finely balanced.

The physical change in the composition of the Lancaster electorate between 1847 and 1848 is summarized in Figure 4.1 and this forms the background to the partisan change shown in Table 4.5. The data suggests that the Liberal advantage in the cohort of new voters was greater

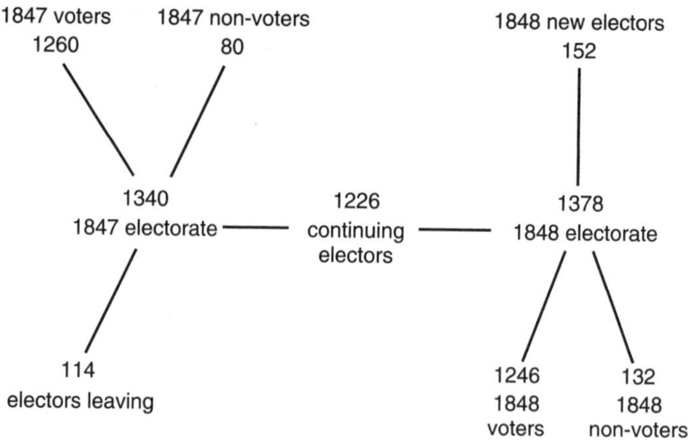

Figure 4.1   Electoral turnover in Lancaster 1847–48
Source: Lancaster poll books for 1847 and 1848.

than their majority in the official results: they won the election by 16 votes but gained 22 more new voters than did their Tory rivals. This advantage in recruitment may not have been the only reason for Liberal success, but it was certainly a significant factor behind Armstrong's victory at the poll.

A total of 114 voters left the electorate between the two elections, 8.5 per cent of the 1847 electorate. They were replaced by 152 new voters, 11 per cent of the 1848 voters. In the seven-month gap between the two elections the electorate grew by about 3 per cent. Turnout was high both amongst 'old' and 'new' voters and, contrary to newspaper reports, a majority of the new voters in 1848 were Liberals. The Tories lost ground in another way too – there were twice as many Tory voters leaving the electorate as there were Liberals. Both of these factors contributed to the Liberal win at the by-election, in addition to the pattern of stability and change in individual voting discussed earlier.[25]

This differential recruitment of new voters reflected organizational activity. Constituency organizers needed detailed local knowledge to recruit new political support, they needed to identify individuals who could pass the property qualification threshold, and who could be influenced to support their party or candidate. We can see how party support was created and maintained from a series of surviving contemporary electoral management notebooks. They show the structured nature of this activity, illustrate some of the procedures involved, and reveal the links between potential electors and the wider community. It is these structural and social factors that provided opportunities for local political organizers.

Of course constituency electoral management was not new, it had existed before reform. What was new after 1832, and even more so after the Registration Act of 1843, was the existence of regularly updated, public, contested, official records of the electorate – and with this annual record keeping came the growth of a group of individuals who specialized in the registration process itself. Initially this coincided with the extensive local political activity just after reform, and in many borough constituencies it was reinforced by the creation of a second level of local political activity after the Municipal Reform Act in 1835.[26]

The small size of the electorate in an urban constituency meant that it was possible for an election agent to know many of the voters personally. The partisan choice of an elector under open voting was public knowledge. His vote could be checked against any pre-election promise and he could be held to account for his actions by family, friends, neighbours, landlord or employer. All these factors – the size of the electorate, open voting, political competition at elections – contributed to the emergence of political organizations and political agents in the period after 1832. In Lancaster the activities of one agent, a 'Wm. Jackson', can be studied in detail.

V

Jackson's activities are recorded in a number of surviving notebooks. Some are manuscript, some printed in a standard format with individual manuscript entries. They provide a systematic record of three different electoral activities – assessing the extent of partisan support through canvassing, recruiting or building political support and maintaining this support.[27]

One notebook is a canvassing book for the St. Ann's ward in 1841 and shows an attempt to gauge the extent of electoral support. It lists individual voters together with personal comments. The format of the book follows that recommended by Cox and Grady, and other contemporary authorities on election campaigning.[28] Individual electors are listed by street, the entries giving details of their occupation and an indication of candidate preference, in many cases the compiler has added comments of a personal or social nature, see Table 4.6.

Table 4.6   Sample entries from a canvass book St. Ann's ward Lancaster 1841

Street	Name	Occupation	Promise	Comment
St Leonard's Gate	Handle, John	Labourer	A	At Thornton's; for Corn Law repeal
Brock Street	Marshall, James	–	A, G	Son of W. Marshall; employed by W. Ward
Brock Street	Raby, Thomas	Cabinet maker	G, M	Now railway; was employed by poor house
Gt. John Street	Parson, Chr.	Whitesmith	A	Admitted by Reform Association 1841
Plumb Street	Minden, Edward	Bookkeeper	A	Stewart* got place at excise
Friar Street	Pinson, Philip	Carpenter	no prom	Wife warm Liberal; he is influenced by Brock
Asylum	Shaw, James	Joiner	A	Shop Nicholas St. R. Simpson says Lib

Notes: A, G, M are the three candidates Armstrong, Greene and Martin. (*) Stewart was an MP for Lancaster 1832–37; unsuccessful candidate 1837.

Source: Ms canvass book, Lancaster 1841.

The systematic nature of the record keeping, the structure of the entries and the comments in the last column, all suggest that electors were identified in terms of social and economic criteria – that is by their work place, family ties or past favours performed by the MP. So James Marshall is listed as the son of W. Marshall and employed by W. Ward; Edward Minden got his job with the 'excise' through the help of Stewart (then the Liberal MP). The comment for Phillip Pinson is particularly interesting: 'wife warm Liberal' as it suggests the influence of a significant group of non-electors.[29]

Table 4.7 Sample entries from Mr Jackson's notebook

Name	Entry
John Wilcock	23 joiner, brother of Tho. Lib not taken up *July 15, 1844 at Hatch's paid
Rob Higgin	Skirton *at Dalston left district
Edward Cotton	Lancaster 2 Market St son Henry at Oxcliffe F. *is put on
Wm Ralph	Painter Bridge Lane now Skirton *left on list
Wm and John Newman	? if can be got on
John Live	Market Sq. relief

Whole page of entries of those 'struck off for relief' 1840–43

Name	Entry
Rd?	Penny St. Struck off rate unpaid
James Rhodes	Penny St. Claim disallowed 1842 as not then on rate *on new list
Joseph Burrow	Left Cheapside now Church St. Pays more than £10
Wm. Dickinson	App(lied) at ? will be admitted next lent. is ? on. son of Rob Dickenson – brother is at W. Dawson *gone to Liverpool
Bousfield	Slip Inn, James St. *Son thinks Tory *on
James Hall	2, Exhouses, Wyerdale. Farmer under D. Hamilton, Catholic *Got on *is on new list
(name illegible)	is not free
James Millany	Cheapside house and shop £18. Not long enough *t(ried?) but not admitted
James Hall	Overton Labourer with R. Barton farmer F(reeman) but not taken up W.J. thinks Lib. Father lives near Betham
Christopherson	Not of the two now on at Lowtray (?). Farmer Aldcliffe not yet admitted.
	Mr Stubs reports that there are no freemen in Clayton over Farleton
Enoch Arden	? Skirton 21 pays his mother 8/- per week for keep and the house. She has got relief when ill, he did not, Enoch then had no work *on

Names should be got on overseers list as well as Town Clerk's on or before 22nd July. Sometime after which the occupiers list goes to print, the list of freemen is not to be printed and alterations may be got in to 21st.

Name	Entry
Wm Greenhall	House and shop Tameside St (rental) £10 *arrears 14/2 fears he cannot pay *paid/on

Note: *indicates a later addition or entry; the text in brackets has been added to make sense of the entry.? indicates either an entry that is difficult to read, or the possible meaning of an abbreviation.

Source: Mr Jackson's notebook 1843–44.

Further evidence comes from a second notebook that gives a detailed record of attempts to qualify individuals as electors. Here the entries are chronological without any reference to street address. Once again the more detailed identification of potential supporters was a first step in recruiting electoral support. 'Jackson' attempted systematically to register potential voters and an outline of the procedures involved can be reconstructed from the notebook. It lists the claims of individuals to be 'on' (the electoral register) together with a later indication of the success of this claim. The period covered is 1843 to 1844. A sample of entries is given in Table 4.7.

The entries, like those from the earlier canvassing book, clearly indicate the importance of ties of kinship and similar links to the local community – Wm. Dickenson is the son of Rob Dickenson, his brother is at W. Dawson; Edward Cotton has a son Henry at Oxcliffe, and so on. The structure and content of entries show that the compiler was also concerned with keeping electors qualified when they moved within the constituency. Other entries note the need to use 'a friendly overseer', indicating the importance of individual political sympathies in this process.

These notebooks show that Jackson was concerned with two aspects of the electoral process: the registration of potential voters and their subsequent voting at an election. In practice these were not wholly distinct, a Liberal activist would be unlikely to expend much effort in trying to register potential Conservative voters – but note the query over 'Bousfield' in Table 4.7.

A third group of records combines these activities and reflects the growth of regular electoral management, further reinforcing the importance of links between the voter/elector and the wider community; these are records of the maintenance of political support.

The Lancaster constituency was divided into five districts or wards in the 1840's. Annual records of electors in each district appear to have been kept in separate notebooks. What has survived is data for some of the districts over the period between 1847–48 and 1851.[30] The format and content of each notebook is identical: electors are listed alphabetically by street with an individual entry covering two pages. The voter's name, occupation and number from the electoral register are entered on one page; on the second page there are three columns to record the vote in 1847 and additional columns headed L, T, and D to record the political tendency of new voters – Liberal, Tory or Doubtful. Electors who have voted previously have their vote recorded. (In the books covering 1847–48 there are columns headed Gregson, Greene and Salisbury.) As before additional space was left for personal comments.

Electors are listed by street address and an agent probably used the list to 'walk' the ward in a similar fashion to a census enumerator.[31] As in the other notebooks, the potential supporter was identified in social terms, and relevant comments are added against his name. The range of personal information recorded includes religious affiliation, employment or kinship ties – information that links the individual to the wider community, to an existing network of multiple social ties and to others with established political loyalties. Once an elector had been identified socially then these personal relationships could be used for communication and influence, to recruit the new elector as a supporter of a particular party or candidate, and to establish his political identity too.

The regular use of the notebooks is indicated by their standardized format and the subsequent addition and deletion of entries. The contents reflect the systematic activity used to assess and maintain partisan support in the 1840's, suggesting that the information was regularly revised and updated. The later books from 1850 or 1851 record the electoral information from the 1848 election in two additional printed columns headed by the initials or names of the candidates, Armstrong and Stanley. In these later books the new electors from 1847–48 have a voting record, their political identity has been established and no additional personal comments are either needed or given.

All of the notebooks appear to have belonged to a 'Wm. Jackson' whose name is in the front of several of them. This may be the same Wm. Jackson referred to in the Lancaster Guardian as canvassing with Gregson in 1847, and as defraying the expenses of Liberal electors in 1848. We may be able to deduce how this material was used, but who was Jackson? There is no mention of anyone of that name in the official report covering the 1847 and 1848 elections although Jackson was a fairly common name in Lancaster: 31 electors with this surname are listed in the 1847 poll book, 32 in 1848. Among this group there were nine William Jacksons. The occupations listed give no clue as to which of them was the compiler of this data and indeed he may not have been a Lancaster elector at all. In one of the books there is a comment stating that a voter was 'carried off by the Tories' which suggests that Wm. Jackson was probably a Liberal organizer.

But if we cannot say much about the individual, we can link the personal data in the notebooks to the printed poll books and explore the process of electoral recruitment and the mobilization of support for candidates. This reveals more about the links between electoral politics and the wider social context, shows the effectiveness of this 'electoral management' and confirms the importance of open voting through which information on the behaviour of individual electors was freely available.

If a party knew the level of its support at the most recent election, and had kept track of subsequent changes in the electorate, then it was possible to estimate the balance of political support for candidates, and to calculate the likely outcome of a forthcoming election. But information was never complete, nor completely accurate, some uncertainty always existed – voters might change their mind or conceal their real intentions. The evidence in Lancaster shows that the political identity of a small number of electors was not established unequivocally, and that even when it had been established an elector might give his support to another candidate or candidates, or even decide not to vote.

VI

What light does this detailed individual level data throw on the Lancaster election of 1848? By linking the data from the two poll books we analysed the behaviour of electors in 1847 and 1848, and identified the pattern of voting behaviour over time, see Table 4.5 and Figure 4.1. We have also found that the recruitment of new voters was an important way of gaining partisan advantage. By linking the new voters in 1848 to the entries in the relevant ward notebook for 1847–48, we can suggest how the process worked, how individual electors were identified, recruited and mobilized.

There are 152 new voters in 1848 distributed across all five electoral districts. The street address in the poll book locates 81 of them in the three districts for which we do have data: No.1 – Town Hall, No.4 – Girl's National School and No.5 – St. Thomas' School. Most of the electors can be traced in the relevant notebook, although there were two voters listed in the notebooks who could not be found in the poll books.[32] Table 4.8 gives details of these 81 voters by district; their vote at the 1848 election has been added from the poll book, and other additional recorded contextual evidence has been noted too.

What can we conclude from this mass of individual biographical data? First, that 'Mr. Jackson' was interested in noting and recording social data relating to new electors. Existing voters have little contextual data, just their vote from the previous election. For the new electors, and for those who have not voted before, the notebooks list the elector's occupation, address, kinship, employer, religion, whether he was a freeman, and other useful information. So, for example, Table 4.8 (a) shows that in the Town Hall Ward Nicholas Drinkall has left,

Table 4.8   New voters Lancaster 1848   (a) No 1 District (Town Hall)

Name	Address	Occupation	Political Affiliation	Vote 1848	Comments
Clarkson, John Jenkinson	Church St Queens Ward		Doubtful	NV	Surgeon; occupier
Drinkall, Nicholas	Church St Castle Ward		Liberal	T	Pike Inn, left occupier
Henderson, Adam	Church St Castle Ward	Shoemaker	Liberal	L	
Mason, Timothy	Church St St. Ann's Ward	Cabinet maker	Tory	T	Voted TT in 47
Manby Charles, Augustus	Church St	Land surveyor		T	[not traced]
Nicholson, James	Church St St. Ann's Ward	Flax dresser	Liberal	L	
Stables, William	Church St St. Ann's Ward		Liberal	L	Livery
Crawford, Robert	Cheapside		Tory	NV	occupier
Wearing, Stephen Wright	Cheapside	Shoemaker	Tory	T	Son of Richard also shoemaker, Cheapside voted TT in 47
Addison, John	St Nicholas St	Labourer	Liberal	L	Scavenger
Harrison, John Hadwen	St Nicholas St	Joiner	Tory	T	
Briscoe, Richard	Damside St	Spinner	Liberal	L	

Continued

Table 4.8 (a) Continued

Name	Address	Occupation	Political Affiliation	Vote 1848	Comments
Letherbarrow, John	Damside St	Stonemason	Liberal	L	Freeman
Scales, John	Damside St	Smith	Liberal	L	Voted LT in 47
Norman, Joseph	Moss Yd Damside St	Boatman	Liberal	L	is Norman, Robert
Barrow, John	Mason St	Draper	Liberal	T	Boatman not in 48. at Barrow's, now King St
Atkinson, Charles	Cable St	Gent	Liberal	NV	Drown'd
Hume, James	Cable St			L	[Not traced]
Lawson, John	Cable St	Land surveyor	Doubtful	NV	partner with McKie was with W. Lamb
Varley, Thomas	Cable St	Painter	Doubtful	T	to Vine St
Harrison, James	Bridgehouse	Whitesmith	Doubtful	T	
Shevson, William	Bridgehouse	Labourer	Liberal	L	Relief
Swain, Lawson Whalley	Bridgehouse		Liberal	L	Beershop
Dobson, Thomas	St George's Quay	Joiner	Tory	T	
Smart, William	St George's Quay			L	[Not traced]
Gregson, Mathew	St George's Quay	Smith	Liberal	L	Freeman, Pothouses

Table 4.8 New Voters Lancaster 1848   (b) No 4 District (Girl's National School)

Name	Address	Occupation	Political Affiliation	Vote 1848	Comments
Christopherson, John	Aldcliffe	Labourer	Liberal	T	Freeman
Armer, Thomas	Cockersham	Husbandman	Tory	T	Son of William
Whiteside, John Snr	Forton	Tailor	Liberal	L	
Whiteside, John Jnr	Forton	Tailor	Liberal	L	
Whiteside, Thomas	Forton	Tailor	Liberal	L	
Welch, Askey	Hay Carr, Ellel	Labourer	Liberal	T	Freeman, illegitimate child
Welch, Richard	Bay Horse, Ellel	Labourer	Liberal	L	
Bleasdale, William	Penny St Queen's Ward	Plasterer	Liberal	L	To China Lane
Fletcher, Joseph	Penny St Ann's Ward	Cabinet maker	Tory	T	
Hovitt, Thomas Jnr.	Penny St Ann's Ward	Surgeon		NV	Now Queen Square; occupier
Kelsall, William	Penny St Queen's Ward	Spirit merchant	Tory	T	occupier
Leeming, Thomas	Penny St Queen's Ward	Printer	Liberal	L	Catholic
Mackerell, Thomas	Penny St St Ann's Ward	Twine spinner		NV	Can't find, no such person
Nicholson, Timothy Jackson	Penny St St Ann's Ward	Cabinet maker	Liberal	L	Freeman

Continued

Table 4.8 (b) Continued

Name	Address	Occupation	Political Affiliation	Vote 1848	Comments
Row, Thomas Bennison	Penny St Queen's Ward	Currier	Liberal	L	
Thompson, Richard	Penny St Queen's Ward		Liberal	L	J. Headdy; hind. occupier
Wilkinson, William	Penny St Queen's Ward		Liberal	L	occupier
Taylor, Miles	Henry St	Labourer	Liberal	L	Freeman
Townley, James	Henry St	Labourer	Liberal	L	
Cleminson, John	Queen St	Whitesmith	Liberal	L	Freeman
Procter, Richard	Queen St	Railway clerk	Liberal	NV	No such person
Procter, Thomas	Queen St	Canal agent	Liberal	L	
Hall, Thomas	Brock St	Chairmaker	Liberal	T	
Pearson, Thomas	Mary St	Mechanic	Liberal	L	
Sanderson, Christopher	Mary St	Smith	Liberal	L	
Bond, Thomas	New Road	Keeper	Tory	T	At Castle; occupier

Table 4.8   New voters, Lancaster 1848   (c) No 5 District St. Thomas School

Name	Address	Occupation	Political Affiliation	Vote 1848	Comments
Battersby, John Jnr	Moor Lane	Cabinet maker	Liberal	T	To J Kirton; 3 others of same name and occupation in Moor Lane. All voted LC
Capstick, John	Moor Lane	Printer	Tory	T	
Hoyle, William	Moor Lane	Upholsterer	Tory	T	
Hudson, William W.	Moor Lane	Painter	Liberal	L	
Shrigley, James	Moor Lane	Cabinet maker	Liberal	L	
Townson, James	Moor Lane	Cabinet maker	Doubtful	L	
Harrison, Thomas	Bath St		Liberal	L	Gent; occupier
Cragg, John	Golgotha	Labourer	Liberal	T	
Shaw, George Lawson	Asylum	Joiner	Liberal	L	To Russell St
Willacy, Henry	Barn Close	Mechanic	Liberal	L	Freeman
Smith, Thomas	Dalton Sq	Servant	Liberal	L	At Mrs Thompson's; to Poulton
Smith, Nicholas	Dalton Sq		Liberal	L	Butcher, Thomas St; to Martin St. occupier
Bradley, William	Thornham St		Liberal	T	

Continued

Table 4.8 (c) Continued

Name	Address	Occupation	Political Affiliation	Vote 1848	Comments
Seal, Thomas	Thornham St		Liberal	L	Railway Clerk
Blackburn, John	Cage St		Tory	NV	Draper
Roper, William	Gt John St	Tobacco manufacturer	Tory	T	
Armson, Thomas	Friar St		Doubtful	L	Rev
Jackson, Henry Coupland	Buck St	Carder	Liberal	L	Freeman;2 other Jacksons also carders in Buck St. both voted LC in 47
Palmer, William	Bulk St	Labourer	Liberal	L	Freeman
Dean, Robert	Monmouth St	Weaver	Liberal	T	
Dawson, William	George St		Liberal	L	Doorkeeper; S & B's; dead
Boardley, William	Marton St	Woolcomber		L	Freeman; to Dolphin Lane
Ellithorn, Abram Henry	St Leonard's Gt St Ann's ward	Railway clerk	Liberal	L	Drown'd
Jenkinson, Richard	St Leonard's Gt St Ann's ward		Liberal	L	Surveyor; occupier
Smith, Joseph	St Leonard's Gt St Ann's ward	Tailor	Liberal	L	
Ireland, Martin	Bulk		Liberal	L	Dunn & Co; occupier

Continued

Table 4.8 (c) Continued

Name	Address	Occupation	Political Affiliation	Vote 1848	Comments
Gregson, Bryan Pagett	Caton	Gent	Liberal	L	
Marshall, Lawrence	Caton	Labourer	Tory	L	Near Holton
Proctor, James	Caton	Smith	Liberal	L	Freeman

Source: Ms Ward notebooks Districts 1, 4 and 5 1847–48; Lancaster 1848 poll book.

Charles Atkinson has drown'd, William Shevson is on relief; all politically relevant information as none of these would now be eligible to vote. In District No.4, Table 4.8 (b), Askey Welch, a freeman, is noted as having an illegitimate child; Thomas Leeming is a Catholic and Thomas Armer is the son of William Armer; again this is all potentially useful information. In the St. Thomas School district, Table 4.8 (c), Abram Henry Ellithorn is recorded as a railway clerk, Martin Ireland is at 'Dunn and Co.' and William Dawson was a doorkeeper at 'S and B's' but is now dead. Such employment information helped to locate individuals within the wider Lancaster community and, in stressing the links to those with an established social and political identity, the information may also have suggested an identity for the new electors.

A definition in social terms was an important step towards establishing a political identity. Political organizers were keen to discover an elector's 'effective social identity' (Moore, 1974, p. 114), they needed to identify the network or group to which an elector belonged. Once this had been done, they could try to translate the social identity into a political identity and electoral support. Within a small community, knowledge about an elector's employer, kin or those with whom he worshipped, could be used to try and influence political choice, indeed it was probably assumed that these factors reflected his political loyalties. None of this was necessarily improper, and the use of social links for political purposes in Lancaster in the 1840s has many similarities with modern techniques for communicating with, targeting and persuading, individual voters.[33] Both the mass of contemporary comment, and the social circumstances of the time, suggest that social ties of any kind could also be used as a channel for 'improper' influence, although the distinction between 'legitimate' and 'illegitimate' influence was a fine one. Contemporary evidence provides examples of employers and landlords coercing or threatening employees and tenants, and networks of relationships could be manipulated by monetary and other means.[34] What is of interest here is the systematic nature of this local party activity, and the organizational consequences that followed from the linkage of an individual to the social context of electoral activity.

If the institutional structure and social context in Lancaster provided information to Wm. Jackson through which he could try to establish the political identity of electors, then he was unsuccessful in only in a very few cases. There are six electors given as 'Doubtful' in Table 4.8, some 7.5 per cent of the new voters. Some of these 'doubtful' entries had no established social identity, others were politically doubtful, some lacked both, but only two of these six new electors failed to vote in 1848. For most electors an identity was established, a political role was defined and the new voter could be added to a known body of political/ electoral support. The systematic keeping of records over a period of years suggests both the continuous use of social and political information, a link to the cycle of change within the constituency, as well as a belief in its effectiveness.

The political affiliation established in this way was not a completely accurate predictor of voting behaviour, and the information from 1847–48 became less accurate over time. Individuals changed their opinions, they might allow personal preference for a particular candidate to influence their vote, or they could become subject to different and competing social influences through a change in employment or residence. In 1848, 13 of the 81 electors, 16 per cent, voted in a way that differed from that recorded by 'Mr Jackson', a comparable level of accuracy to canvassing in other constituencies.[35] Fifty of these new voters from 1848 were still electors in 1852. Some 18 electors (36 per cent) gave a vote at that election for a candidate of a different party to the one they had supported in 1848 – a higher level of individual electoral change than is found in other constituencies.

Perhaps the number of 'floating' voters in Lancaster was a result of the corruption to which Dod refers, and that was the subject of the parliamentary enquiry in 1847. But it may also reflect the rapidly changing nature of the social environment and genuine changes in political opinion or personal circumstances. However by 1865 electoral abuse was sufficiently widespread for the report of the Royal Commission to comment on the long history of such behaviour, and recommend the disenfranchisement of the constituency.

VII

Although not conclusive, this qualitative evidence suggests that in the mid-1840s, political recruitment and electoral management in Lancaster depended upon establishing social ties between new electors and existing social networks. It also suggests the importance of activists and organization in mapping and managing electoral support, as well as the systematic use of individual information, and the structure of social relationships, to build and maintain it. If Wm. Jackson used the connections between social context and electoral behaviour to help the local Liberal party and Liberal candidates, then his Tory equivalent, of whom we have no record, probably operated in much the same way.

The analysis has wider implications. Similar conditions for registration and political campaigning existed in many constituencies, particularly in the smaller borough seats. The lack of electoral secrecy was general, and all constituencies had an annual registration that produced a regular, updated record of electors. Although the local social conditions may have varied, the register was open to similar investigation, mapping and use for electoral purposes in all borough constituencies. The size of the electorate and the balance of support for differing political tendencies varied but it was probably everywhere assumed that social ties influenced or determined an elector's political choice. So in many constituencies it would have been possible for an agent to calculate the level of political support for a particular party or candidate, over both the short and long terms, in a similar manner.

This was an environment in which the size and composition of the electorate changed through political and demographic processes. If a local party was to win or retain a seat then the nature of change implied that recruiting new supporters was a constant process, organizing the electorate was a continuing activity. After 1832 this created opportunities for political agents and organizers to operate in other constituencies like 'Mr. Jackson'. In Lancaster we have analysed electoral change only in the short term in the mid-1840's. In the next chapter we examine the implications of the same processes for electoral behaviour and local political organizations in the longer term, over the whole period between the First and Second Reform Bills.

5
Electoral Change in Bedford 1832–68

The shifting fortunes of candidates and parties in Lancaster resulted from changes in individual behaviour and turnover in the electorate. Successive election results reflected stability and change in individual voting together with the effects of electoral demography. Both were linked to the underlying social context, and so electoral change was linked to it too.

These changes in electoral behaviour, and in the electorate, had implications for local agents, constituency organizations and the conduct of election campaigns. Parties needed to retain the support of electors who had voted for them at the previous election, and to recruit new voters to replace those who had left the electorate. The evidence in Lancaster suggested that new electors were identified in social terms and that there was a connection between such links and electoral behaviour – if you could identify someone socially then you had identified them politically as well.

That analysis was for two elections only but the underlying processes occurred in all constituencies and resemble patterns identified elsewhere and by others. Extending the analysis to a series of elections outlines the long-term consequences of change and reinforces the importance of electoral turnover under partial enfranchisement between the First and Second Reform Bills – and the partisan effects that flowed from it. The shifting pattern of support and party advantage had consequences for local political organizers and for political campaigning.

To examine the processes in detail we need to disaggregate the constituency electorate into sets of voters by the date of their first potential vote (or non-vote). At any election, the electorate is composed of electors who are qualified for the first time, those for a second time, a third time and so on. Each of these groups of electors is a separate cohort, and we can refer to those first entering the electorate for any election at time (t) as C(t). The cohort at the next election (t +1) will be C(t + 1), those at the election after that C(t + 2), etc.[1] Similarly the cohorts of new voters at the previous elections are C(t – 1), C(t – 2) etc. The total electorate at any time (t) is made up of the new voters, C(t), together with those remaining from previous cohorts – it is a set of cohorts, the total electorate being the sum of C(t) + C(t – 1) + C(t – 2) + C(t – 3)…+ C (t–n), see Figure 5.1.

As in Lancaster, the electorate changes as voters leave and new electors are added to the register. The number of electors remaining in a cohort decreases over time as individuals leave the electorate and the cohort decays, it decreases in size as it loses members. The process of cohort decay, and the recruitment of new cohorts, results in turnover in the electorate. However the total aggregate electorate may remain roughly constant as a new cohort at any time (t + 1), (t + 2), (t + 3) etc. may replace the total

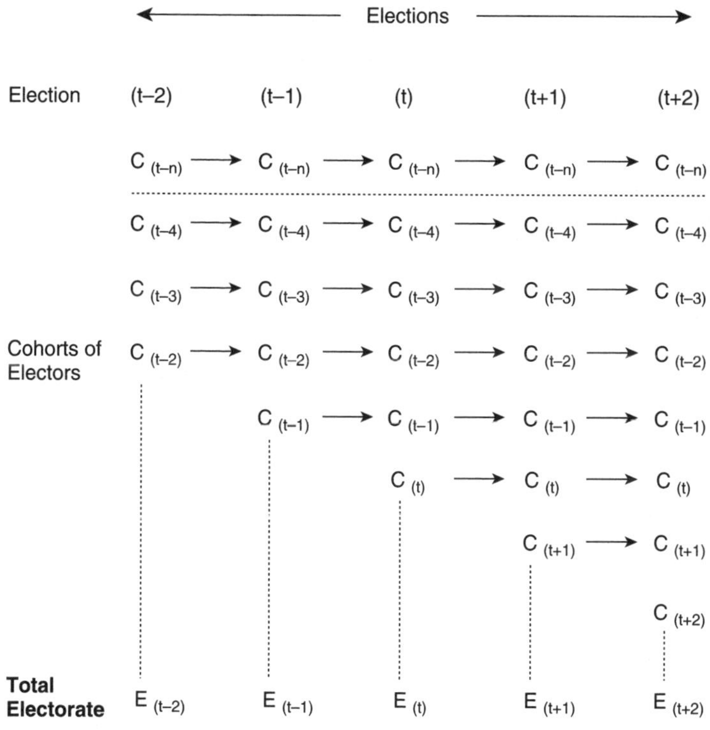

Figure 5.1   The composition of the electorate in cohorts

number leaving from all previous cohorts. But whether the electorate increases in size, decreases or remains the same, will depend on the balance between the number of electors leaving and the number of new electors added. By separating the electorate into cohorts we can map the overall turnover in electors, follow changes in the composition and behaviour of each cohort over time, and identify differences between cohorts.

I

A party agent trying to estimate the level of support for a candidate could divide electors into four groups: those who had voted for 'his' candidate or party at the last election and would do so again; those who had voted for the opposition at the last election and would do so again; those electors who had not voted; and those whose vote was uncertain. The recruitment of electoral support involved the qualification of new voters, the partisan recruitment of voters who had previously voted for other candidates and the politicization and mobilization of electors who had not voted before. Behind the aggregate change in the electorate, and in electoral behaviour, we can identify four distinct processes, two associated with continuing political or party support, and two with changes in the voting behaviour of individual electors.

1. *Recruitment*: A party gained electoral advantage by qualifying more new supporters than the opposition. At the Lancaster election of 1848 more new voters supported the Liberal candidate rather than the Tory (see Table 4.5). If one party had a continuing advantage in recruiting new voters over time, this could change the political complexion of a constituency – it might start as finely balanced electorally and evolve into a safe seat for one or the other of the parties.
2. *Defection*: A small number of voters changed their vote at successive elections and one party might benefit differentially from such changes. Amongst those who voted at the Lancaster election of 1847, the number of Conservative voters who subsequently voted Liberal in 1848 was larger than the number of Liberals who voted Tory.
3. *Differential participation*: Electors could register disapproval for a party or candidate by not voting as well as by changing their partisan choice. In Cambridge at the 1841 election 1,430 electors voted; in 1852, 1,546 did so, but in 1847 only 1,205 voted, and there were 300 non-voters. This was a much higher level of non-voting than was usual at Cambridge elections in this period. A total of 71 per cent of the non-voters in 1847 were previously consistent

Conservative voters; only 22 per cent were previously consistent Liberals. If they were still in the electorate in 1852, most of the 1847 non-voters voted for their 'usual' party at the next general election. The withdrawal of support in 1847 was a temporary expression of political disaffection. The large number of Conservative voters within this group of non-voters suggests that it may have been the policy position of the Conservative candidate over the Corn Laws that was the major reason for their action.[2]

4. *Critical issues*: External events could influence electors to change their vote. Mitchell and Cornford identified 114 Conservative voters in Cambridge whose voting behaviour changed during the period 1832–52. More than half of them did so in 1847, following the crisis in the parliamentary Tory party over the Corn Laws. Similar behaviour occurred in other constituencies. The Canterbury poll book for the 1847 election notes:

> the extraordinary change of principle manifested by certain electors... [who]... at the election of 1841, and on previous occasions, enrolled on the Conservative side; some from a new light having broken in upon them – others for pique, envy, jealousy, or malice – have cast their consistency overboard, and aided Whigs, and men of no principle at all to usurp the representation. (Canterbury poll book for 1847, p. 36)

Important national issues had an effect at the constituency level and could influence both those who had voted before and the new cohort of voters.

These four processes define the major electoral activities of local party organizations – the mobilization of 'your' supporters and the need to make sure they go to the poll and vote, and the de-mobilizing of your opponents, sometimes even physically preventing them from voting; registering 'your' new supporters, and trying to disqualify potential new supporters of your opponent; trying to change an elector's vote through 'influence' or other means; and manipulating political issues to partisan advantage.

The balance between recruiting new voters and seeking to change the vote of existing electors depended upon constituency circumstances. It was possible to estimate the effect of the physical change in the electorate but there was always some uncertainty about the behaviour of new voters, and to a lesser extent that of previous supporters too. At the Lancaster election in 1848 the new voters for the two parties out-numbered those who changed their vote between the Liberal and Tory candidates; there were 138 new partisan electors in 1848 but only 28 party voters changed their partisan behaviour between 1847 and 1848 (see Table 4.5).

Disaggregating a constituency electorate into cohorts helps to identify the relative importance of each of these four processes, and extends the analysis of short-term change over a longer period. Longitudinal data provides both information about individual voting over time and a more detailed picture of long-term electoral change. It outlines the structure of constraints and opportunities for those organizing electoral support – election agents and parliamentary candidates – and reinforces the previous arguments made in Lancaster about the origins of local party organization.

II

Bedford, a two-member borough, was contested at all ten general elections between 1832 and 1868. Before the First Reform Bill it had been a patron borough but this was no longer the case after 1832. Dod comments that 'the Duke of Bedford can usually return one member, and the Whitbread family have had much influence, but the interest of both has materially declined'. The population of about seven thousand was 'engaged in the corn and timber trades, in lace, shoe and straw-plait making' (Dod, 1853, p. 19). It was a relatively small market and county town and, while the population grew steadily between 1831 and 1871, the size of the electorate was roughly constant for much of the period, although it doubled after the Second Reform Bill, see Table. 5.1.

Table 5.1 Population and electorate in Bedford 1832–68

Year	Population	Year	Electorate
1831	6,959	1832	1,029[a]
1851	11,693	1852	870
1861	13,143	1865	1,049
1871	16,850	1868	2,124

Note: (a) The figure for the electorate in 1832 is an estimate.

Source: Population – McCalmont (1971); Electorate – Bedford Poll Books.

It is an example of the type of constituency that Vincent sees as the central element of the electoral system in this period: a 'medium sized…market, county or cathedral town…' (Vincent, 1967, p. 4). However it is less typical in being contested at all ten elections between 1832 and 1868, other boroughs of its size did not have such a continuous pattern of contestation. Politically the representation of Bedford's two seats changed from Liberal to Conservative to Liberal again between 1832 and 1868, see Table 5.2.

In Bedford, as in some other constituencies, the Tories recovered soon after Reform. In 1835 they gained one seat and both at the next election in 1837. One of the seats was lost in 1847 but it was not until 1857 that the Liberals again won both seats.

This Liberal dominance was brief, in 1859 and 1865 the representation was divided between the parties. The Second Reform Act doubled the size of the electorate and the Liberals won both seats by a comfortable margin in 1868. Except for this last election, all the contests were close. However when two candidates were standing from the same 'party', the second candidate sometimes received many fewer votes than his running mate. In 1852 the second Liberal candidate received less than half the number of votes of his party colleague, as did the second Tory in 1857. Clearly the pattern of individual voting was more complex than the aggregate figures suggest.

Table 5.2   Bedford election results 1832–68

1832		1835		1837		1841		1847	
L_1	599	T	490	T_1	467	T_1	433	L	453
L_2	486	L_1	403	T_2	419	T_2	421	T_1	432
T	483	L_2	383	L	412	L	410	T_2	392

1852		1857		1859		1865		1868	
T	535	L_1	452	L_1	455	L_1	574	L_1	1311
L_1	514	L_2	435	T_1	449	T	476	L_2	1242
L_2	252	T_1	375	T_2	427	L_2	345	T_1	769
		T_2	179	L_2	427			T_2	491

Source: McCalmont (1971).[3]

But were these fluctuations in voting caused by changes in individual behaviour, by changes in the electorate or by a combination of the two? The linkage of successive pairs of poll books identifies the separate cohorts of Bedford voters at the elections between 1832 and 1868. The resulting data on voting and electoral change can be used to help answer these questions, and the collective biography of the electorate shows the relative importance of the two processes of electoral change in determining election outcomes.[4] Similar changes in electoral support occurred in all constituencies, and had similar consequences for party agents and local organizers – particularly in the smaller and more contested English, urban seats.[5] So this analysis is of wider relevance, and illustrates the general effects of continuous change in constituency electorates over the period; it makes possible a detailed analysis of the interaction between electoral turnover and the changes in individual behaviour that lay behind election results in Bedford between the First and Second Reform Bills.

III

The Bedford poll books are the source for this longitudinal data. These usually list both voters and non-voters at each election, together with their occupation and vote.[6] By linking poll books for two successive elections, we can partition the total electorate at the two elections into three disjoint sub-sets – those electors common to the electorate for both elections, those who left after the first election, and the cohort of new voters at the second election. We can then analyse the electoral behaviour of each group separately.[7] By extending the linkage process to the series of poll books, the total electorate over the period 1832–68 can be disaggregated into ten cohorts of voters – those who were electors in 1832 and the new voters at each subsequent election from 1835 onwards.[8] Changes in the composition of the separate cohorts reflect the demographic changes in Bedford between 1832 and 1868, and the aggregate of the changes in all cohorts gives the total change between elections. This changing physical composition of the electorate forms the background to the activity of the two parties and is summarized in Figure 5.2.

Figure 5.2 shows that in 1832 there were 961 electors in Bedford and 857 electors at the next election in 1835; 90 of the electors in 1835 were new voters, 10.5 per cent of the electorate; the remaining 767 had also been electors in 1832. Some seven hundred and sixty two members of the 1835 electorate were still voters in 1837, and so on. The balance

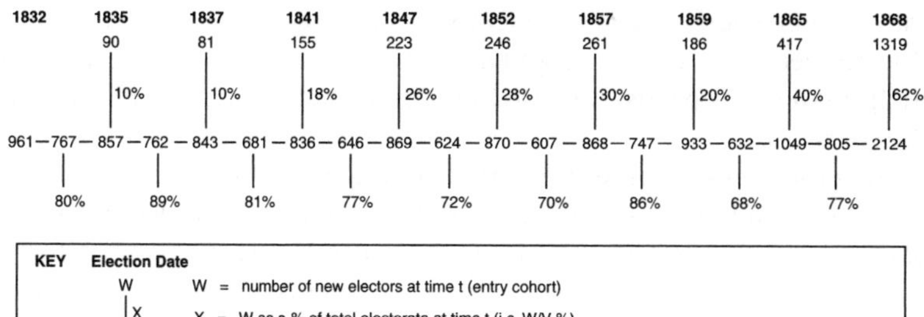

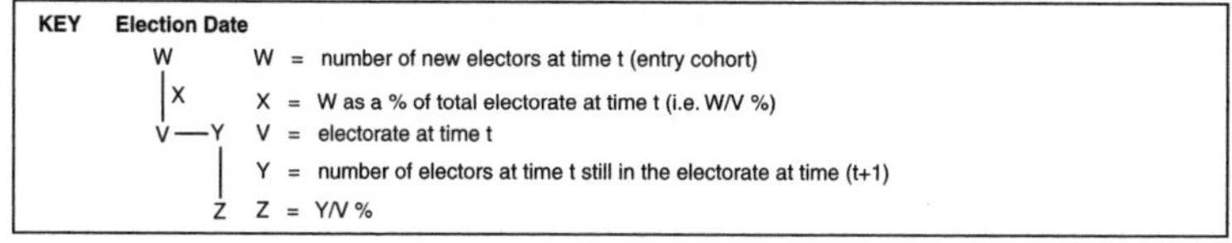

Figure 5.2   Electoral turnover in Bedford 1832–68[9]

between new and continuing electors varied over time. The total number of electors decreased between 1832 and 1835, remained roughly constant from 1835 to 1857, and then increased again until 1865. The Second Reform Act in 1867 more than doubled the size of the electorate. The appearance of little or no aggregate change is deceptive; there was continuous turnover, a regular pattern of electoral change and renewal.

The contribution of each new cohort to the total electorate varied, from 1 in 10 electors in 1835 and 1837, to 2 out of 5 in 1865, and 3 out of 5 in 1868. Until 1868 a majority of the electorate at any one election went on to vote at the next election, when they also usually formed a majority of the electors. This changed after the Second Reform Bill – new voters made up 62 per cent of the electorate in 1868. Between 1832 and 1868 the turnover in the Bedford electorate was higher than that found in the United Kingdom electorate today. This higher nineteenth century figure is a reflection of effects of partial enfranchisement and demographic change, together with mobility between constituencies and mortality within the constituency.[10]

What was the partisan impact of this continuous change? To some extent this depends on the nature of voting behaviour itself. If electoral preference did not change after initial partisan commitment, then the implications for party agents and election management were clear. In a constituency like Bedford, where the opinions of electors were relatively evenly divided between the two parties, electoral success would depend upon recruiting new voters and retaining the loyalty of those already in the electorate.[11] If voting was closely linked to social factors, then it may have been easier to recruit new electors than to persuade continuing electors to change their vote from election to election – although given the fine balance of electoral forces such changes in partisan behaviour could have made a difference at the margins.

The processes that gave rise to this demographically related change – death and migration – are continuous and relatively independent of political activity, so some of the variation in the size of new cohorts may result from the variation in the time period between successive general elections. If we look at the change in the electorate over time, we find that the rates of electoral recruitment and decay fluctuate within relatively narrow limits, see Table 5.3.

The 'recruitment' at any time (t) refers to the number of new electors who have joined the electorate between that election (t) and the proceeding one (t–1). 'Decay' is the number of electors who leave the electorate between the election (t) and the next election (t+1). In both cases the time period between elections is measured in months. So, on average, 8.1 electors per month left the electorate between 1832 and 1835, and new electors were added at the rate of 3.7 electors per month over the same period.

Unfortunately, we do not know the actual pattern of demographic change in the Bedford population at this time and so we cannot estimate the contribution that changes in the underlying community made to the processes summarized in Table 5.3. Although some of the turnover resulted from population change, part of the variation was caused by the partisan activity surrounding the annual registration process. Such activity could increase both the underlying rate of recruitment – by registering more voters – and the rate of decay, by increasing the number of successful objections to other electors, the difference between recruitment and decay determining the net change in the total electorate.

As in Lancaster, recruitment was the process by which electors became absorbed into political networks. How did this happen? Some potential electors may have served a 'political apprenticeship' before getting on to the register, possibly building up a stock of 'political capital' and

Table 5.3   Recruitment and decay in the Bedford electorate 1832–68

Year	1832	1835	1837	1841	1847	1852	1857	1859	1865	1868
Recruitment		3.7	3.9	3.3	3.0	5.0	5.8	7.4	5.6	33.0
Decay	8.1	4.5	3.4	2.6	5.0	5.8	4.8	4.0	6.1	

Source: Bedford poll books; canvass book for 1835.

establishing their 'soundness' before local party activists would allow their name to go forward for registration. Theoretically an individual could vote at 21, but how old was an elector when he first voted? After 1835 did he first have to qualify as a municipal elector and only later become a parliamentary elector? What was the connection between the two levels of electoral activity? At present we have little or no information on the overlap, if any, between the municipal and parliamentary electorates and no answer to these questions.[12] However, even without it we can say more about the pattern of demographic change amongst Bedford voters and its electoral consequences.

Electors left the register through death, migration or disqualification. The disqualification of electors is sometimes noted in the poll books, but evidence is not available on a systematic basis. Migration is also an extremely difficult problem and cannot be treated systematically either.[13] So for a more detailed analysis of electoral demography we will assume that death was the most important reason an elector left the Bedford electorate in this period. This allows us to analyse regularities in the pattern of change summarized in Figure 5.3.

Record linkage generates a life history of the electorate both individually and collectively. From the linked data we can follow individual behaviour from election to election and the change in the cohorts of voters into which the electorate has been partitioned. The changes for all the cohorts between 1832 and 1868 are summarized in Table 5.4. The row entries of the table show the initial number of electors in each

Table 5.4   Electoral cohorts in Bedford 1832–68

	1832	1835	1837	1841	1847	1852	1857	1859	1865	1868
1832	961	767	689	568	446	342	253	225	141	104
1835		90	73	57	45	31	23	20	13	10
1837			81	56	42	35	26	24	19	12
1841				155	113	81	64	57	49	42
1847					223	135	97	87	67	59
1852						246	144	128	94	77
1857							261	206	140	116
1859								186	109	84
1865									417	301
1868										1,319
Total	961	857	843	836	869	870	868	933	1,049	2,124

Source: Linked Bedford poll books, 1835 canvass book.

cohort, the column entries the numbers remaining at each subsequent election; the sum of a column gives the number of potential voters at each election, the total electorate at that time.

From Table 5.4, we can see that the 1847 cohort contained 223 electors; of these 135 were still electors in 1852, 97 remained in 1857, 87 in 1859 and so on. There were 870 electors in 1852; 135 first entered the electorate in 1847, 81 in 1841, 35 in 1837 etc. Since each cohort enters the electorate at a different time, it is a different political 'generation'. As a result, the electoral behaviour of each cohort could differ as it may have been shaped initially by different formative political events and issues with each cohort being socialized into a different political environment. The 1832 cohort was probably most influenced by events surrounding Reform, while the new electors in 1847 might be more concerned with the Repeal of the Corn Laws or the Maynooth controversy. Table 5.4 shows that the largest group was the 'Reform Generation' of 1832 (apart from those who qualified as electors in 1867).[14] This group dominated the Bedford electorate after 1832 and for much of the 1840s. It still formed over half of the electorate in 1847 but by 1852 its numerical dominance had declined. No other group is as important until the Second Reform Act when the cohort of new electors made up over two-thirds of the electorate at the 1868 election.

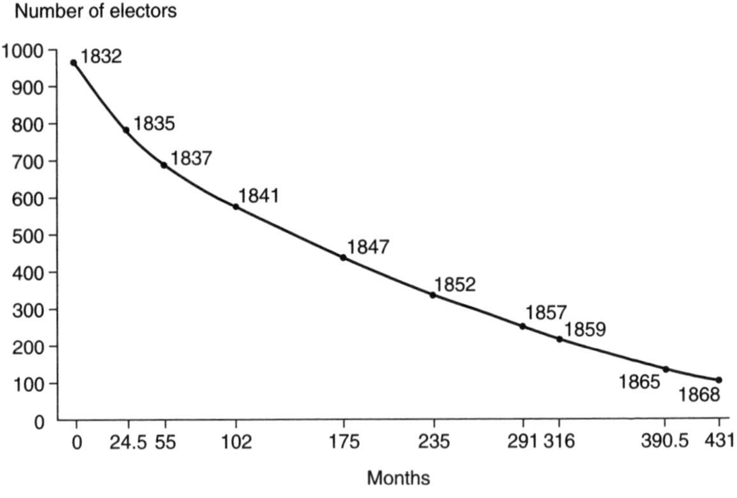

Figure 5.3   Electoral decay – the 1832 cohort of Bedford electors

The changing numbers in the 1832 cohort over time are shown in Figure 5.3; the other cohorts exhibit a similar pattern of change and decay.

Assuming that the decay is continuous and exponential, the data can be used to estimate how long individuals continued as electors in Bedford in the mid-nineteenth century, and the summary statistics for all the cohorts between 1832 and 1857 are given in Table 5.5. The data suggests that all the cohorts of Bedford electors changed at roughly the same rate. The 1835 cohort had a half-life of 10.4 years: that is after 10 years and 4 months we would expect half of the 90 electors in this cohort to have left the electorate; by the end of a further 10 years and 4 months, a half of these surviving electors should have left, and so on. The half-life of all the cohorts between 1832 and 1857 varies little with a mean value of 11 years and 2 months. (Only the 1841 cohort is significantly different.[15]) Overall the figures reinforce the impression of stability in electoral politics in Bedford, at least in terms of the regularity of the physical change in the electorate.[16]

Disqualification and migration contributed to cohort decay. Such processes affected living electors. If more individuals left or were disqualified this would *increase* the apparent rate of decay resulting from mortality alone. Unfortunately the separate effects of these processes cannot be estimated independently. No records of the annual decisions of the revising barristers were kept and although incomplete records sometimes appear in local papers, these reports are usually coloured by the political inclinations of the paper concerned.[17] Partisan activity

Table 5.5   Cohort half-life in the Bedford Electorate 1832–57

	Half-life	
Cohort	Months	Years
1832	136	11 years 4 months
1835	124	10 years 4 months
1837	141	11 years 9 months
1841	161	13 years 5 months
1847	128	10 years 8 months
1852	122	10 years 2 months
1857	124	10 years 4 months

Source: Table 5.4.

should increase both the number of electors disqualified and the number put on the register, so increasing both electoral turnover and the rate of cohort decay. However while the individual effect of such processes may be unknown, the collective picture is still of a constituency with a constant and fairly regular turnover in the electorate.

A comparison of the change in the electorate with the election results shows just how important electoral turnover could be. With the exception of the 1857 election, the number of electors in each new cohort of electors was greater than the margin of votes between the successful second candidate and the unsuccessful third candidate. So it was always important to recruit new voters to try to influence the outcome of the next election. But at the same time success depended upon retaining support from the previous election. At the 1841 election there were 681 electors who had voted in 1837, some 81 per cent of them voted for the same 'party' at both elections. So the Bedford data, in particular the presence or absence of stability in voting behaviour over time, can be used to explore the nature of individual and collective choice, and their contribution to the electoral fortunes of parties and candidates. It can show whether the Bedford electors voted consistently for parties and candidates between 1832 and 1868.

IV

The battle over registration was one influence on the origin of local parties as constituency organizations were formed to recruit new electors and to maintain existing support, but what was the extent of partisan loyalty amongst the electors who voted at successive elections? Today we might classify an elector who voted for the same party at every election as a *strong* or a *consistent* party voter. One who occasionally voted for another party or abstained, but who supported one party more often than not, might be called a *weak* or inconsistent party voter. An elector, whose voting history showed no consistency and was characterized by frequent changes in partisan choice, could be called an *independent* voter.

This is straightforward when the elector has only one vote but in Bedford, as in other two-member seats in this period, the elector could use their two votes in a variety of ways. The only restriction was that they could not give both votes to the same candidate. Of course the voter need not use both votes and could choose to use only one vote, or not vote at all. This decision might be influenced by the number of candidates standing – there were not necessarily two candidates on both sides at every Bedford election. In fact most of the Bedford elections in this period were three-cornered contests where two candidates from one party faced a single candidate from the other party, see Table 5.2. In this situation the voter who normally supported the party that was putting up only one candidate was faced with a dilemma: what should he do with his second vote?

Suppose that there were three candidates standing and that there were two Tory candidates – T_1 and T_2 – and only one Liberal – L. Then four of the six possible votes (T_1, T_2, T_1T_2 and L) are for candidates of one party only – and are consistent with party voting or partisan loyalty. The other two available votes – LT_1 and LT_2 – are split between candidates of the two parties. When there were four candidates, two from each party, there were six possible 'party' votes and four possible split votes.[18] The variation in the number of candidates, and in the possible individual votes, makes the analysis of voting behaviour between successive elections in two-member seats more complex than it is for single member constituencies. Only at the elections in 1857, 1859 and 1868 were there four candidates in Bedford, two from each party. On all the other occasions two candidates from one party were opposed by one candidate from the other and this gave rise to strategic possibilities for both voters and parties.[19]

How are we to categorize voting behaviour under these conditions? Consider an elector who gives a double vote for the two Conservative candidates when that was possible, but a split vote between a Conservative and a Liberal candidate when there was only one Conservative standing. Is such a voter an independent voter because he voted for candidates from both parties? Or a weak Conservative because he voted for a Liberal candidate on at least one occasion? Or indeed a strong Conservative as he always gave the maximum possible number of votes to a Tory? If we take non-voting into account, the problems of classification become even more difficult.

The multiple vote was used by some electors at the Lancaster election of 1847 to differentiate between candidates who were both (nominally) Conservatives, to express a degree of approval or disapproval over policies or candidates. At some Bedford elections, even when there were two candidates for each party, a number of electors gave only a single vote for one candidate. Does this behaviour imply anything about the strength of partisan commitment? Does it imply a judgement by the elector on the relative merits of the two candidates of a party?[20]

In the absence of other information, the following categorization has been used for the analysis of long-term voting behaviour in Bedford: a *party* voter is a Conservative (or Liberal) elector who gives his initial vote, or votes, for a Conservative (or Liberal) candidate or candidates. He may give only a single vote when two candidates of the same party are standing; he may refrain from voting on one or more subsequent occasion; he may give a double vote split between candidates from the two parties when there was only one candidate of 'his' party standing. But having first voted for party-A he does not vote only for a candidate or candidates of party-B at any subsequent election, nor does he give a vote of the type AB when there were two candidates of party-A standing. (Note that he would still be classified as a party voter if he votes initially for party-A and subsequently votes AB where there was only one candidate standing from party-A, or where he gives a single vote when there are two candidates from 'his' party).

This is fairly weak requirement. It allows partial but not complete political dissent. A Bedford voter classified as a Liberal could have voted in any one of the following ways over the series of elections between 1835 and 1857 (from the many possible)

	1835	1837	1841	1847	1852	1857
Candidates	2L/1T	2L/1T	2T/1L	2T/1L	2L/1T	2L/2T
Votes	LL	L	L	L	LL	LL
	L_2	L	LT_2	NV	LL	L_1
	L_1	L_2	LT_1	LT_2	LL	L_1
	L_1	L_1	NV	NV	L_1	L_1

But not one of the following:

	1835	1837	1841	1847	1852	1857
	LL	L	L	LT_1	$\underline{L_1}T$	LL
	LL	LT_1	LT_2	LT_1	$\underline{T}$	LL

For these last two voting sequences the disqualifying vote is underlined. In the first case he voted for a Tory when there were two Liberals standing; in the second example he voted for a Tory after previously voting Liberal – although he had split his votes across party lines when there was only one Liberal candidate. To summarize, this classification places no restriction on the use of the second vote when there is only one candidate standing from the party of initial choice.

An *independent* elector is one whose voting pattern does not conform to that of a party voter. This implies either some degree of vote splitting – a lack of party voting by the individual – or a change in partisan choice between elections. As such it conflates two quite distinct patterns of electoral behaviour. A truly independent voter is one who is not influenced by party labels but votes for the candidate or candidates that he considers the 'best' either in personality or policy terms, or in terms of inducements – he is a rational voter in his own terms. But this categorization also includes cases of partisan conversion – electors who vote for party-A up to one election and for party-B thereafter.[21] (Note too that a voter is not necessarily characterized as independent because he gives his second vote to a candidate of another party on one or more occasions.)

If an elector first gives a vote split between the two parties, LT, then he is classified as a voter for the party for which he first gives an undivided vote. An elector whose votes on three successive occasions are LT – T – T would be classified as a Tory; LT – L – L as a Liberal, and LT – T – L as an independent voter. There are a few Bedford voters who consistently give a split vote, and they are classified as cross-party voters– X – as are those who vote LT at one election and then leave the electorate. Electors who enter the electorate as non-voters are classified in a similar manner: by the party of their first partisan vote. There is a very small group of persistent non-voters.

Table 5.6 summarizes the voting of all Bedford electors between 1832 and 1868. It shows, for example, that the 1847 cohort contained 223 electors, 88 of these (39.5 per cent) were Tory voters, 92 (41 per cent) were Liberals, 26 (12 per cent) were cross-party voters and 17 (about 8 per cent) did not vote. Some 16 (18 per cent) of the Tory voters subsequently voted for another party on one or more occasions, as did some 21 (23 per cent) of the Liberal voters. A total of 44 electors in this cohort (20 per cent) were independent voters and subsequently changed their vote from the one they first gave.

Overall the data in Table 5.6 suggests that most electors in Bedford supported one party consistently over time, that is they were *party* voters. There seems to be a fairly high occurrence of stability in voting behaviour with only 444 from the total of 3,939 voters (11 per cent) classified as independent voters. However the incidence of non-party or independent voting was higher than this figure suggests. The 1,319 new voters in 1868 only voted once and we have no information on the consistency of their electoral behaviour over time. Similarly 708 electors from the earlier cohorts left the electorate after only one election and so cannot be categorized either. The remaining 1,912 electors voted more than once between 1832 and 1868 and of these almost a quarter, some 444 (23 per cent) were not party voters. Interestingly such electors were concentrated in the 'Reform' generation – 247 of the 'independent'

Table 5.6 Electoral Recruitment in Bedford 1832–68

Cohort	Partisan composition of cohorts									Electors who subsequently changed their partisanship									
	T	%	L	%	X	%	NV	%	Total	T	%	L	%	X	%	NV	%	Total	%
1832	344	35.8	478	49.7	139	14.5	*	*	961	71	20.6	112	23.4	64	46.0	*	*	247	25.5
1835	41	45.6	26	28.9	12	13.3	11	12.2	90	4	9.6	9	34.6	2	16.7	1	9.1	16	17.8
1837	33	40.7	34	42.0	8	9.9	6	7.4	81	4	12.1	4	11.8	2	25.0	1	16.7	11	13.6
1841	69	44.5	75	48.4	7	4.5	4	2.6	155	12	17.4	15	20.0	1	14.3	0	0	28	18.1
1847	88	39.5	92	41.3	26	11.7	17	7.6	223	16	18.2	21	22.8	5	19.2	2	11.8	44	19.7
1852	40	16.3	82	33.3	93	37.8	31	12.6	246	9	22.5	9	11.0	15	16.1	1	3.2	34	13.8
1857	80	30.7	122	46.7	27	10.3	32	12.3	261	9	11.3	12	9.8	0	0	4	12.5	25	9.6
1859	73	39.2	87	46.8	13	6.9	13	6.9	186	12	16.4	6	6.9	0	0	1	7.7	19	10.2
1865	131	31.4	182	43.6	59	14.1	45	10.8	417	15	11.5	5	2.7	0	0	0	0	20	4.8
1868	324	24.6	750	56.9	143	10.8	102	7.7	1319	*	*	*	*	*	*	*	*	*	*
Total	1223	31.0	1928	48.9	527	13.4	260	6.6	3939	152	12.4	193	10.0	89	16.9	10	3.8	444	

Note: * indicates unavailable data.

Source: Bedford poll books 1835–1868; Bedford canvass book for 1835.

electors (56 per cent) were from the cohort that first voted at the 1832 election. Perhaps they were uncertain about their loyalty in this new political world, perhaps there was a delay in establishing a long-term partisan commitment after the excitement and uncertainty of the Reform period had died down. There are some parallels here with the voters in Cambridge where many new electors in 1832 gave one vote for Reform, and became Tory supporters only at a subsequent election.[22]

Apart from 'the Reform cohort' only 10 per cent of electors changed the party they supported, after 1832 electors who cast a partisan vote at one election were increasingly likely to vote the same way at successive elections. The proportion of electors who changed their vote certainly decreased after 1852, see Table 5.6, but there were fewer opportunities to do so. Overall it was Tory voters who were more likely to change their partisanship, but before 1852 this was truer of Liberals.[23]

But did one party enjoy a consistent electoral advantage amongst new voters? The data shows that each new cohort of voters usually had more Liberals than Tories. Only in 1835 did a plurality of a cohort initially support the Tory candidate(s). So Tory success in Bedford must have come from the recruitment of support from former Liberals, from those who gave a split vote, or from electors who had not voted previously.

One aspect of voting in multi-member constituencies has been the subject of earlier analysis. This is the extent of split voting where a voter gives his two votes to candidates from different parties. Both Mitchell and Cox have suggested that the level of party voting increased in two-member constituencies after 1832 and that by 1841 it had reached a consistently high level with a relatively small number of electors in most constituencies giving a double vote split between candidates from two different parties. In Lancaster the division within the Conservative party over the Corn Laws helped to produce confusion over candidates and policies at the 1847 election; there was a sharp decline in party voting and a corresponding increase in cross voting and plumping, see Table 4.3. By 1852 individual voting along party lines was once again at a high level in the constituency. But such behaviour was not confined to Lancaster; there was a general increase in split voting at the 1847 election.[24]

Table 5.7   Party voting (%) at Bedford elections 1832–68

1832	1835	1837	1841	1847	1852	1857	1859	1865	1868
86	81	89	93	90	48	90	92	85	89

Sources: 1835–68 Bedford poll books; 1832 Smith (1844–50 Volume 1).

Table 5.8 Voting at Bedford elections 1832–68: Aggregate figures and vote breakdown[25]

			Total votes				Double votes (Party votes / Split votes)							Single votes						
Year	Electors	Voted	T_1	T_2	L_1	L_2	T_1T_2	L_1L_2	L_1T_1	L_1T_2	L_2T_1	L_2T_2	T_1	T_2	L_1	L_2	NV	PP %	Split vote %	Turnout %
1832	*	961	483	–	599	486	–	468	124	–	15	–	344	–	7	3	*	1.0	14.5	–
1835	857	834	490	–	403	383	–	282	78	–	82	–	330	–	43	19	23	7.4	19.2	97.3
1837	846	817	467	419	412	–	391	–	70	22	–	–	6	6	320	–	29	1.5	11.3	96.6
1841	828	806	433	421	410	–	393	–	37	22	–	–	0	5	349	–	22	0.6	7.3	97.3
1847	873	836	432	392	453	–	361	–	52	28	–	–	19	3	373	–	37	2.6	7.2	95.8
1852	869	794	517	–	435	252	–	36	223	–	151	–	143	–	176	65	75	30.4	47.1	91.4
1857	869	793	376	176	452	435	164	399	46	2	30	5	136	5	5	1	76	17.3	10.5	91.3
1859	932	882	449	427	455	427	401	407	35	12	11	9	2	4	1	0	50	0.8	7.6	94.6
1865	1059	955	478	–	574	345	–	295	113	–	32	–	331	–	166	18	104	18.2	13.7	90.2
1868	2124	1955	769	494	1311	1242	494	1154	151	0	62	0	62	0	6	26	169	4.8	10.9	92.0

Note: PP – preferential plumping – is defined in Appendix 2.

Source: 1832 election – Smith (1842); 1835–68 – Bedford poll books.

Bedford does not conform to this pattern. There was a small increase in the number of split votes at the 1847 election, but party voting was still high – only 3 per cent of all the votes at this election were given across party lines. The major change in the aggregate pattern of electoral behaviour came in 1852 when the level of party voting decreased to 48 per cent, see Table 5.7.

The full breakdown of the vote by ballot type for each election is given in Table 5.8. The figures show a decline in party voting in 1852 and an increase in the number of cross votes. Some 30 per cent of all the votes at this election were preferential plumpers for one or the other of the two Liberal candidates, rather than a double vote for both.

At most Bedford elections split voting and plumping were unimportant. The level of preferential plumping between 1832 and 1868 varies between 0.8 per cent in 1841 to 7.4 per cent in 1835, and apart from 1852, it was higher – over 10 per cent of all ballots – in only two elections: 17.3 per cent in 1857 and 18.2 per cent in 1865. At the 1852 election all three candidates received a significant number of single votes and only 36 electors voted for both Liberal candidates. The new electors showed a similar pattern of behaviour with 38 per cent of them voting across party lines, a much higher proportion than in any other cohort.

However, the extent of split voting, and measures of individual voting stability, tell us little about the effects of permanent political conversion. All electors who change their vote are grouped together in Table 5.6. Someone who votes L in 1832, 1835 and 1837 and then T in 1841, 1847 and 1852 is classified as an independent voter but in partisan terms he is a party voter both before and after 1841; he has however changed the party that he supported. To analyse the effects of such short-term change we need to look at the detailed pattern of voting between successive elections.

Voting between any two elections can be summarized in a transition table similar to Table 4.5 (see Appendix 3, Table A3.1). From these tables we can calculate an index of vote stability, a measure of the extent to which those who voted at two successive elections, supported the same party on both occasions.[26] Table 5.9 shows the variation in this index across pairs of successive Bedford elections. The level of stability in electoral behaviour over pairs of successive elections in Bedford was high, although not as consistently high as Mitchell and Cornford found over a series of elections in Cambridge for the same period. For all except three pairs of adjacent elections there, vote stability ranged between

Table 5.9   Aggregate vote stability at Bedford elections 1832–68

32/35	35/37	37/41	41/47	47/52	52/57	57/59	59/65	65/68
0.81	0.75	0.81	0.81	0.50	0.51	0.82	0.74	0.69

Source: 1835 canvass book; linked Bedford individual electoral data.

0.76 and 0.89.[27] This is a higher level of stability than was found by Elklit for open voting in Denmark at elections in Fredericia between 1890 and 1898, higher than that estimated for the Swedish electorate in the early phases of party formation and probably higher than at successive elections in Britain today.[28]

Any measure of the extent of stability, and/or volatility, in the British electorate today is more uncertain. Part of the problem is methodological – measures of stability have to be derived from survey data and self-reported political preferences rather than from the known political preferences of open voting. So Heath et al., 1991

> estimate that, out of the people who were eligible to vote in 1983 or 1987, 20% voted Conservative on both occasions, 9% voted Alliance on both occasions, 13% voted Labour on both occasions, and 11% abstained on both times… [so] we find that 53% voted the same way at both elections

(Heath et al., 1991, pp. 18–20).

This is lower than the figures for most Bedford elections as shown in Table 5.9. They go on to recalculate the figure excluding those who did not vote – on the grounds that non-voting was a largely chance or involuntary act. 'Stability among those who actually did manage to vote… between 1983 and 1987 was 81%' – and they report the reverse, the percentage of voters who changed over pairs of elections: 1959–1964, 18%; 1966–1970, 16 per cent; 1970–February 1974, 24 per cent; October 1974–1979, 22 per cent; 1979–1983, 23 per cent, and 1983–1987, 19 per cent.[29]

It would be possible to recalculate the figures for Bedford excluding the non-voters and this would increase the overall figures for stability. However under open voting the decision not to vote was probably a much more conscious decision than it is for the contemporary voter, it was the (non) expression of partisan preference, and so it has been included in all the calculations of vote stability before 1872.[30]

At elections between 1832 and 1847, and from 1857 to 1865, aggregate stability was high, ranging from 0.74 to 0.82, suggesting that most electors voted the same way at successive elections. This is consistent with an assumption that parties had a core of stable electoral support carried over from a previous election. The low figures for 1847–52 and 1852–57 confirm the evidence from split voting and preferential plumping about the unusual nature of the 1852 election. Aggregate vote stability decreased from 0.81 between the elections of 1841 and 1847 to 0.50 between 1847 and 1852, indicating that more electors than usual changed their pattern of voting between these last two elections. The index is similarly low between 1852 and 1857 when a high level of party voting was re-established.

A more detailed picture of aggregate voting stability over time comes from extending the transition table analysis to each pair of successive elections in Bedford between 1832 and 1868, see Table 5.10. These detailed figures provide more information about voting when the pattern of support for party candidates changed, as occurred at the election of 1852.

V

The data in Table 5.10 support the conclusion that there was fairly strong partisan stability between most pairs of successive Bedford elections. In addition the tables give more detail about the behaviour of groups of voters. In particular note the T–T or L–L cells in Tables 5.10(a)–5.10(d) and 5.10(f)–5.10(g), indicating the extent to which an elector gave a vote for the same 'party' at two successive elections. They show, for example, that between 1832 and 1835 some 86 per cent of those who gave a Liberal vote in 1832 voted the same way three years later, as did 84 per cent of Tory voters. Similarly 94 per cent of those who voted Conservative in 1857 supported the same party in 1859. This was a slightly higher figure than for the Liberal party where only 88 per cent were consistent in their party support. The non-party voters do not show the same pattern. The equivalent figure for persistent split voting ranges from 67 per cent, between 1847 and 1852, to a low of 15 per cent between 1852 and 1857.

There was some persistent non-voting too. Between 1865 and 1868 it was 16 per cent, although it fell as low as 4 per cent between the elections of 1847–52, 1841–47 and 1857–59. The data reinforces the earlier analysis that suggested that most voters were loyal to a particular political party from election to election. But there were exceptions, and

Table 5.10   Electoral change at Bedford elections 1832–68[31]

		1835								1837				
		L	T	X	NV	% total			L	T	X	NV	% total
1832	L	86	3	10	2	46	1835	L	83	6	8	3	41
	T	2	84	12	1	38		T	2	91	6	1	38
	X	7	29	62	1	16		X	15	53	29	3	19
	NV	*	*	*	*	*		NV	19	50	–	31	2
						(767)							(762)

10(a): 1832–35   10(b): 1835–37

		1841								1847				
		L	T	X	NV	% total			L	T	X	NV	% total
1837	L	90	5	3	2	38	1841	L	89	4	7	1	42
	T	4	89	5	2	48		T	5	86	6	2	48
	X	36	24	36	3	9		X	41	27	27	6	8
	NV	28	39	11	22	3		NV	29	29	–	41	3
						(681)							(646)

10(c): 1837–41   10(d): 1841–47

		1852								1857				
		L	T	X	NV	% total			L	T	X	NV	% total
1847	L	63	0	30	6	44	1852	L	89	4	3	4	32
	T	3	34	57	5	46		T	3	87	3	7	16
	X	20	2	67	11	7		X	35	43	15	7	46
	NV	16	5	37	42	3		NV	29	32	12	27	6
						(624)							(607)

10(e): 1847–52   10(f): 1852–57

Continued

Table 5.10 Continued

		1859						1865				
1857		L	T	X	NV	% total	1859		L	T	X	NV	% total
	L	88	5	5	2	47		L	82	3	8	6	47
	T	1	94	2	2	36		T	10	66	16	8	43
	X	7	49	39	3	10		X	25	9	61	5	7
	NV	10	42	6	42	7		NV	43	24	10	24	3
						(747)							(632)

10(g):1857–59   10(h): 1859–65

		1868				
1865		L	T	X	NV	Total
	L	88	3	3	6	47
	T	10	71	11	7	32
	X	48	18	20	14	15
	NV	45	26	13	16	6
						(805)

10(i): 1865–68

between 1847 and 1852, and to a lesser extent 1852 and 1857, the tables show that there was a breakdown in the 'usual' pattern of voting at these elections.

So what did happen at the 1852 election? The two tables 5.10(e) and 5.10(f) summarize the behaviour of electors at the three elections between 1847 and 1857. Note that one Liberal and two Conservative candidates contested the three elections before 1847. In 1837 and 1841 both Tories were elected but in 1847 the Liberal came top of the poll. At the next election in 1852 the situation was reversed, with two Liberal candidates and only one Tory, and at this election there was an almost complete disintegration of party loyalty in the voting for the two Liberals. This change was to the advantage of the Tory candidate who picked up the second vote of many Liberal electors, see Table 5.11 for a breakdown of the aggregate voting into ballot types for this election

Table 5.11 Vote composition Bedford 1852

	T	L_1	L_2
T	143	223	151
L_1		176	36
L_2			65

Source: Bedford poll book for 1852.

The more detailed analysis of voting change between 1847 and 1852 shows that almost one-third of the Liberal electors from 1847 gave a split vote in 1852, 58 per cent a Liberal plumper for one or other Liberal candidate, with only 10 per cent voting for both Liberal candidates, see Table 5.12.

Table 5.12 Liberal voters Bedford 1847–52 (%)

				1852		
		L_1	L_2	L_1L_2	L_1T	L_2T
1847	L	46	12	10	18	14

Source: Linked individual level Bedford electoral data.

If electors did not defect and support the Tory candidate, they registered their protest by voting in other ways, see Table 5.10.e. However, it was not only the Liberal vote that fragmented, the Tory vote did too. Table 5.10(e) shows that very few Tory supporters from 1847 voted for both Liberals in 1852. There was little partisan defection; the majority, some 57 per cent, gave a split vote which was almost evenly divided between the two Liberal candidates, with only 37 per cent giving a single vote to the Conservative candidate, see Table 5.13.

Why did this breakdown in party voting happen? The change in the number of candidates on both sides may have presented strategic opportunities for a Conservative candidate who was uncertain of the level of his support in the constituency, but a similar reversal in the pattern of candidature between the elections of 1835 and 1837 did not have the same effect upon individual voting behaviour. At most elections the two candidates of the same party campaigned together but in 1852 the single Tory was able to capitalize on a lack of co-operation between the two Liberals, and the local press hints at a tacit campaign coalition between

Table 5.13 Tory voters Bedford
1847–52 (%)[32]

	1852		
	T	L_1T	L_2T
1847 T	37	33	30

Source: Linked individual level
Bedford electoral data.

the Conservative and one of the Liberals. So this was an election in which voters used their double vote, or preferentially plumped, to distinguish between two candidates of the same party who appear to have had policy differences.

Whatever the cause, the 'deviating' character of the 1852 election is confirmed by the voting at the next election in 1857, and the pattern of change between the two elections. At this later election there were four candidates, two from each party. If 1852 was a 'deviating election' with little agreement between the two Liberal candidates and a decline in party voting amongst electors, then 1857 was a 'realigning' one.[33] The previous high level of party voting was restored, as is shown by the voting figures (Table 5.8), the level of party voting (Table 5.7) and a more detailed look at the changes of Liberal and split voters between the two elections. The flow of the vote is shown in Table 5.10(f) with more details in Tables 5.14 and 5.15. However the complete re-establishment of voting along partisan lines at the later election was complicated by the campaign of the second Conservative candidate who stood as a Tory-Radical and differentiated himself from the other Conservative.

So, either through confusion or political disaffection, many Conservative voters in 1857 gave only a single vote for one candidate, rather than a double vote for the two Tory candidates. Some 87 per cent of those supporting a Conservative at both elections gave either a single vote for the leading Tory candidate or a double vote for him and the 'Tory-Radical'. The two types of ballots occurred in the ratio of 51:49 T_1: T_1T_2, see Table 5.16 that refers to the votes of the 87 per cent of all the Tory supporters from 1852 who voted in the 1857 election.

Those who split their votes across party lines in 1852 returned to party voting in 1857, see Tables 5.10(f) and 5.15. It is interesting to note that 50 per cent of the L_1T voters from 1852 voted L_1L_2 in 1857 but 51 per cent of the L_2T voters switched to voting T_1T_2, see Table 5.15.

Table 5.14 The composition of the Bedford Liberal vote in 1857(%)

		1857
		L_1L_2
	L_1	41
	L_2	15
1852	L_1L_2	8
	L_1T	22
	L_2T	14

Source: Linked individual level Bedford electoral data.

Table 5.15   The re-establishment of party voting from split votes, Bedford 1852–57

		1857			
		T_1	T_1T_2	L_1L_2	
1852	L_1T	28	22	50	(71% of all linked L_1T voters)
	L_2T	10	51	39	(86% of all linked L_2T voters)

Source: Linked individual level Bedford electoral data.

Table 5.16   Lack of cohesion in the Tory vote, Bedford 1857

		1857	
		T_1	T_1T_2
1852	T	51	49

Source: Linked individual level Bedford electoral data.

The high level of individual partisan voting found between 1837 and 1841 was re-established in 1859. At this election there was no disagreement between the two Conservative candidates and the solidarity of the Tory vote was restored, see Tables 5.8, 5.10(g) and 5.17 (which includes 77 per cent of all linked Tory voters at these elections).

Table 5.17   The re-establishment of
the Tory vote in Bedford 1857–59

		1859
		T_1T_2
1857	T_1T_2	57
	T_1	43

Source: Linked individual level Bedford
electoral data.

To summarize, the overall pattern of change: 283 (45 per cent) of the 624 electors who participated in the elections of 1847 and 1852 split their votes across party lines in 1852. The composition of the split vote, in terms of their 1847 vote, is shown in Figure 5.4.

A total of 58 per cent of the split votes in 1852 came from those who had voted Tory in 1847, 29 per cent from those who had supported the Liberals, and so on. Similarly, 42 per cent of those who had given a split vote (X) in 1852, voted Tory in 1857, 35 per cent voted Liberal, 17 per cent gave a split vote, and 6 per cent did not vote at all. If an elector 'defected' in 1852, most of those who voted at all three elections returned to the party of their original choice at the third election. The dominant pathways of change over 1847–1852–1857 were T–X–T (81) and L–X–L (48); voters changing from Conservative to Liberal, pathways of the type T–X–L, out-numbered changes in the other direction, Liberal to Tory – L–X–T, by 18:6.

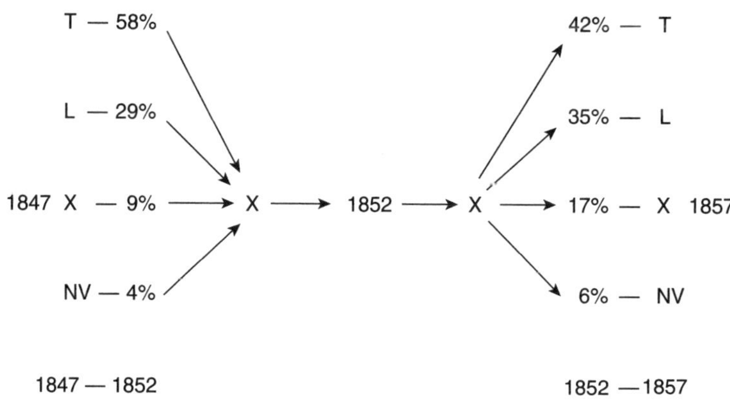

Figure 5.4   Ballot change in Bedford 1847–52 and 1852–57

The disintegration of the Liberal vote in this period can be outlined from the same data; there were three possible patterns of behaviour for those voting Liberal in 1847 and 1852 – (a) $L\rightarrow L_1$, (b) $L\rightarrow L_2$; and (c) $L\rightarrow L_1L_2$. The number of electors who voted in each of these three ways were respectively: 116 (67 per cent), 31 (18 per cent) and 25 (15 per cent); 99 from this group of voters were still electors in 1857 and at that election all but one of them voted for both Liberal candidates. This pattern of a lack of electoral cohesion in the support for candidates of the same party at one election, and subsequent agreement at the next, suggests that it was policy differences between the two Liberal candidates that caused the breakdown of strict partisanship and the diversity of behaviour in 1852.[34] In many constituencies there was a similar pattern of change in the pattern of voting along party lines at the previous election in 1847. Then it was often over the Corn Law issue. It is doubtful if this was the problem at Bedford in 1852. At this election local issues and local candidates were more obviously important than strictly national partisan concerns although at other Bedford elections, such as 1832, national issues appear to have had more of an impact on the constituency electorate. But are these relatively coherent patterns of disruption evidence of rationality and calculation on the part of the electorate? Or the result of the confusion that followed the breakdown of the normal pattern of electoral and partisan cues in 1852, so producing a weakened sense of partisan loyalty, with 'normal' electoral politics returning in 1857.

The election of 1852 was not the only one at which the level of party voting decreased in Bedford. This also happened at the 1865 election, see Table 5.10(h). This later election had some features in common with 1852. In 1865 there was only one Conservative candidate, and some Tory voters gave one of their two votes to a Liberal – see the relatively low figure (66 per cent) in the T–T cell in Table 5.10 (h). At the same time the high degree of stability in the Liberal vote masks a lack of support for the second Liberal candidate. This lack of co-operation between the two Liberals is confirmed by the figure for preferential plumping, and Table 5.18 shows the behaviour of the 81 per cent of the 1859 L_1L_2 voters who voted in 1865. As in 1857, the Liberal electors returned to voting along party lines at the next election in 1868, see Table 5.10 (i).

The lower aggregate stability between the elections before and after the Second Reform Bill, 1865–68, shows a drift of voters towards the Liberals. But in 1867 the change in the franchise doubled the number of electors and altered the basic parameters of the system.[35]

Table 5.18   Liberal votes at Bedford
1859–65 (%)

		1865	
		L_1	L_1L_2
1859	L_1L_2	40	60

Source: Linked individual level Bedford
electoral data.

VI

How typical was Bedford of borough constituencies over this period? It had a smaller electorate than other frequently contested seats and a lower rate of population growth than the more industrial constituencies. But similar electoral turnover occurred in all borough seats and the patterns of change in electoral behaviour, and in the composition of the Bedford electorate, illustrate the pressures that influenced the electoral calculations of party agents and candidates in many constituencies, not only those that were contested at each election.

The analysis shows that with an even division of opinion, and a high level of partisan loyalty, both parties could win elections in Bedford. So, as in Lancaster, political organizers will have tried to use the underlying changes in the electorate to influence election outcomes. Regular contests had other consequence. The results of an election confirmed the accuracy of the information available to a party about the extent of its support in the constituency – the loyalty of the electorate – and the success of their campaign of electoral recruitment. With no contest, the party agent or constituency organizer had less accurate information on voter behaviour both individually and in the aggregate. A series of uncontested elections would increase the level of uncertainty and the regular turnover in the electorate would increase the proportion of those with no previous voting record. So uncontested elections decreased the reliability of social and electoral information and increased uncertainty about electoral outcomes.

The Bedford data shows that an elector in this period could expect to remain in the electorate for between fifteen and nineteen and a half years (see Appendix 3 Table A3.2). By 1852 the Reform cohort of electors was no longer a majority in the electorate and its influence had declined. The data also shows that most electors were loyal to the party for which they first voted, and that aggregate stability in voting behaviour was usually high. If few electors changed their political allegiance, a party organizer needed to recruit new voters for electoral success. In 1841 there were 681 electors still in the electorate from 1837; some four out of five of them voted the same way at both these elections, one in five did not. In 1837 the margin between the losing candidate and the successful second candidate was only seven votes. In 1841 it was eleven votes. We know that 155 new voters were registered between the two elections, see Figure 5.2 and Table 5.4. Of these new electors 69 voted Tory, 75 Liberal, 7 split their votes between the two parties and 4 did not vote (see Table 5.6). There was little partisan change between the parties, although the Liberal candidate gained more from those who had previously split their votes – see Table 5.10c – but this was not enough to win a seat. The even division of opinion reinforced the pressure on local parties to recruit and retain support, and if social ties were important for establishing political identity, the fine balance of partisan support would have helped to maintain the politicization of the electoral community.

In Lancaster new voters were identified and recruited on the basis of personal information. 'Mr Jackson' was able to locate many electors in both social and political terms. Since the two constituencies were comparable in size, it is possible that an election agent operated a similar system to recruit and organize new electors in Bedford. Some partial confirmation of this can be found in a canvass book for the Bedford election of 1835.[36] Then the Conservatives put up one candidate and received cross votes from supporters of both Liberals. The Tory came top of the poll with 490 votes. The two Liberals received 403 and 383 votes respectively; the detailed voting analysis for 1835 shows that 160 electors split their votes across party lines and a further 62 gave only a single vote to one or other Liberal candidate, see Table 5.19.

In 1835 there were 78 electors who voted L_1T, 82 electors voted L_2T, as well as 43 single votes for one Liberal (L_1) and 19 for the other (L_2). If the local party organization had been able to turn Liberal plumpers, or the split votes, into a double ballot for both Liberals then they would have had enough electoral support to win both seats. But did the Liberal election manager know this before the election? How accurate was his knowledge of party support, and of the strength of the opposition? Did a party lose because electors did not vote as they had promised or because they did not vote at all? Was one party, rather than its opponents, able to persuade more voters to defect?

Parties canvassed electors about their voting intention before the poll and the surviving canvass book for the 1835 election gives an indication of the accuracy of the information available. The correspondence between promise and vote is shown in Table 5.20.

Table 5.19   The composition of the Bedford vote in 1835

	T	L_1	L_2
T	330	78	82
L_1		43	282
L_2		–	19

Source: Bedford poll book for the 1835 election.

Table 5.20   The accuracy of canvassing, Bedford 1835

		Vote in 1835					
		T	L_1L_2	L	X	NV	Defectors
	T	305	2	0	53	5	(60)
Promise	L_1L_2	0	244	42	13	3	(58)
	L	0	2	1	1	0	(3)
	X	17	1	2	73	1	(21)/(142)
	no promise	11	33	14	19	(14)	

Source: Canvass book for the 1835 election.

Before the election, 365 votes were promised to the Conservative, 302 votes to both Liberals, 94 electors indicated that they intended to split their votes and a further 91 made no promise. The evidence suggests that most electors voted as they promised – 84 per cent of Tories and 80 per cent of all Liberals. If the Liberals could have gained the support of the undecided voters and persuaded the split voters to support both Liberal candidates, then they might have been able to elect two MP's. (Very few voters are recorded as promising only a single Liberal vote.) The Conservatives benefited marginally from the split votes, and the Liberals recruited more of those who gave no pre-election promise. The two parties were equally affected by defections – 60 Tory voters and 58 Liberals did not vote as they had promised, but the Liberals gained more from the split votes of Tory promises. However, overall, local party organizers had fairly accurate information on the level of their support – and that of their opponents.

All this evidence – on electoral turnover, on change between elections, on individual voting and on the accuracy of the knowledge that an agent or party could have about the nature of partisan support in the electorate – suggests a relatively stable and predictable electoral environment. This impression is reinforced by the analysis of electoral behaviour over time, and such diachronic analysis helps to explain the result of the 1852 election when party loyalty declined. Even with substantial short-term change in individual voting behaviour there is still a degree of partisan consistency. Over the three elections between 1847 and 1857 some 129 out of 153 voters, 84 per cent, returned to their 'normal' party after a temporary change in voting behaviour. Similar 'defections' from one or the other party occurred at other Bedford elections and, as in 1852, it allowed a candidate of the other party to win a seat.

VII

The Second Reform Act changed the electoral environment, further enlarging the franchise and doubling the number of electors in Bedford. In 1868 almost two out of every three voters were newly enfranchised, although voter loyalty continued at a high level amongst those who had voted before – see Table 4.10(i). As in 1832 the Liberals enjoyed an overwhelming advantage in the 1868 cohort of new voters, and there were also a significant number of new voters who split their votes across party lines (see Table 5.6).

In the period immediately after the First Reform Bill there had been an improvement in Conservative electoral fortunes, and something similar seems to have occurred after 1868 with the Tories winning one of the Bedford seats in 1874. We have seen that the first two or three elections after 1832 were characterized by a growing stability in party voting and the development of party organization. Following the passage of the Ballot Act in 1872 it is no longer possible to obtain information on individual voting for elections in Bedford after 1868 so we cannot analyse the consequences of this second enfranchisement in the same detail. We cannot map the behaviour that produced Tory success in 1874. As in 1832, the underlying social context probably did not change as rapidly as the electoral context immediately after 1867 – although the Second Reform Bill may have brought a significant change in the relationship of electors to non-electors. With a greater proportion of the community now enfranchised, the possession of the vote became more widespread. As the vote itself became a less scarce social good, the relative social status of an elector may have been reduced.

In this enlarged electorate each voter would now interact more frequently with other voters, and so the social constraints acting on the individual elector changed. He was now part of a more inclusive and wider electoral community, and a more extensive social and political network. The problem of organizing the vote increased in scale for a local party organization, particularly in urban seats where electorates grew dramatically, some now had more than 35,000 electors. The methods of social identification and recruitment used in Lancaster, and possibly in Bedford too, could function well with a relatively low turn-over of electors, a low rate of population growth, and a small electorate where all electors could be known personally to party organizers. After 1868 this would not be the case in urban constituencies with large or very large electorates.

For much of the period after 1832 the electoral community in Bedford was fairly stable with a low turnover in the electorate – the rate of electoral recruitment between 1832 and 1865 was 5–6 voters a month, see Table 5.3. The increase between 1865 and 1868 averages out at 33.0 electors per month and most of this increase probably occurred after the passing of the Reform Bill. If the rate of change remained con-stant before the Second Reform Act, then the subsequent growth in Bedford after 1867 was of the order of more than 70 electors per month. This is a very much higher rate than before and would have posed prob-lems of a different order in terms of social/political identification and electoral recruitment.

The reduction in the relative social status of an elector and a decrease in intra-group social distance, combined with 'over-load' on the mecha-nisms for recruiting voters, may have weakened the strength and impor-tance of hierarchical social linkages. At the same time the changes in the franchise increased the 'horizontal' pressures on electors, such as those of class or peer group. Direct evidence is not available but it is clear that cumulatively such changes may have lead to the development of new mechanisms for organizing voters in large urban constituencies. This can be seen explicitly in three member seats like Birmingham where the minority representation clause applied after 1867, and where the Liberal party caucus so effectively linked local politics to the organ-ization of parliamentary elections.[37]

VIII

The Bedford data has shown how one electorate voted and how it changed over a long period. It has illustrated some of the consequences of electoral demography, and of the continuous turnover in the elector-ate that linked electoral politics to wider social changes and to the local social context. The political changes that followed reform in 1832 interacted with the particular constituency context to create a stable electoral environment – stable in terms of the behaviour of the electorate and its regular change. It also created a structure of opportunities for political agents, and a relatively bounded set of social relationships within which political behaviour occurred. Above all it produced a set of expectations that encouraged party agents and election managers to create institutions for organizing and channelling the behaviour of voters. Over time such institutions became a structural influence on constituency politics. In Bedford the population and the electorate grew relatively slowly for much of the period between 1832 and 1867, the consequences of electoral turnover would have been more extensive in constituencies that had either a larger electorate or a more rapidly growing population, or both.

The detailed analysis of individual and aggregate behaviour suggests a high degree of stability in voting, although there were limits to this stability with some responsiveness to issues and candidates. National issues, or a local disagreement between candidates, could create electoral uncertainty. As in Lancaster, the basis of recruitment may well have been personal social information, and so behind the actions of election agents and party organizers there is a link between the social context and the behaviour of electors. What was the nature of this link? Was open voting based on class, community or corruption? Did religious affiliation play a role? These questions are central to any account of Victorian voting. So the next chapter looks at the dynamics of mid-nineteenth century electoral behaviour in the light of the evidence on electoral recruitment in Lancaster, and the pattern of long-term electoral change found in Bedford between 1832 and 1868. It outlines one possible set of links between the social context and voting, links that have implications both for party organization and for electoral behaviour under open voting.

6
The Voter and the Electoral Community

Studies of elections between 1832 and 1868 do not suggest a single explanation of open voting but they do provide a body of evidence for analysis. A general explanation of electoral behaviour between the First and Second Reform Bills has to take this evidence into account, as well as the indirect relationship that existed between political and social development over this period.

The political context after 1832 was one of relative institutional stability. In parliament the party system fragmented in the mid-1840s, but a two party alignment began to evolve by the end of the 1850's. This stabilized with the emergence of the Gladstonian Liberal coalition, and with Disraeli's consolidation of his position within the Tory party. Immediately after 1832 constituency contests were often between 'Reformers' and 'Anti-reformers', but over the period up to 1868 candidates became increasingly identified – and identified themselves – as Liberals or Conservatives.[1]

The social context of electoral behaviour in this period is more uncertain. Social changes helped to produce the 'viable class society'[2] of the late nineteenth century but this makes any social explanation of voting in the mid-nineteenth century more problematic. If electoral behaviour was linked to social structural conditions then changes in the class structure should have been reflected either in changes in the pattern of voting or in changes in the relationship between class and vote, or both. If these social changes occurred independently, then class may have been a less important influence on voting – and the relationship between voting and the underlying social structure in the mid-nineteenth century may have been very different to the one that developed later. Any growth in class voting was further complicated by variations in the constituency social context and by differences in the pattern of change as well. The 'modern' social structure did not evolve uniformly across constituencies, there was a pattern of leads and lags with some constituencies changing early and rapidly, others later or more slowly.

The end of the process – the outline of the modern class structure – is known in some detail. We can also sketch something of the pre-existing 'world we have lost'[3], but the details of the transitional period, when both the class structure and the relationship between class and vote began to assume something like their modern form, are more uncertain. Partly this is due to a lack of detailed investigation but there was also local and regional variation. Overall it is doubtful if any general statements on the relationship between class and vote can be made for this period.[4] Finally, the transition from non-class politics to class politics at the end of the nineteenth century and the beginning of the twentieth century was rapid with little electoral discontinuity; it was helped by continuities in political leadership, in party organization and a partial continuity in the electorate too.[5]

One explanation of the relationship between class and vote is contained in the suggestion by Perkin that at the mass level: 'class was latent...in the politics of the old society. It was overlaid by powerful bonds and loyalties that effectively prevented its overt expression. The explanation lies in the total situation of the individual.' (Perkin, 1969, p. 37). So to understand electoral behaviour we need to re-examine this 'total situation' and the relationship between the voter and the electoral community.

For the elector the relationship had several defining characteristics. First, there was the institutional structure of politics within the local community, although this differed between borough and county constituencies. Second, there was only partial enfranchisement. About one in five adult males had the vote and this inequality of political status, this 'electoral stratification' may have influenced the relationship between an elector and the community of which he was a member. Many of those with whom he regularly interacted were not themselves enfranchised.[6] The right to vote was both a relatively scarce social resource – with status implications – and a potential economic resource as well. Conversely, even though most adults were non-electors and excluded from the formal electoral process, they were not 'depoliticized' but could participate in and influence constituency political life. Politics in a broader sense was more inclusive than is narrowly defined by the possession of the franchise alone, or the irregular occurrence of parliamentary elections.[7] Finally, voting was open and the lack of secrecy had consequences for individuals, party organizations and the electoral process.

I

After 1832 the formal barriers to the franchise were one stimulus for partisan organization. In many constituencies committees were created to manage the register on a regular and continuing basis, not just before an election. Experts were retained to give legal advice and defend a party's interests at the annual registration. As in Lancaster, partisan advantage came through lodging claims and objections before the revising barrister, by adding the supporters of one party to the register – and having the supporters of the opposition struck off. The annual revisions became surrogate elections and 'the entire period between 1832 and 1847 can be interpreted as a continuous registration battle'.[8]

These battles are reported in the intensely partisan local press. In Cambridge the Chronicle commented in 1838 that 'the results of the grand battles of the registration courts are so far decidedly in favour of the Conservative party', and a year later the Advertiser confirmed a similar advantage at the 1839 revision.[9] Registration activity overlapped with the use of illegal or dubious tactics. In 1839 the Independent reported that a number of voters had their rates paid by the local Conservative agent. This was done without their knowledge and the votes were disallowed; Mr Jackson had tried to make a similar use of the annual revision in Lancaster.[10]

The local battles continued in Cambridge with further Tory gains in 1841 but a fairly even contest was reported in 1843 with full-scale objections to individual electors being put on a retaliatory basis by both parties. After this the Tories seemed to lose heart; in 1846 they were not very active and the following year they were not represented at all and left the field to the Liberals. The Tories revived in the late 1840s, but were at a disadvantage after the Cambridge bribery case of 1852–3 and were not professionally represented at the 1853 revision. Subsequently they revived once more but party activity, and party feeling generally, was not as intense after 1854 as in the period from 1838 to 1843.[11]

But local politics often went further than the politicization of the annual revision. In many urban constituencies the Municipal Reform Act in 1835 had created elected local councils with annual elections. There was considerable overlap between the elections at municipal and parliamentary levels and Fraser has suggested that, in many parliamentary borough seats, general political features were reflected in the annual municipal elections and council politics.[12] The Liberals monopolized council offices and local patronage in Cambridge in the period immediately after 1835. By the late 1830's the Tories had gained ground in the council elections, and in 1839 they took control of the town council. In the same year, they contested the mayoralty for the first time, as well as the elections for Poor Law Guardians. The pattern of party activity is similar to that shown by the registration battles, and to that found in other constituencies. The Tory party disintegrated locally in the mid-1840s but revived in 1849 when they made economy an issue in local government. The next local elections in 1850 were hotly contested, and the Tories made further gains in 1851 and 1852. After this the political temperature cooled, but revived periodically as in the Tory offensive of 1857.

Several points emerge from this cursory glance at Cambridge local politics. Parliamentary election results reflected the pattern of activity at the municipal level, and successes at the parliamentary level are the culmination of local activities over the previous three or four years. Following Reform the Liberals took both Cambridge parliamentary seats at the elections of 1832, 1835 and 1837. The Tories won by-elections in 1839 and 1840, reflecting their municipal successes, and both of the seats at the 1841 general election. When the Tories regained their confidence in the later 1830s, they campaigned actively in all spheres of political life and forced the reformers onto the defensive. The Advertiser's comments on the municipal election of 1840 sums it up well: 'we have witnessed with equal surprise and pain that as Toryism has exhibited boldness, daring and organisation the leaders of the Reform party have become submissive, inert and disunited'.[13]

Voter apathy and non-participation, and the ever-present possibility of a split between the Radicals and Whigs in their ranks, hampered the leaders of the Reform party. Apathy was constantly used as an explanation for Tory success and Liberal failure. After the Tory victory at the 1839 Cambridge by-election, the Independent claimed that 108 out of 170 non-voters were reformers. Following more Tory success in 1840, the Advertiser analysed the non-voters as '125 Reformers, 20 Tories and 23 persons who never vote'. In the late 1850s and early 1860s the same paper regularly saw every Tory victory as resulting from Liberal abstention.

Some non-participation may have been tactical behaviour reflecting the deep policy disagreements within the local Liberal party, usually between the leaders but sometimes affecting the rank and file supporters as well. So, for example, some of the Radicals abstained at the 1857 election because Adair, the sitting Liberal member, supported

Palmerston, of whom they were critical.[14] The local Liberal party had a long history of such Whig–Radical disagreement. In the late 1830s the Radicals were dissatisfied with Pryme, the Whig MP, and in 1841 prominent Whigs registered their protests by failing to turn up for Liberal election meetings.

On the town council it was Tory policy to try to separate the Whigs from their Radical allies. This policy paid off with the Whigs voting on the same side as the Tories, and against the Radicals, over the proposed settlement between the town and the University in 1850. This split was most visible during periods of Liberal success; the Whig–Radical alliance reformed when the Tories were in control.

The two levels of political activity, parliamentary and municipal, reinforced one another.[15] There is a difference here between urban and rural areas. In the more important towns the reform of the municipal corporations had taken control of the local administration away from bodies that were often oligarchic and self-perpetuating, and placed these powers in the hands of annually elected town councils. The government of the counties was not reformed until the 1880s and so politics in county constituencies lacked a second level of activity, organization and competition.[16] The reformed corporations also provided office and small-scale rewards – patronage for successful parties and politicians.

Taken together these factors suggest that the organizational form of local parties in constituencies with regular municipal contests was of a modified machine type. A political machine in this context is a 'non-ideological organization interested less in political principle than in securing and retaining political office for its leaders and distributing income to those who run it and work for it' (Scott, 1972, p. 108). There was a link between the administrative authorities, in this case the local council with its control of local resources, and a partisan segment of the local community. The group in control used the council and its resources to differentially reward their own supporters and to reinforce the link between them. Scott suggests a set of minimal conditions for the emergence of such a form of local political control: 'the selection of authorities through elections; mass adult suffrage; a relatively high degree of political competition over time. These conditions reflect the fact that machine politics represents a distinctive way of mobilising voters, it arises only in systems where getting out the vote is essential to gaining control.'(Scott, 1972, p. 107).

Two of these conditions are unproblematic – local councils were selected through elections and immediately after municipal reform there was a high degree of competition at the annual elections. The franchise barrier for local elections was lower than for parliamentary elections: enfranchisement was still partial but, as with parliamentary elections, political participation – as opposed to mere voting – was not confined to those who were formally enfranchised. Control of the local council gave access to financial and political resources. Particularistic rewards were used as pay-offs that included money, office at different levels of the system or favours similar to those provided for their constituents by MPs.[17] Municipal reform gave reformers access to a wide range of such small-scale rewards. Scott suggests that 'the classical machine faces a social context in which narrow community and family orientation are most decisive' (Scott, 1972, p. 110). This was certainly true in Cambridge where issues from outside the community seldom influenced local and constituency politics. In this social setting individuals were constrained and influenced by personal ties – which made the electoral community fertile ground for a style of politics that was determined by narrow localistic and individual concerns rather than broader social and political forces and ideas. Similar conditions existed in many urban constituencies with reformed corporations.

Cornford and Mitchell identified a set of ward committees in Cambridge that existed in the late 1830s and early 1840s to contest the local elections and to organize party activity. These had no dues paying membership and were financed from 'above'. There was a presumption that the individual elector would see his vote as a resource that he could realize for money, so the organization of bribery may have helped create a skeletal organizational structure too. The exchange was more subtle than a simple money for votes transaction; what was involved was bargaining for the spoils that were provided through the fiscal powers vested in the reformed corporation. These rewards acted as the cement for the patron/client relationships of politics within the local political community.

Vincent noted that the existence of the spoils of the game at the parliamentary level performed an equivalent function to those at the municipal level. He suggested that there were 'a variety of personal rewards located at all levels of the political system' and went on to note 'the creative function they performed...in inducing local notables to tether themselves to one or other of the parliamentary parties'. At this level 'magistracies formed the small change in which debts between notables and the national party were adjusted'. (Vincent, 1966, p. 161 and p. 171). The spoils of municipal control extended this practice to the lower levels of the political system and linked it to the emerging organizational structure of parliamentary politics in the constituencies.[18]

In Cambridge the division of the spoils was reflected in partisan bias in the awarding of corporation contracts – a report in a local paper suggested that the surgeon to the gaol had been dismissed by the Liberal council allegedly for voting Conservative at the recent election. After the Liberals had won the first municipal elections in 1835, they made a clean sweep of the Tory appointees, filling posts such as the Town Clerk and the aldermanic bench with their own men. Four years later these appointments were reversed after the Conservatives regained control.[19]

II

The entry requirements for the franchise were not the only barriers to wider popular participation. There were other barriers of exclusion, not for party organization as such, but for parties organized from below with popular support. These took several forms: financial thresholds such as the property qualification required of an MP or town council-lor, and the opportunity costs of political activity in terms of time and skills, as well as the pressure of social dependence.

However such pressure could operate in two directions. As not all adult males had the vote, partial enfranchisement gave the individual elector added status and differentiated him from his non-elector neigh-bour. It provided him with a resource – his vote – that could be exchanged for money or payment in kind. But the elector was in a minority within the constituency and, for those lower down the social scale, within his immediate social environment too. He may have been dependent economically, or in other ways, on his social superiors, but he was also vulnerable to pressure from his peers. The threat of violence was used in some constituencies to reverse the pattern of social dependence and to ensure that electors followed the wishes of the more numerous lower status non-voters.[20] Pressure was not only applied to voters, it was also directed at representatives to censure them for their past behaviour, with the implicit threat that future support was conditional upon specific approved actions. As noted earlier, the division between the Whigs and the Radicals in Cambridge was a constant source of tension. On May 30 1839 the Chronicle reported that Henry Gunning, a Whig councillor, was attacked by the electors of Barnwell, a predominantly Radical area, for taking patronage and for not voting in favour of a resolution on police expenditure, as well as for supporting an increase in the salary of the local Recorder.

Such pressure was neither undirected nor wholly spontaneous. It was channelled through the ward-level political organizations. In Cambridge their activities are well covered in the local press between 1832 and 1852. The Independent in 1840 had regular reports of the Castle District Reform Association and of the East and West Barnwell Reform Associations too. On the 4 of March 1843 the Chronicle reported that Councillor H.S. Foster was attacked at a Radical meeting in East Barnwell for collaborating with the Tories, and especially for his attitude to police expenditure. In 1846 the Independent noted that the Castle District Reform Association had passed a resolution asking for two Reform candidates to stand in the forthcoming parliamentary election. They suspected that the Whigs might favour an agreement to share the representation with the Tories without a contest.

Parallel organizations existed on the Conservative side. In 1837 the Chronicle reported that a Conservative Association had been established, had held an annual meeting and had insisted that a second Conservative candidate contest the parliamentary seat at the next election. There were also reports of a Conservative Mechanics Festival in 1841 – 'an excellent repast' – which suggests that leading Conservatives were also trying to use local organizations to mobilize and consolidate potential support. These seem to have been initiated from above, rather than from the grass roots as was partially the case with those on the Reform side. Taken as a whole the evidence supports Fraser's view that: 'politics intruded into the whole urban experience and the limited political world of parliamentary elections identified by many historians as the stuff of urban politics was not a political boundary recognised by contemporaries'(Fraser, 1976, p. 9).

What was important was the stratified nature of political activity, and the interdependence between the levels of the system. Parliamentary elections saw the formation of election committees of local notables and political leaders that were dependent upon the continuing activity at the annual registration. Such committees also served as a conduit for the money that was needed to finance electoral activity, and these resources were channelled by activists to lower level ward politicians.

The ward politicians were active on a regular basis for the annual municipal elections. Lower level political actors inhabited a geographically smaller and socially more homogeneous political environment. For Cambridge in the late 1830s and early 1840s, the surviving comments suggest that there was more activity on the Liberal/Radical/Whig/Reform side, as well as confirming a continuing dissenting connection.[21] This was the 'old opposition' in Cambridge town politics and it emerged actively once more over questions such as disestablishment, Catholic and Jewish emancipation, or church rates. The evidence is consistent with Fraser's archaeological model which 'conceives of layers of political activity at different levels of urban life, with political issues taking on the character of bore holes penetrating each stratum'(Fraser, 1976, p. 9).

Mass involvement over political issues had been a feature of the larger open constituencies before Reform. The 1832 Act extended popular involvement by increasing the size of the electorate in many urban constituencies, and the Municipal Corporations Act of 1835 reinforced tendencies towards wider and more frequent popular involvement. The Act came into force soon after 1832, when reform issues were still controversial, and this helped to structure local, municipal political activity along similar lines to national and parliamentary politics with the annual town council elections maintaining political competition between parliamentary elections.[22]

So after 1835 a pattern of political competition existed between the parties that appealed to an enlarged electorate on a basis that was both stratified and mutually reinforcing between the distinct levels of activity. Stratified in that competition took place both for parliamentary and municipal elections – at least in urban constituencies with reformed corporations – as well as in a surrogate form at the annual revision. Also it was mutually reinforcing as the parties at the two levels of popular elections came to have the same attitudes over issues, as well as the same local activists, organizations and methods of electioneering.[23]

The electoral qualifications for municipal and parliamentary elections were not identical although there was considerable overlap in the electorates.[24] This overlap was not complete but was sufficient to reinforce the link of personnel and organizations. The same local political leaders were involved in both municipal and parliamentary politics, there was the same structure of election committees and ward associations and the electorate reacted in the same way to issues at both levels. While there was a difference between the parties – the Conservatives were less 'democratic' – overall there was a clear connection between ward-level politics and the activities of the constituency election committees.

Within this framework there were recognized relationships between representatives and constituents for both town councillors and MPs. Both were held accountable for their actions and were closely scrutinized by constituents. Representatives, particularly on the Liberal side, felt it necessary to account publicly for their actions. The mechanism of control by the whole electorate was acknowledged, as was control through nomination within parties.

This was all maintained by the regularity of political competition, and by the strength of partisan feeling. Local politics in Cambridge was extremely rancorous just after Reform. There was high feeling amongst the reformers against the 'old corruption' and against the Conservative monopoly of office and reward in the old corporation. After 1835 a 'winner takes all' attitude dominated council politics and it took 20 years for there to be a move towards non-partisan appointments to municipal office.

This structure of political activity, organization and principle was also held together by the rewards available, some coming from control of the municipal administration – the small change of political patronage – and some from the higher levels of the political system as it had in the past. These were used to reinforce continuing political support. The analysis of the behaviour of the electorates in Bedford and Lancaster showed that the voting behaviour of the majority was generally stable from election to election. Partisan advantage came through registering new electors, rather than from persuading existing electors to change their vote. Support was maintained through control of the spoils of office and the use of social pressure. So while politics took place in a context that varied across constituencies, it had some common social and structural elements. It also took place under open voting that provided party organizations with relatively accurate electoral information about potential supporters – reinforcing the links between social relationships and political action – and helped to maintain the overall structure of activity and organization.[25]

III

The 1832 Reform Act may have extended the parliamentary franchise but electors were still a minority of the adult population. Partial enfranchisement meant that electors interacted with non-electors. The franchise did not coincide with other social divisions,[26] and the existence of open voting ensured that an elector was unable to keep his political preferences a private matter – apart from the small number of persistent non-voters. So electors existed within a web of inter-personal relations, a network of interactions with others, many of whom did not themselves possess the same formal political rights and were not full members of the electoral community. The behaviour of an elector was structured and influenced by this network of personal relationships. So to understand nineteenth-century electoral behaviour and its social constraints, we need to analyse the context in which such behaviour was embedded, and of which it was itself a constituent element.

The idea of a social network has already been introduced to explain electoral recruitment, the process through which a potential voter was registered as an elector:

> whoever was qualified to be registered, registration was not automatic; someone had to take the initiative. Sometimes this someone was the voter himself. As a rule, however, it was the leader of the social group or network to which the prospective voter belonged, the man who expected to benefit individually from the prospective voter's vote, or someone associated with him.(Moore, 1975, p. 101)

This was very much the way that 'Mr. Jackson' operated in Lancaster, locating potential partisans through their links to individuals who had a known political identity. Nossiter suggests a similar process when discussing local party activity and the position of the individual in the community: 'the one central institution was the canvass buttressed by the immutable poll book. In this conception of what politics was about, the elector was encouraged to take his total social situation into account and by his vote express the network of influences of which he was a part' (Nossiter, 1975, p. 6).

More generally one can understand such a network as: 'an interconnected chain or system of immaterial things...it contains as much as possible about the whole of the social life of the community to which it corresponds'(Barnes, 1969, p. 56). It is a 'general social matrix out of which various forms of quasi-group, and eventually group and corporate group, may be differentiated'.[27] As such it is defined by interactional criteria, rather than by structural characteristics, and is a more general 'meta-structure' than class or group. However, if it persists over time, elements of a network may acquire structural permanence and evolve into other social institutions.

A brief discussion of some characteristics of social networks, and their implications, will help in understanding the electoral process in nineteenth-century England. This is not an exhaustive discussion and draws on other sources, particularly those that have used the network idea to analyse small face to face communities. Partly because the analogy has often been used metaphorically, there is a degree of terminological confusion that Mitchell has attempted to clarify.[28] He draws a useful distinction between the morphological characteristics of networks, 'the patterning of the links in the network in respect to one another' (Mitchell, 1969b, p. 12), and their interactional criteria – the nature of the links themselves. (The two are related, the interactions give rise to the patterning of links; the institutionalization of such links transforms an interactional 'pattern' into a social structure).

Two network concepts seem particularly relevant in the nineteenth-century electoral context – reachability and range. The first, *reachability*, refers to the links between individuals, and the use of these links to influence actions or behaviour:

> the degree to which a person's behaviour is influenced by his relationships with others often turns on the extent to which he can use these relationships to contact people who are important to him or alternatively, the extent to which people who are important to him can contact him through these relationships... the sociological significance of the notion of reachability lies in the way in which the links in a person's networks may be channels for the transmission of information, including judgements and opinions especially when these serve to reinforce norms and bring pressure to bear on some specified person. (Mitchell, 1969b, p. 15–17)

Most borough electorates were small although some were part of a large urban community. So it was possible for an election agent to know many, if not all, of the electors in 'his' constituency. The surviving canvass books and electoral management notebooks in Lancaster reveal just such a degree of personal knowledge, and the use of social links for transmitting information or influencing behaviour. The same process occurred when landlords exercised, or tried to exercise, 'influence' over their tenants.

The second concept, that of *range*, relates to the scale of personal contacts, the number of persons that an individual knows: 'Some persons may have many direct contacts while others have few. The first order range or number of persons in direct contact with the person...is likely to be a significant feature of a personal network...if the emphasis is on mobilising support for the individual' (Mitchell, 1969b, p. 19).

The idea can be extended to a second order range – those in contact with people in the first order range of an individual and so on. The first order range may be quite small: 'in general it appears that there is probably a limit to the number of people with whom an individual might be in direct and regular contact' (Mitchell, 1969b, pp. 19–20).

In an urban environment this limit may be about thirty persons. But even if one person knows only thirty others, and each of these in their turn knows a further thirty, then one individual could reach around nine hundred individuals (or electors) through his second order range – those at one remove from himself. (Although there may be some overlap and redundancy in a small community). In 1832 about half of the English borough constituencies had fewer than 700 electors and so the problems of 'knowing' or 'influencing' the political behaviour of the electorate in a borough of this size, the problem of organizing the vote, was possibly manageable by a single individual. As a result the political organization of many English borough constituencies in the period between 1832 and 1868 may well have been carried out by a small, or very small, group of political activists.

While these characteristics suggest an underlying structure to the social context of electoral behaviour, they are no more than a useful analogy without some indication of 'how the system worked'. What was the nature of the interactions that define and constitute the network links between individuals? Here again Mitchell's analysis is suggestive – what are important are the meanings that individual actors give to the nature of the link between them, their *content*:

> [Content]: concerns the meanings which persons in the network attribute to their relationships. The links between an individual and the people with whom he interacts come into being for some purpose or because of some interest which either or both of the parties consciously recognise. We may speak then of the content of the links in a person's network. This content may be, among other possibilities, economic assistance, kinship, obligation, religious co-operation or it may be simply friendship. (Mitchell, 1969b, p. 20)

There is an obvious parallel with Nossiter's comments that: 'the working class tenement was at the centre of a vast web of influence in which his employer, union leader, minister, publican, doctor and landlord were caught up as much as he was' (Nossiter, 1975, p. 159).

The analysis of canvassing and electoral management in Lancaster shows striking parallels – individual electors were identified as much by their relationships to others as by whom they were themselves. The content of links between individuals need not have been simple and could arise from more than one form of interaction, as when a relationship was both economic and with kin, with an employer who was also a co-religionist and so on.[29]

For any one individual their total network will describe or contain all the interactions they have with other individuals. It will be based upon many types of criteria or content – social, economic and so on. However if we look at relationships with others in terms of only one criterion then we are describing a partial network such as that containing just co-religionists or only kin. Every individual has a set of such partial networks, each one based on a different criterion – kinship, friendship, economic relations, religious observance and so on – each one relating to a different social role.

A personal network persists through time and an individual may mobilize part of their network for a specific purpose, at a specific time. They might use kinship as a means of obtaining employment or as a mechanism for mobilizing voters for electoral purposes. When he supported a particular candidate an elector might try to persuade others in his personal network to support the same candidate at an election too. Such a grouping of individuals is an 'action set' – a sub-set of individuals derived from a network in a particular context for a particular purpose.[30] An action set is not the same as a partial network. It is not a permanent set of individuals and is defined only by its external purpose rather than by the content of personal interactions. Once the purpose has been realized – or not – the action set ceases to have a function and dissolves back into the general set of social relations.

The post-1832 English electorate comprised roughly 1 in 5 of the adult males in an overwhelmingly pre-industrial population. Each individual, whether or not they were an elector, was at the centre of his or her own individual network. The linkages to others in such networks can be defined in terms of various contents. These other individuals are in turn linked to more individuals by a variety of ties – kinship, an employment relationship, religious sympathy, a social obligation and so on. These are the second order range of the original individual, and they in turn are linked to others, the whole ramifying outwards to encompass, indirectly, many of the actors in a particular social setting.

Obviously the question of 'boundedness' is important. Are there limits to the extent or range of an individual's network? Theoretically the total population could be encompassed by the nth order range of a given individual but, for most purposes most relevant actors will exist within a bounded arena – such as a parliamentary constituency, a parish in county divisions or a ward in a municipal election. Most individuals functioned within a relatively small, fixed and bounded social world. Their network was composed of those with whom they interacted regularly, although some will have important linkages to actors outside this primary arena. In this way, any social setting can be conceptualized as a series of partially overlapping personal networks, and the total social setting is a system of relatively independent, stratified networks – stratified not just in terms of locality but also perhaps in terms of the social status of the constituent individuals and the frequency of the social interactions involved.

From such a network one could extract the personal network of an individual in which the content of individual linkages could be specified. Note that this exists independently of 'politics' although 'politics' may be an important defining element, it may be the content of a link between individuals. Importantly the network of an elector included others who were not electors. Nevertheless these individuals could still serve important functions both socially and politically, and may have shaped or influenced both the perceptions that an elector had of his own interest, and his political behaviour. Women are a particularly important example. If politics were discussed within a household then the elector's wife could play an important part in the informal political process.[31]

Some qualifications need to be made – no network is isolated, it has links with the wider community, and, particularly for activists and party organizers, there is a structural parallel with the developing network of party organization. Finally, the electoral process itself, or rather its institutional setting, imposed other constraints. Partial enfranchisement has already been discussed but the lack of secrecy was important too. Open voting created a system that was potentially one of full information for parties and organizations, and imposed constraints on individual electors that reinforced the political consequences of their personal relationships.

IV

In his account of political development in Western Europe, Rokkan discussed some of the consequences of the introduction of secret voting. He argued that secrecy under full suffrage differentiated voting from other political acts in three ways: universality of access, equality of influence and the privacy and irresponsibility of the participant act.[32] All three were essential for the development of modern party systems and mass democracy. The three factors are distinct but related. In Britain, secrecy at elections was introduced by the Ballot Act in 1872. Before then, elections under open voting had the inverse characteristics – they were characterized by restricted access, inequality of influence and the public and accountable nature of the voting act.

The restriction of access has been mentioned as one aspect of partial enfranchisement. Full enfranchisement came in stages with equal adult suffrage not achieved until 1948. Women were disfranchised until 1918 although they could exercise political influence in other ways.[33] The franchise was linked to a property qualification, a particular definition of political rights. It does not appear to have been directly class related in the period between 1832 and 1868 and cut across other social divisions.[34]

Inequality of influence was related to restricted access. There were recognized leaders or influentials within the enfranchised stratum whose social dominance was often accepted as legitimate in politics too. The restriction of access was a justification for the inequality of influence not only between the enfranchised and the unenfranchised, but within the established electoral community too. However, it is the third aspect of open voting, its public nature and direct accountability that had most consequences for the individual elector.

Voters were affected in several ways. First, the criteria for electoral inclusion remained at the local level and were administered there. This effectively reinforced the importance of local authorities and structures, and limited the ability of the political to transcend the local, inhibiting the emergence of national patterns of political activity whether by politicians, parties or individual electors in the aggregate. As already noted, there was a difference between urban constituencies, where the structure of local authority was reformed in 1835, and the counties in which local government and administration was not reformed until later in the century. The provision of a second level of urban electoral activity – in which voting was also open – reinforced the politicization of constituency activity. In the absence of parliamentary elections, or between them, the annual electoral activity at municipal elections helped to maintain the underlying structure of local political competition.

More importantly for the individual – and maintaining this structural effect – under open voting the voter was constrained by his roles in the other systems of the household, the neighbourhood, the work place, the church, the civil association, the kin group and so on. When acting as a member of the local political sub-system there was feedback from activity in any public role to activity in all other roles. The voter had to take responsibility for the act of voting in his other everyday interactions in his regular environment. This is of course the opposite of the privatization and separation of the political role from other roles that takes place under secret voting. With electoral secrecy it is possible either to conceal or make public one's political preferences. Under open voting it is not possible to conceal them, political partisanship was public knowledge and information on voting behaviour was often available in printed poll books. Where a printed record was not published, the local parties may have had an equivalent record in the form of checklists taken at the time of an election.[35] In either case this increased the pressure on the individual elector to keep any promise of a vote or political support.

All of which suggests that without secrecy the political role was not differentiated from other roles, and emphasizes the possible pressures for conformity, whether 'vertical' in the traditional sense of the influence of social superiors, or 'horizontal' as with kin, neighbourhood or peer group. Much of the discussion of 'influence' has assumed that it was a 'vertical' relationship based upon inequality and social deference, but it could also have been based on relationships of exchange between social equals. As Hoppen suggests when referring to a particularly important group of social intermediaries, 'the integration of shopkeepers within local communities which laid them open to pressure also ensured that many were able to assume positions of influence and power. Buying and selling are reciprocal acts and, more often that not, involve a set of mutual rather than merely one-sided obligations' (Hoppen, 1984, p. 56).

This mutuality and exchange applied to others too and was a major mechanism for political influence and for social integration more generally. This reinforces the suggestion that the political role was only one role embedded in a total network of social relationships, and that 'politics' could not be separated from other social activities. It implies too that, in the mid-nineteenth century electoral community, all forms of social activity could be equivalent to, or substitutable for, 'politics'. So everyday life necessarily became highly politicized. The equivalence between the 'economic' and the 'political' can be seen both in the use of the vote as an economic good – selling it and establishing a market in votes – and in the use of economic power for political purposes – as in exclusive dealing. This interdependence of politics and social life, with the politicization of the social sphere, made for intense political debate and intensely felt political issues and partisan differences.

In such an environment the resolution of conflicting role expectations would tend to be a once and for all process for an elector. To change your vote or political allegiance publicly would mean establishing a new role equilibrium – and possibly bearing substantial social costs – with the constraints of a different set of sanctions and rewards, the establishment of new personal relationships and the potential loss of old ones. So we would expect a high degree of stability in individual political preferences under open voting.[36] This had obvious conse-quences for party organizations and electioneering. Most of those who supported a particular party at one election, and were still in the elec-torate at the next election, would continue to support the same party. So local parties could rely on a large fixed element of support, as in Bedford, with all the implications that were discussed in the analysis of electoral politics there.

There were of course those who did change their vote. Some electors might change over a highly salient issue, such as the Corn Laws. Others would be able to tolerate the social costs incurred – those who were either financially or socially independent. Out-voters in county seats, not resident in the place where they were qualified to vote, might be socially isolated or only weakly linked to the existing community social networks and so might be relatively independent of community social pressures. But there are also those voters who were totally dependent, whose vote in effect was not their own and who bowed to the 'legiti-mate influence' of their betters. Finally, there were always some venal voters who sold to the highest bidder.

There is little direct evidence on individual vote stability over long periods. Davis found that only 18 per cent of his population of voters in Aylesbury could be classified as true floating voters over the period 1847–1859, which implies that the remaining 80+ per cent voted consistently for one or other party. This is about the same level that was found in the Bedford electorate between 1832 and 1868.[37]

Mitchell and Cornford found that stability was even higher in Cambridge parliamentary elections between 1834 and 1847. In the 11 cohorts of elec-tors who entered the electorate between 1834 and 1847, the percentage of electors who voted consistently ranged between 82 per cent and 91 per cent of each cohort, averaging 89 per cent for those electors who partici-pated in more than one election.[38] Such evidence is suggestive, rather than conclusive, of a stability and continuity in political behaviour. It does not, by itself, necessarily confirm the embedding of a political role as one role within a total network of social relationships.

However, if open voting reinforced an interdependent relationship between the social and the political, then this has consequences both for party organizations and for the individual elector. With secrecy there is an asymmetric relationship between voting and public knowledge – electors may reveal how they vote, but they need not do so. There is another discontinuity too: a party organization or candidate cannot link the promise of support to an actual vote. So for parties and candidates there is always a degree of uncertainty about the extent and reliability of their support. This was less the case under open voting, a situation of more complete information. Not only was the past behaviour of an elector known, but a party or candidate could link the promise of support to the actual vote, and sanctions could be invoked if a voter reneged on a pre-election promise or previous vote. This helped to reinforce stability in voting and meant that party organizations could obtain relatively accurate information on their level of support before an election.

Surviving canvassing returns recording the promises made by electors before voting confirm the predictability of voting behaviour, and the overall stability of the electoral environment. The Bedford canvass book analysed in Table 5.20 showed that before the 1835 election the compiler had fairly accurate information; some 83 per cent of the electors voted as they had promised. Other data for urban constituencies confirms that this level of accuracy was not unusual. At Durham City in 1868 three candidates contested the two-member seat, and a surviving canvass return is summarized in Table 6.1 which shows that 89 per cent of electors voted as they had promised.

Table 6.1   The accuracy of canvassing – Durham City 1868

		VOTES					
		T	LL	L	X	NV	Changers
	T	550	8	1	10	22	41
	LL	35	728	3	12	17	67
PROMISES	L	4	4	10	6	0	14
	X	29	7	4	40	1	41
No promise		39	16	0	5	45	

Source: Durham canvass book 1868.

Even in the notoriously corrupt constituency of Sudbury the party agents had relatively accurate information. Sudbury was eventually disfranchised in 1844 but even with extensive corruption there was a fairly reliable connection between promise and vote. The poll book for the 1837 by-election contains the following comments:

Number of votes promised	Bagshaw 317	Smith 306
Number of votes polled	Bagshaw 284	Smith 278
Number of votes promised and not polled	Bagshaw 10	Smith 11
Number of voters who violated their promises	Bagshaw 23	Smith 17

All promises in this list were made by persons upon whom the committee believed reliance might have been placed' (Sudbury, 1837 poll book, p. 21). Ignoring the potential arithmetical and linguistic confusion, some 90 per cent of the electorate – 562 out of 623 electors – voted as they had promised.

Regular elections were important. The absence of a contest may reflect the successful elite management of constituency politics, but after a series of uncontested elections the party managers had less accurate information on the relationship of promise to vote, less accurate knowledge on the extent and reliability of their support. When there were long intervals between elections, politics in a formal sense may have been only a minor part of everyday social interactions and electors may not have known their 'correct' political behaviour. Those to whom they looked for political cues may also have been unused to exercising social and political leadership. As a result electors would have little idea of how they 'ought' to vote, and the general problems of electoral management would have been reinforced by the lack of information on the past behaviour of voters. So regular elections were necessary for the 'system' to work and perhaps, as Dahl suggests, political competition was a necessary condition for political organization and control.[39]

In many urban constituencies the evidence of canvass books show that it was possible for party managers to have fairly accurate knowledge of the level of their support. Open voting and the growth of systematic record keeping enabled party managers to go further. Over a series of elections they could build up a picture of the dynamics of constituency electoral change and, as in Lancaster, the information could be used to maximize the electoral success of a constituency party organization.[40]

V

We have seen that the related influences of electoral turnover, kinship, religious affiliation, and employment structured electoral politics and channelled individual political behaviour in urban constituencies. Local politics could also provide rewards to help sustain individual loyalty. Partial enfranchisement, and the small size of many electoral communities, located electors within social networks with known connections between the members of such networks. The lack of secrecy gave party managers accurate information on individual behaviour and the overall distribution of party support. The behaviour of an elector could be linked to his immediate social environment and electoral support could be identified and replaced. The voter was constrained in voting by its publicness and accountability, as well as by his network of personal connections. Together these various elements formed a mutually reinforcing system which linked individuals, social context and constituency organization.

But how did this 'system' function in an election? One possible outline of the processes involved is suggested by the dynamics of politics in contemporary small-scale societies where social relations are similarly structured, and in which there are parallel links between social and political organization. Indeed the dynamics of electioneering and political behaviour in nineteenth-century England appear strikingly similar to those outlined in one study of a modern election in an India state:

> the link between the individuals (sometimes groups) are distinguished by their content i.e., these vary between one or more of the following kinship, occupational...economic, religious links and so on.... while the outgoing relationships may be diverse, the incoming links all have the same content – support for the candidate in the election (Mitchell, 1969b, p. 21).

Compare this with Hoppen's comments on elections in Ireland in the mid-nineteenth century:

> electoral influence functioned not only by means of party organisation or individual relationships...but through the more complex mechanisms of groups of people bound together by mutual interests, shared obligations, or family bonds. Given sufficient time, political connections, even if built on the shifting sands of cash and favours, could sometimes achieve a remarkably coherent momentum of their own. Most obviously impressive were the large connections managed by landlords in the countryside or by wealthy merchants and urban proprietors in the towns. The latter were able to dominate some of the smaller boroughs virtually unaided, at least for short periods (Hoppen, 1984, p. 63).

The parallel between the two, the management of elections in India in the 1950's and in Ireland in the mid-nineteenth century, is suggestive. In both cases the content of the links between individuals, the separate elements of a personal network, were used to mobilize political support. An action set was activated within an existing social network. A grouping emerged for one specific purpose, it was created to mobilize electoral support for a candidate or organization. In the Indian context Mayer 'traced the chains of influence through which a candidate in an election solicited support and how the successful candidate was able to reach a particularly extensive body of potential supporters in this way'.[41] Similarly in his survey of politics at the micro-level Barnes noted that:

> these lower level, or local level, political processes occur within institutions that fulfil many functions that are not themselves political. Political behaviour is here intimately bound up with activities that are aimed at other non-political ends and can be isolated from the other aspects only analytically, not in terms of space, time or personnel. (Barnes, 1969, p. 51)

Both Mayer and Barnes were discussing contemporary non-European politics – in India and Africa – but the processes involved are similar to those that occurred under open voting in nineteenth-century England between 1832 and 1868. In both communities politics was part of a general set of social relations, not something that had become differentiated and distinct. So the dynamics of the action set in the Dewas election are probably similar to the social processes that underpinned electioneering under open voting in England. In both situations political action was closely linked to personal relationships. Mayer suggests that one or more individuals could mobilize political support through their social networks using links that had other social contents. It was a dynamic process in which:

> a) Many different outgoing links were mobilised but incoming relationships were all the same, viz, electoral support...; b) the links were sometimes based on group membership, e.g....a group of religious worshippers, but they might have been distant kinship...some links were between employer and employee, creditor-debtor or storekeeper-customer; c) it contains intermediaries or paths of linkages leading out from ego; d) it is a bounded entity, unlike the total network. It ends with the voters in the wards; and finally, e) it is not a permanent entity, it exists only until the election.[42]

Since all electors are already members of networks, the functioning of a similar system in English nineteenth-century elections under open voting is straightforward. The potential voters or supporters are located socially mostly in the first or second order range of a party activist. Each party will try to win support through the 'cashing' of obligations or the manipulation of favourable relationships – friendship, kinship, common residence, common workplace or religion and so on. An action set is produced, originating with an individual who, by activating one or more of the relationships that form the linkages in his personal network, builds political support for 'his' candidate. Those in his first order range use these relationships in a similar manner – they make up the original individual's second order range. This process can be repeated in others steps, through other relationships, as required. These activated relationships may well be based on multiple criteria and structurally the end result can be represented in a 'cascade' or 'tree' form as in Figure 6.1. In this process of serial activation the terminal respondents – the voters – need not themselves form a group; there are not necessarily any horizontal, cross-linkages between individuals.[43]

This process of the activation of linkages produces 'political' networks with two characteristics. Although the end product is political support – votes – which can be considered as 'flowing upwards', the balancing flows in the reverse direction need not all be the same, political interactions are not necessarily symmetric. In such interactions a social link has been transformed into a political one. This reinforces

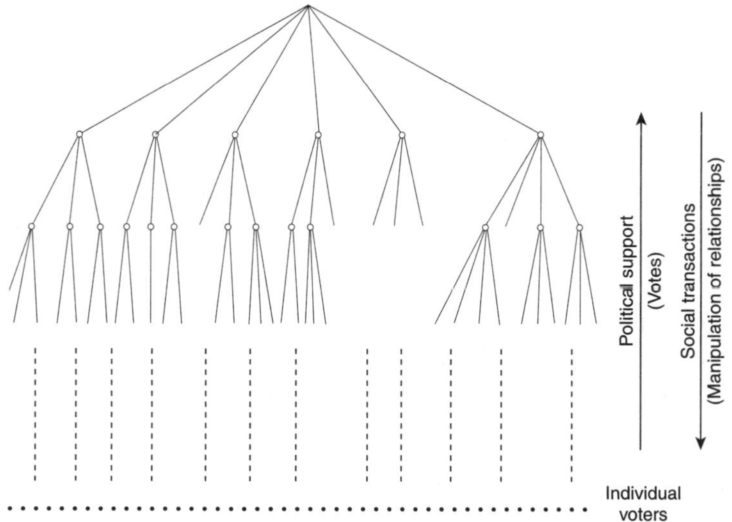

Figure 6.1   The mobilization of political support

the consequences of politics as public knowledge and a public activity. Under open voting, there is only a very limited separation of the private and the public realm. Finally, because there is a limit to the number of individuals with whom one can interact and influence, and this limit may be small compared to the total number of electors involved, there will be an element of organization or differentiation within the total network in terms of activism.

It is unlikely that the total mobilization of support for one party or candidate originates with one person. There may well be activists who mobilize different strata of the community. Cambridge was divided into wards for elections, each one with its own organization. Similarly, county constituencies were often divided according to the estates of large landowners. Within the different strata – the 'upper crust', 'respectables', 'lower orders' etc. – activists would initiate support within their own social networks. These activists might well form a meta-network of party electoral managers, ward bosses and local political figures of influence. In such a structure there would be a link between the MP and his agent, a relationship that links the constituency to the supra-system of all the constituencies, the local agent to the national agent.[44]

Such political networks would not need to be created afresh at each election. They would be latent in the everyday social life of the community. Latent and at the same time subject to change. Change both in the content of interpersonal linkages – friendships may end, religion may diminish in personal importance, or the pattern of economic activity and employment may change – and there may also be the physical replacement of individual members of a network. The loss of one individual could disrupt the chain of influence within a network, organization or constituency and add to the problems of recruitment that follow from the turnover in the electorate.

Nor were networks politically neutral structures. The new elector joined through establishing links with other individuals, and these social links were used at an election to channel support for one or other candidate. Individuals interacted with others similar to themselves in terms of social position, economic standing, religion, workplace or residence. This similarity may have extended to political partisanship too and, over time, many of these supposedly independent social factors varied together and this could establish a permanent bias in a network. Political inclination would increasingly tend to co-vary with this bias. The mere fact of being A's son or B's employee or going to church with C would mean that an individual also probably shared A, B or C's political opinions. Drawing on such bias the local political activist would tend to qualify only those who supported 'his' party, as Moore put it, 'principally these men [nineteenth-century election managers] were concerned to identify each prospective voter in terms of his membership in a specific group or network' (Moore, 1974, p. 108).

The social conditions under open voting between 1832 and 1868 certainly allowed, and perhaps encouraged, the equivalence of social and political links in a manner very similar to that described by Mayer in Dewas. The parallel is plausible. The existing accounts of constituency politics in the nineteenth century also show how non-political relationships could be 'cashed' in exchange for political support. So clearly the social environment between 1832 and 1868 could be mobilized for electoral purposes in a manner that can be described in network terms. However, beyond the accounts of the use of influence to solicit votes, either directly or more usually through the use of intermediaries, there is little direct evidence of political mobilization through networks in the Reform system. Other evidence is in Mr Jackson's notebooks for Lancaster, the analysis of Irish politics by Hoppen, the data from the canvass books discussed earlier, as well as many contemporary novels and memoirs.[45]

VI

But there are other, theoretical, advantages to an explanation of voting based on social networks. Previous studies advancing the claims of class, religion or other social factors are not necessarily mutually exclusive or incompatible; they have all been examining only one partial aspect of the total network involved, or analysing one specific content from the many that existed in the linkages between individuals. As a result, whether they emphasize the economic transactions of the vote market or the hierarchical relationship of social and political dependence, these explanations are necessarily partial. In addition, if there were 'leads' and 'lags' across the constituencies in the process of electoral and social change, then the importance of a particular content within a social network might also vary, depending on the pattern of change within the constituency.

This suggests that the four models of open voting outlined in Chapter 1 can be subsumed within a more general social network explanation, and that in stressing the relative importance of a single social factor such as religious affiliation, or social dependence, other accounts have been examining only one partial network.

A social network was not only a mechanism through which electors could be mobilized, it also provided a channel of influence and a potential distribution structure for bribery and the rewards of office. Theoretical discussions of social networks draw a distinction between the flow of goods and services through a network, and the flow of communication. In urban settings the development of multiple nodes suggests a stratification of individual electors in terms of activism. Davis, for example, found that of the electors in Buckingham who changed their vote between the parties:

> fourteen…followed remarkably closely the shifts and turns of Humphrey Bull, and for nine of them at least there is reason to believe that this was no coincidence, all of them being his neighbours and the sort of small farmer and tradesman over whom his particular kind of influence might have been effective. (Davis, 1972, p. 182)

There is an echo here of Hoppen's comments that 'publicans without votes could still "command" others to do as they required and men who could influence publicans themselves were men of influence indeed' (Hoppen, 1984, pp. 54–5).

More generally within this framework one can accept the existence of a political class, in Vincent's terms, as a core of activists mobilizing, and interacting with, fringes of supporters – an alternative formulation of the same social situation and the same political process.[46]

Recruitment and the inherent bias of networks have been mentioned earlier. In many cases there were no doubts about new voters 'it is clear that individuals recruit people to networks on the basis of many different relationships and that further, the types of relationship for which they use recruitment to networks varies with their social situation and their social position'(Mitchell, 1969b, p. 41).

But there were cases where the qualified individuals might be linked to an existing network only weakly. This is the problem noted by Moore in discussing the comment 'doubtful' which is found referring to individuals in canvassing returns: 'the "doubtful" were not the "don't knows"…of present day electoral behaviour. Rather, they were the ones whose effective social identity had yet to be discovered, and whose behaviour could not be predicted as the behaviour of others, presumably, could be predicted' (Moore, 1974, p. 109).

Such an explanation also helps to account for larger continuities in electoral behaviour in the nineteenth century, linking behaviour before and after the expansion of the suffrage. Following the Second Reform Bill in 1867 the new electors were not suddenly absorbed into social networks and then mobilized to vote. They were already located within a web of personal relationships and were already politicized. After 1867 they were enfranchised too and so became formal participants in the electoral process.

This interpretation of the link between social life and electoral behaviour, does broadly agree with the available evidence on electoral behaviour for the period between 1832 and 1868.[47] It provides a feasible interpretation of electioneering, and of the relationship between the voter and his social environment. It accounts too for the continuities in electoral behaviour and, in the absence of direct evidence, the network interpretation can be advanced for its overall plausibility, its more parsimonious fit with a wide and diverse set of facts, and its compatibility with alternative explanations. And it suggests a different understanding of the effects of the changes that followed further enfranchisement and the later introduction of electoral secrecy in 1872 when:

> politics for more than twenty years after the 1867 Reform Act became the central preoccupation of the nation. The party system was remodelled to encourage popular participation on an unprecedented scale. The number of votes cast in general elections rose rapidly, each party gaining over a million votes for the first time in the general election of 1874. (Hanham, 1978, p. xi)

Or, as with the development of the party system in the United States, 'the salient characteristic of the … party system was the mobilisation of mass participation in elections' (Chambers, 1967, p. 11). The pattern of electioneering, and the relationship between the elector and his social community, that had developed under restricted enfranchisement between the First and Second Reform Bills, together with local constituency institutions and organizations, provided a framework for the later growth of a mass party system following the further expansions of the suffrage after 1867.

7
After the Second Reform Bill

After 1832 electoral behaviour was influenced by three related factors – partial enfranchisement, the social relations within the electoral community and the public nature of open voting. In borough constituencies there was a link between the elector and the social environment that can be described in terms of social networks. Such networks were used to influence the behaviour of electors and, with the institutional structure created by the Reform Bill, contributed to the development and growth of local party organization.

Political partisanship was public knowledge under open voting. A change in political behaviour, such as voting for a candidate or party other than the one to whom support had been promised, could incur social costs. Partly as a result, electoral preferences tended to be stable over time with the electorate changing as voters left the electorate and new electors were registered. The extent of electoral turnover varied between constituencies and the links between 'new' electors and existing social networks were used to influence, and to maintain, the underlying constituency pattern of electoral behaviour. Parliamentary candidates, and local party organizations, could rely on a core of known support within the electorate and concentrated on establishing the political identity of new electors. The accuracy of political information was confirmed through canvassing, and by the knowledge of voting available from poll books and other sources. As a result, within the small and restricted local electoral community of most borough electorates, there could be both a consistent pattern of political campaigning and a relatively stable structure of electoral behaviour individually and collectively.

In 1867, before the passage of the Second Reform Bill, about one in five of the adult male population were enfranchised; 20 years later this had increased to approximately two out of every three. More importantly, 'with the extension of the suffrage, class was becoming the most important single factor in deciding political allegiance' (Cornford, 1963, p. 37). By the end of the 1880s mass electoral behaviour had become increasingly class based, a major change from the earlier period between the First and Second Reform Bills.

The social and political changes that came after 1867 modified patterns of individual electoral behaviour, and the organizational activity of constituency parties. The Second Reform Bill doubled the number of electors and, five years later, the passing of the Ballot Act altered the conditions that had sustained the link between voting and the social context. The 1872 act introduced the secret ballot and ended the 'full information' character of elections, voting became an increasingly private and individual act, with consequences for party organizations, individual electors and political campaigning.[1]

Within constituencies the relationship between electors, and between electors and non-electors, had already been altered by the extension of the franchise in 1867. The Ballot Act brought other changes, and the transformation of voting and political campaigning was completed by the further alterations in the franchise, and in the structure of constituencies, that followed the Third Reform Bill in 1884/85.[2] These later changes were accompanied by attempts to control and eliminate electoral corruption, and the transformation of the social context of voting was completed by the emergence of a mature class society in the last quarter of the nineteenth century.[3]

By the end of the nineteenth century a majority of the electors in England lived in urban and suburban areas, so the typical social context of voting was no longer that of the medium-sized market town that had been the main element of electoral system between 1832 and 1867. In addition not only had the class system changed but so had the relationship between class and vote. Finally, as the franchise widened, the context of electoral politics became increasingly nationalized.[4] General elections became general, with campaigns that concentrated on party leaders and party policy, as compared to the previous focus on mainly local concerns. So in a relatively short period after 1867, successive changes had a major effect on electoral behaviour, and, as a result, electoral politics after 1885 were qualitatively different to those found within the more restricted electorate of the period between 1832 and 1868.

I

The passing of the Second Reform Act in 1867 extended the right to vote and 'overturned the principle ... that property was the sole indication of fitness to vote' (Smith, 1966, p. 2). The Act introduced household suffrage and a lodger franchise in the boroughs, but the twelve-pound tenancy qualification in the counties enfranchised fewer new electors in rural areas, making the increase in the electorate smaller in county constituencies.[5] The borough electorate grew by 134 per cent between 1866 and 1869, the county electorate by only 37 per cent; overall the number of electors doubled, (see Table 2.2).[6] There was some redrawing of the boundaries of county constituencies and new boroughs were created, particularly in the north of England. However, unlike the changes brought by the First Reform Bill in 1832, few constituencies were abolished. Some of the larger urban constituencies now returned three members but overall the distribution of seats in relation to both electorates and population remained skewed with the counties still over represented.[7]

As in 1832, there was an increase in the number of contests after the Reform Bill and the growth in the borough electorate increased the number of first time voters at the general election in 1868. The local impact in Bedford can be seen in Table 5.1 and Figure 5.2 that show that some 62 per cent of the constituency electorate voted for the first time in 1868. Between 1832 and 1865 the number of new voters in Bedford had averaged between 5 and 6 electors a month (Table 5.3). After 1865 the rate increased to 33 per month. The change in the franchise probably meant that most of the new voters in 1868 were registered after the passing of the bill and before the election. So the rate of increase between 1867 and the election in 1868 was probably even higher, perhaps about 70 per month.[8] This would have strained the existing constituency party organization – the sheer number of new electors to be registered in a relatively short period posed problems of social and political identification. In some boroughs the level of enfranchisement after 1867 approached about 1 in 2 adult males and, as more individuals became electors, it became increasingly likely that an elector had social links to others with different political preferences. In modern terms more electors would be cross-pressured.[9] Perhaps as a result the local party organization would have found more electors with a political identity that was 'doubtful'.

But how typical was Bedford of borough constituencies? It is difficult to say. We know that in 1832 borough seats varied in terms of population and electorate (see Table 3.3), and although the Bedford electorate grew by about 102 per cent between 1865 and 1868, this was less than the national average of 134 per cent. This overall figure disguises significant regional variations; industrial areas, such as Lancashire and

Table 7.1   The increase in English borough electors after the Second Reform Bill, by region[10]

Region	% increase in borough electors
North of England	282
Lancashire	194
Yorkshire	296
East Midlands	169
West Midlands	240
East Anglia	125
Central Region	137
Bristol Region	102
South East Region	67
Wessex	103
Cornwall and Devon	71

the West Midlands, saw an above average increase in the number of electors; in areas with less industrialization, such as Wessex or Cornwall and Devon, the increase was below average, see Table 7.1.

The figures in this table should be treated with caution because of the inaccuracies in recording the number of electors, and as some constituency boundaries were redrawn to incorporate areas from the surrounding counties.[11] So while the official figures give the increase in the electorates at Bedford, Hereford, Ipswich, and Gloucester as 93, 95, 152, and 160 per cent respectively, the data in poll books for these constituencies suggests increases of 102, 101, 165 and 174 per cent. The overall accuracy of the figures may be questionable but they do illustrate the range of variation that occurred across the English regions, and that underlay differences in politicization and contestation.[12]

The changes in 1867 affected the size of the electorate, the behaviour of electors and the number of contests. At the 1868 election the Liberals gained seats – in 1865 there were 359 Liberal MPs and 299 Conservatives; after 1868 there were 379 Liberal and 270 Conservative MPs. There were few changes in those seats that were nominally contested in the same way, and the balance of party representation was largely preserved in the one and two-member seats where the net gain to the Conservatives was three seats. So despite the increase in the number of electors there was a substantial degree of continuity in party representation between 1865 and 1868.[13]

However these were changes at the aggregate level. We can examine individual and constituency level changes through the linkage of poll book data to give a more detailed picture of the effects of enfranchisement, and an indication of the extent of continuity and change in the electorate, and in electoral behaviour.

II

Some of the effects can be seen in five constituencies – Bedford, Cambridge, Gloucester, Hereford and Ipswich – all two-member boroughs. These were medium-sized county towns, the most typical element of the electoral system between 1832 and 1868. According to Hanham, three of these constituencies – Gloucester, Hereford and Ipswich – possessed a corrupt element between 1865 and 1868. Gloucester and Hereford were 'extremely corrupt', and he notes that in Gloucester corruption was 'an integral part of the political life of the community', but adds that the elections of 1865 and 1868 were 'comparatively pure' despite this 'long history of corruption' (Hanham, 1959, pp. 263–70).

Data for the five constituencies is summarized in Table 7.2. The table shows the electorate and population before and after 1867 as well as the percentage increase in both. The percentage of electors in 1865 who were still electors three years later identifies the level of continuity in the electorate. The table also gives the extent of party voting at both

Table 7.2   Electoral data for five borough constituencies 1865–68

	Pop 61	Pop 71	I %	E65	E68	EI %	L	P^1	P^2	S	T^1	T^2
Bedford	13,413	16,850	41	1,049	2,124	102	77	66	82	69	90	92
Cambridge	26,361	33,996	29	1,793	3,852	115	79	98	97	86	84	84
Gloucester	16,512	31,804	93	1,615	4,431	174	69	92	96	71	93	79
Hereford	15,585	18,347	15	1,094	2,195	101	66	95	93	81	90	91
Ipswich	37,950	42,947	12	2,044	5,418	165	66	91	94	75	90	81

Key: Pop – population 1861,1871; I – increase in population; E65, E68 – electorate 1865, 1868; EI – increase in constituency electorate 1865–68; L (linked electors) – % of 1865 electorate who were still electors in 1868; P_1, P_2 – extent of party voting at 1865 (P_1) and 1868 (P_2) elections; S – stability in voting of those electors who voted at both elections; T_1, T_2 – participation rates for 1865 (T_1) and 1868 (T_2) elections.

Source: Constituency poll books; McCalmont (1971).

elections, the pattern of behaviour amongst electors voting in both 1865 and 1868, the turnout at the two elections and the percentage of the electorate voting for the first time in 1868.

The similarities across the five constituencies are striking. Despite the increase in the electorate for the second election, voting was still very much along party lines in 1868. Over ninety per cent of the electors in the four largest boroughs gave a party vote even when there were only three candidates standing, as at Gloucester and Hereford in 1865, and Ipswich in 1868. This is an impressive display of consistent behaviour, particularly as most electors were new voters in 1868 – between 62 and 75 per cent across the five constituencies.[14] In Cambridge only 13 electors cast a split vote in 1868 – less than 0.5 per cent of those voting. Turnout was high despite the increase in the number of electors although it decreased in the two con-stituencies where the electorate grew most, Gloucester and Ipswich. In the other three seats the turnout increased or stayed the same.

Did enfranchisement have other effects on voting behaviour? 'Vote stability' between 1865 and 1868, that is the proportion of electors voting for the same party at both elections, varied between 69 and 86 per cent in the five constituencies, see Table 7.2. This level of stability is comparable to that found for many pairs of 'normal' elections in the period before 1867.[15] Importantly, the new voters voted along party lines to a similar extent to those who had voted previously. Only in Bedford did a significant number of the newly enfranchised vote across party lines – 10.8 per cent of new Bedford electors give a split vote in 1868, see Table 7.3.[16] The table indicates that the extent of split voting

Table 7.3   The voting behaviour of new electors in five borough constituencies 1868

	New voters as a % of the 1868 electorate	Voting of new electors in 1868 (%)			
		L	T	X	NV
Bedford	62.1	56.9	24.6	10.8	7.7
Cambridge	62.0	52.9	32.1	0.4	14.5
Gloucester	75.0	49.7	40.2	1.5	8.5
Hereford	67.0	45.7	43.2	2.6	8.5
Ipswich	75.0	43.2	35.5	1.8	19.5

Note: L, T, X, NV refer to those voting Liberal, Tory, giving a vote across party lines, or Non-voting respectively.

Source: Constituency poll books.

in the other four constituencies was lower than that found in Cambridge after the Reform Bill in 1832.[17] So we can, perhaps, conclude that the voting behaviour of the new voters in these constituencies was not significantly different to that of electors who had voted before.

In all five seats the Liberals had a partisan advantage amongst new voters; this varied from a lead of 2.5 per cent over the Tories in Hereford, to 20.8 per cent in Cambridge and 32.3 per cent in Bedford. But we cannot base general conclusions on the evidence from these five constituencies alone. The Second Reform Bill gave a greater weight to the industrial towns rather than the 'provincial backwaters', so these five towns were now less typical of the electoral system as a whole than they had been between 1832 and 1867. But the high level of voting along party lines does suggest that the mechanisms for electoral recruitment and campaigning outlined in the previous chapters were probably still in place, at least in the smaller towns such as Bedford and Hereford. Perhaps the higher level of non-voting in Gloucester and Ipswich, where the increase in the number of electors was greater, is some indication that local organization there was functioning less effectively than it did before 1867. But the passing of the Ballot Act in 1872 makes it impossible to carry out individual level analysis for later general elections, and we cannot outline the longer-term effects of enfranchisement in the same detail as we could for the 1832 Reform Bill.

Although there was some continuity in electoral behaviour, the Second Reform Bill began to undermine the existing social mechanisms for recruiting and maintaining partisan support. Even though the electorate doubled in size, the enfranchised were still a minority in many constituencies after 1867. The increase in the number of electors posed problems for constituency organizations, particularly in urban constituencies. It may have been possible to use network links to establish the social and political identity of the new electors, and to recruit their partisan support, but the sheer number of new voters posed a problem. (As we have seen, the rate of electoral recruitment possibly increased almost tenfold in Bedford after 1867.[18])

So even if a political identity could be established for all the new voters, it is possible that there was increased uncertainty about the reliability or accuracy of this information, and canvassing may have recorded more 'doubtful' voters than previously. In many constituencies there would be increasing uncertainty about the overall level of partisan support. One party agent, in discussing the difference between votes promised and votes recorded, reported after the 1868 election that 'at the last election exceptionally we lost 11¼ per cent' – normally he would have expected to 'lose' 5 per cent of promised support.[19]

In a small electorate one individual or agent could know many of the electorate himself or could reach them through one intermediary – all electors would be in his first or second order range. But after 1868 the electorate in Leeds was over 37,000, in Liverpool over 39,000, in Birmingham over 42,000, in Manchester over 48,000, in Glasgow about the same. In all these constituencies the total number of electors was now well beyond even the third order range of one individual. In these large borough constituencies, the growth in the number of electors posed general problems for constituency party organizations both in identifying new supporters and in 'getting out the vote' at an election, and existing social mechanisms and social networks might no longer function as effectively as before.[20]

There were other consequences for the electors themselves. They were already members of existing networks when they were enfranchised, and were located within an established web of social relationships. They were probably politicized and possibly mobilized too.[21] So enfranchisement after 1867 involved relatively little social or political change for new electors and there could be a substantial degree of continuity in electoral behaviour before and after the Second Reform Bill. The extension of the franchise did not alter personal relationships, although it may have changed the balance between electors and non-electors, and for most electors there were now more individuals who were also electors within their personal networks. This changing balance, in conjunction with the increased uncertainty about political behaviour in the enlarged electorate, may itself have altered the pattern of behaviour within social networks. It could have decreased the effectiveness of hierarchical influence on individual electors and, at the same time, increased peer group pressure. There could now be a greater exercise of influence by other electors within the immediate social environment and 'horizontal' pressure from electors who were social equals might, to some extent, replace 'vertical' influence from social superiors.

III

What was the relationship between the electorate and the underlying social structure, between enfranchisement and social stratification in the enlarged electorate? We know that the enfranchised stratum increased in size after 1867, but know very little about the relationship between enfranchisement and the evolving class system – the relationship of electoral stratification to social stratification. So, for example, we do not know whether the distinction between an elector and a non-elector was related to other existing social differences within a constituency. The earlier discussion has suggested that 'class' was not a primary factor in influencing voting behaviour before 1867. But we do not have an agreed picture of social stratification in the wider society for much of the period after 1832. In some constituencies we have occupational evidence about the electorate from poll books, but the most thorough survey of this evidence concludes that, in most constituencies, 'the political society was pre-industrial'(Vincent, 1967, p. 24). The rise of a modern-class society in Britain has been dated to about 1880, after the Second Reform Bill and almost coincident with the Third Reform Act in 1885.[22]

Other factors also make any general statement about the relationship between class and vote problematic. One was the cross-local variation in the development of the stratification system itself. As well as local and regional differences across communities, under partial enfranchise-ment there was also variation in the relationship between the franchise and local social structural conditions within constituencies. We know that the proportion of the adult male population enfranchised varied considerably across constituencies, so even if the social structure was everywhere the same, we cannot infer that the relationship between it and enfranchisement was everywhere identical. The possession of the vote might well be a contributory factor to local differences, particu-larly if it was dependent on variation in property qualifications or local rights to freemanship.

But, while we know little about the relationship between enfranchise-ment and social structure between the First and Second Reform Bills, we do know that as the suffrage was further extended, social stratification within society and within the electorate converged, although there would continue to be some differences between the two until full adult suffrage was achieved. We also know the later importance of class for voting in Britain under universal suffrage.[23] More speculatively we might suggest that, under full adult suffrage, the range of independent variation along any one dimension of class is small across constituencies and so local differences in social stratification became less important. Being an elec-tor today does not, of itself, confer higher status or lead to variation in an individual's social location. But this may not have been the case within the more restricted electorate that existed between 1832 and 1868.[24]

Because of the later importance of class to electoral behaviour under full enfranchisement, the extent of the suffrage amongst the working

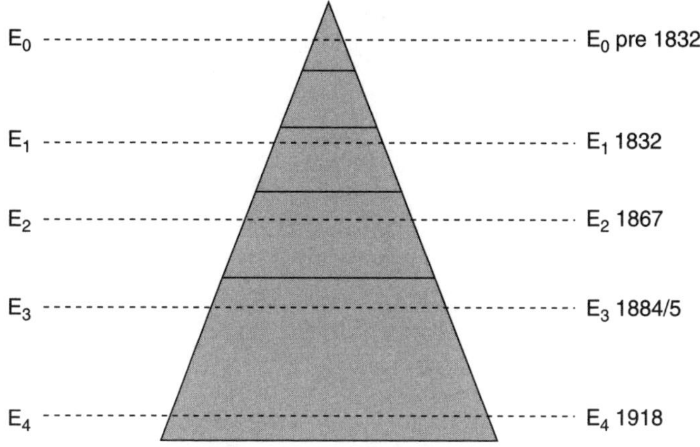

Figure 7.1   Electoral stratification and the extension of the suffrage[25]
Source: Mitchell, 1982b.

class after 1867 is particularly interesting. Even if we do not know the outline of the stratification in any detail, we know that mid-nineteenth century society was stratified. It is quite possible that there were no working-class electors at all after 1832, and that working-class enfranchisement followed the later changes in 1867 and 1885. If we represent the class system in the mid-nineteenth century as a simple stratified pyramid (Figure 7.1), and if electoral stratification was similar to social stratification, then the pre-Reform electorate may only have included those individuals above the dotted line E_0E_0 in Figure 7.1. In that case, the relationship of electors to non-electors would be one of strict class opposition. The successive enfranchisements in 1832, 1867, 1884/85 and 1918 could have increased the number of electors but maintained the relationship between electoral and social stratification, that is the class 'antagonism' of electors to non-electors. This is shown diagrammatically in Figure 7.1 with the dotted lines E_1E_1, E_2E_2, E_3E_3, and E_4E_4, representing the successive enfranchisements of the Reform Bills between 1832 and 1918.

But, even if the outline of the stratification system is not known in any great detail, we do know that there were some electors classified as working class by contemporaries, both before and after 1832. So Figure 7.1 cannot accurately reflect the relationship between electoral

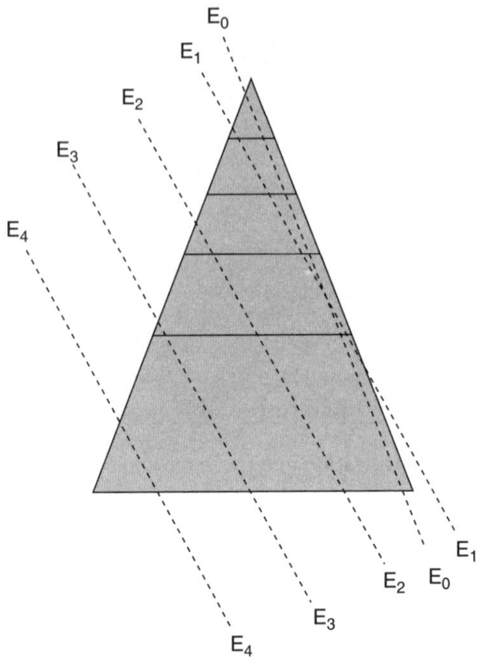

Figure 7.2   Electoral stratification and suffrage extension – a reticulated model
Source: Mitchell, 1982b.

and social stratification – it was probably a more crosscutting one that is represented in the reticulated form of Figure 7.2.

In Figure 7.2, as before, the pre-1832 electors are those above E_0E_0, and the later changes in the suffrage are shown by the lines E_1E_1, E_2E_2, E_3E_3, E_4E_4. The exact nature of the reticulation is uncertain although we know that the 1832 Bill may have decreased working-class representation.[26] A study of the electorate in Cambridge between 1832 and 1868 found that non-electors were drawn from a similar range on the social scale to electors, suggesting that electoral stratification did not follow the lines of social stratification. If social and political divisions were partially crosscutting, this would have reduced the potential for conflict within the system, as reflected in Vincent's comments on the 'classlessness' of political society at this time – a classlessness that coexisted with a high degree of 'social' class consciousness.[27] However this raises a further question: if electoral behaviour before 1868 was not related to 'class', and if after 1885 it is characterized by a growing relationship between class and vote, then how and when did this relationship develop?

This will depend too on the development of the class system. Perkin suggests that a modern-class system has at least two essential characteristics, a 'vertical antagonism between a small number of horizontal groups', and a degree of solidarity, of common interests, within such horizontal groups.[28] British society was certainly hierarchical and stratified in status terms in the nineteenth century but it is questionable whether that stratification was necessarily antagonistic or whether there was solidarity within existing social strata. Many stress the role of industrialization in generating economic conflicts, and urbanization in producing new and larger communities with common interests. But, as Hoppen notes, until late in the nineteenth century workshops remained small and 'the extent to which the workforce felt a sense of sameness, of unity...is likely to have been limited' (Hoppen, 1998, pp. 59–60). It is only later that there was the development of common interests between workers in different industries, or indeed collaboration between different occupational hierarchies within the same industry. The development of a wider sense of class consciousness followed the growth in the size of industrial undertakings, the growth of labour organizations and the articulation of common grievances. All these changes could have interacted with, and influenced, the replacement of earlier social hierarchies by 'the small number of horizontal groups' – characteristic of the later British class system, but the process of change was not well advanced until the later decades of the nineteenth century.

Some of the necessary conditions may have existed in a few large, urban seats by 1867, for example in constituencies such as Leeds, Glasgow or Manchester. But, as noted earlier, electoral politics in these places already required an alternative organizational basis to the one operating in most small borough electorates before 1867. Foster has argued that class was the basis of electoral politics in Oldham from 1832 until the 1850s.[29] However his analysis applies only to that constituency as the general conditions for class-based electoral politics did not exist until after the growth in the electorate in 1867, and the further increase that followed the third Reform Bill in 1884/85.

During the debate over the extension of the franchise in the 1860s there was an inquiry into the extent of working-class representation in the electorate. In 1866, just before the Second Reform Act, the parliamentary returns classified some 26 per cent of the borough electorate as working class, but found substantial variation in the concentration of working-class voters across the constituencies, from 2.6 per cent in

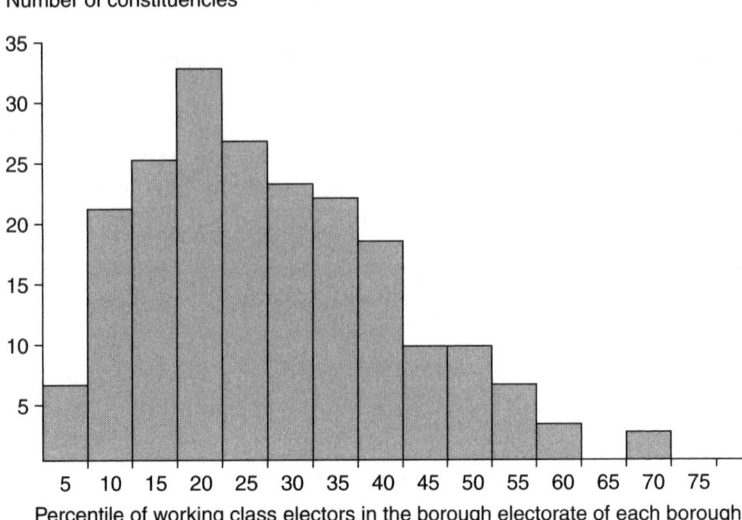

Figure 7.3   The distribution of working-class borough electors, England and Wales 1866

Source: Drake and Mitchell, 1982.

Buckingham to 69.8 per cent in Coventry, see Figure 7.3.[30] This variation in prior working-class representation within constituency electorates would have affected the incorporation and mobilization of new voters *after* the extension of the franchise in 1867, and the social relationships between electors too.

Whilst the local variation in the enfranchisement of working-class electors in 1868 is debatable, the changing balance between electors and non-electors after the Second Reform Bill, and even more so after the Third Reform Bill, is not. In the short term the increase may have stimulated local party activity, and in the longer term helped to alter both electoral campaigning and local party organization. After 1885 most adult males would be electors. So, in theory, the number of 'political' interactions between electors should have increased as well, and increased the level of politicization in all constituencies. However, after 1872 the vote was secret and, as a consequence, the nature of political partisanship and of the relationships between individuals within social networks, changed too.

IV

Open voting had consequences for the voter. His political identity was public knowledge and there was a close connection between 'politics' and other areas of social life. The political role was not, in general, differentiated from other roles and political control could be exercised by the manipulation, or the threatened manipulation, of social relationships. The pressures for conformity remained fairly constant within the small electorates of most borough seats before 1867, at least in the short run. This suggests that the relationship of individual electors to their community remained fixed and that both individual and collective partisan choice was relatively stable. The importance of this stability for party organizations, and for political activity generally, has been one of the themes of earlier chapters. However the relationship between politics and urban social life was complex – the community constrained participation and, as Fraser, noted 'politics intruded into the whole urban experience' (Fraser, 1976, p. 9).

The Municipal Corporations Act of 1835 had further blurred this boundary by creating a second level of political activity in many towns. The relationship between the electorates for municipal and parliamentary elections is unclear, but council elections took place on an annual basis, more frequently than the irregularly spaced parliamentary elections.[31] Coming close in time to the controversies surrounding Reform at the beginning of the 1830s, political competition at this second level of activity rapidly became structured along similar partisan lines. The political activists at the local level were frequently the same for both parliamentary and municipal elections and this further reinforced the interdependence of the two levels. The system was structured and maintained by the regularity of political competition, and by the rewards available through control of municipal administration – the small change of patronage.

Political activity took place at other levels beyond these two formal channels. Some of these were official, such as the world of the vestry explored by Fraser and touched on by Foster, but other political activities could fall outside the electoral community.[32] One such area was the emerging world of pressure group activity that in time interacted with the developing organizational structures of political parties. Between 1832 and 1868 there were a succession of popular causes that enlisted mass support over issues such as the Corn Laws or Chartism.[33] All may have had effects at the local level. The petitions and demonstrations of the Chartists shaded over into the other forms of political action that were traditionally available to those formally excluded from the political nation as narrowly defined by the parliamentary franchise – the riot, demonstrations and other forms of public disorder.[34]

In a setting where politics was both a public activity and a public entertainment, the stratified levels of political activity continuously influenced each other.[35] One major interaction was between electors and non-electors. As Foster has emphasized, before 1867 the non-elector was not necessarily a passive spectator of the political game. The non-electorate was politicized and partisan too. W.A. Abrams vividly describes one type of participation open to non-electors in a Lancashire election of the 1860s:

> at a contested election in a Lancashire borough, one may see the entire body of workers at two rival factories pitted against each other, like hostile armies, and the deeds of prowess performed by each are proudly rehearsed by every man and boy, by every woman and girl, attached to the establishment. Politics resolve themselves into partisan warfare, and the real objects of political parties are totally forgotten in the zest of local clanship.[36]

Such intense partisan divisions helped to produce and maintain social or group solidarity – reinforced by the public knowledge of the partisan preferences of the electors within the group. The lack of secrecy imposed structural constraints upon individual behaviour and reinforced the political consequences of the pre-modern social structure. But there were other consequences for electoral politics and for party organizations. While it left the voter subject to 'influence', open voting also made an election campaign into a political game with full information. The introduction of secrecy did not change this immediately; there was a period of adjustment when secrecy was evaded to a greater or lesser extent, before political actors had fully realized its implications. But over time electoral secrecy produced changes for the individual elector and for local constituency political parties too.

For the elector there was a change in social constraints. The voter need no longer be subject to influence from his other roles within the community. The political role need no longer co-vary with them; indeed there could now be a distinct and separate political role. So secrecy may have limited or even diminished social and group solidarity. After its introduction there is an asymmetry in political information – an elector could, if he wished, reveal his political preferences, but he did not need to, it could remain 'private knowledge'. In turn this could lead to a depoliticization of relationships within personal networks as every interaction need no longer be 'equivalent' to a political interaction or have 'political' consequences.

Secrecy reduced or eliminated the social costs of a change in partisan behaviour for the individual elector, and it created greater uncertainty and a loss of information for local party organizations. Importantly, the vote ceased to be an economic good – an elector might still wish to sell his vote but it was now irrational for a buyer to purchase it as he (the buyer) could no longer establish after an election that the contract had been honoured. Bribery should therefore have decreased, although this too did not happen immediately.[37]

As a result the introduction of secrecy changed constituency electoral campaigning. Under open voting a party had a core of known partisan support. With partial enfranchisement there was a regular renewal of the electorate. In most boroughs all electors could be in the first or second order range of one individual. With a core of known support, 'Wm. Jackson' in Lancaster concentrated on recruiting new electors to replace those who had left the electorate. After the Second Reform Bill in 1867, and even more so after the Ballot Act in 1872, this was no longer an effective strategy. The number of electors increased, and perhaps 'overloaded' personal networks, but, more importantly, after 1872 an agent or party organization now had increasingly less reliable information about the intended behaviour of both 'new' and 'old' electors.

With the elector protected by secrecy, there was now no systematic way to link a promise of electoral support to the actual vote. The accuracy of the information about the partisanship of electors became more uncertain, and the total information on the balance of political opinion in the constituency became less reliable. A party could no longer rely as much as before on a known core of support. Recruiting new electors would no longer be sufficient to change or maintain the pattern of partisanship within a constituency. Parties would now have to campaign to retain the support of all 'their' electors, and at the same time try and persuade other existing electors to vote for them too. They would now have to campaign across the whole electorate and, although they would continue to canvass political opinion, this information would become less reliable without any means to confirm its accuracy after an election.

In Bedford the electorate increased from 2,144 in 1868 to 2,255 in 1874. The margin between the second elected Liberal MP and the losing Tory candidate in 1868 was 573 votes. In 1874 one Liberal and one Tory were elected. The two Liberals received 1,155 and 1,006 votes; the Tory candidate, 1,010 votes. Behind this result the voting patterns identified for the period between 1832 and 1868 probably changed in 1874 with party voting for the two Liberal candidates decreasing. It is unlikely that the increase in Tory support came only from recruiting new voters and if this was the case, then this too would imply a major change in the pattern of electoral recruitment. So there must have been a change in the core of Liberal party support – secrecy enabled a Liberal voter to give a split vote for the Tory too. Not only did secrecy allow the development of the politics of individual opinion, to use Nossiter's phrase, it also allowed electors to vote against their 'objective' interests and to evade group or community pressure for political conformity. In time this lead to the development of a significant level of working-class support for the Conservative party.[38]

However if electoral campaigning became more extensive, covering the whole of a now larger constituency electorate rather than concentrating on new electors only, this would require a more extensive local organization. The increased personnel could be drawn from the membership of the local constituency party organization and was probably no longer supplied by just a small group of activists. As a result local organizations would need more available members to maintain a continuing institutional presence in the constituency.

Individual electors were still located within personal networks but under secrecy there would now be no necessary reason for political bias in such networks. Friends could now more easily have different political loyalties, and social or economic connections need have no political content. However this change should be qualified in two ways. At first, after 1872, many individuals would still have a known political preference and the asymmetry introduced by secrecy could lead to a stratification of the political community in terms of activism.[39] We would expect activists to have 'biased' personal networks, but other structural elements would, over time, become more important as the determinants of political behaviour since the number of such activists would be small in relation to the total electorate.

For electors this change in social constraints had several consequences. As the political role was now differentiated from other roles, it was no longer necessary to establish a new role equilibrium after 'changing sides' and supporting a different candidate or party. Such a decrease in individual social costs could well have produced two other effects on political campaigning. There may have been a general drop in the level of turnout – the pressure to vote was decreased – and the volatility of individual opinion could increase as voting was no longer as constrained, as role determined, as it had been under open voting. There would no longer be as large a fixed or known core of party support; the basis of support becomes more uncertain and the 'electoral game' becomes one of incomplete information and greater uncertainty.

The removal of the link between an electoral promise and a confirmable vote has other effects too. With the decline of the previous mechanisms of political persuasion, it became important to establish a greater organizational presence for political recruitment and mobilization. So there was a growth in constituency organization and activity, and also a growth of secondary political organizations such as Liberal and Conservative Working Men's Clubs. These other organizations carried out some of the recruiting and socialization functions that were unnecessary under open voting, and 'in many parts of the country the political associations to which such men belonged almost imperceptibly became social organizations as well' (Hanham, 1978, p. xiv).[40]

We can go further and suggest two other effects of the change from open to secret voting. First, the differences between rural and urban constituencies diminished. In rural constituencies the social networks could be characterized as relatively close knit, whilst in urban constituencies they were more differentiated and interpersonal linkages were of a less multiplex character. Again the differentiation of a distinct political role brought a convergence between the two social settings and should gradually have eliminated the hierarchical dominance that was characteristic of some rural communities. This process was accelerated by the change from multi-member to single member seats that came with the Third Reform Act in 1885, together with a redrawing of constituency boundaries. In most constituencies the elector could no longer cast two votes, possibly across party lines, and now had to vote for a single party or candidate. But, second, the individual elector would now, in the act of voting, be in direct, unmediated communication with 'the state'. This would further help 'politics' to transcend the local to a greater extent than was possible previously. Finally, the new pattern of electoral mobilization was helped by interactions with the changing structure of party organization and the rise of a viable class society.

Taken together this suggests a developmental sequence for the origin of class-based mass electoral politics in the last third of the nineteenth century, a process that accelerated after the Fourth Reform Act in 1918. Up to 1868 'party', either as an organization or in terms of the elector's vote, was related in many of the small or medium sized borough constituencies to the network-based structure of political action. This network acquired class bias with the development of the system of social stratification, and with the relative decline in the salience of other elements of the multiplex linkages between individuals, together with the increasing interaction of an elector with other electors in his immediate environment. Increased social mobility also reduced hierarchical influence, particularly in urban constituencies. Finally, the introduction of secrecy and the privatization of individual political opinion brought a decline in the importance of the total network, and left 'party' directly related to a more fully evolved system of social stratification as the main mediating structure for the individual.

The evolution of class voting varied across the constituencies as it was influenced by local and regional differences. Substantial differences in the extent of working-class enfranchisement existed before the Second Reform Bill (see Figure 7.3) and this affected the growing salience of class for electoral behaviour. In the short term other factors within social networks continued to influence voting behaviour – so, for example, one would expect that denominational attachments would continue to influence behaviour in Quaker Darlington after 1872. Indeed, given the nature of network ties, in some constituencies religion could well affect the voting behaviour of electors until the expansion of the suffrage in 1918.[41]

While the process of evolution is controversial, Clarke may well be correct in asserting that 'class politics in much their modern form appeared in England before the First World War and were the force behind the Liberal election victories of 1910' (Clarke, 1972, p. 52).[42] Any subsequent changes or realignments of the party system in the first half of the twentieth century were merely adjustments to an already existing pattern.[43] But, even if the links between class and vote evolved with great rapidity during and after the 1880s, the initial stages of the process still show the influence of electoral practices from the preceding period. Changes in the electoral community, and the partisan behaviour of individual electors, were then both constrained and influenced by open voting within the restricted electorate. The legacy of this earlier organization of opinion established under open voting can be seen in the form and practice of constituency organization and electioneering in the early phases of mass politics after 1868.

8
The Organization of Opinion

The requirements of electoral registration after the 1832 Reform Bill combined with the regular change in the electorate, and the social consequences of open voting, to produce an identifiable pattern of electoral organization in many English borough constituencies. For party agents, the situation was one of relatively full information and the existing social constraints and incentives could act, as in Bedford, to produce a high level of stability in individual voting. This had important consequences for the organization of electoral activity. The stability in electoral behaviour, and the regular change in the electorate, could provide candidates with an accurate idea of the division of opinion in a constituency, of the extent of their support, and the possible outcome of an election too.

In addition, this underlying stability meant that much regular electoral activity, as in Lancaster, revolved around attempts to gain partisan advantage by recruiting new supporters, by identifying and registering electors. 'Mr Jackson' tried to establish a political identity for any potential new voter, and then attempted to add them to the electoral register. At the same time he objected to the registration of individuals who might support another party or an opposition candidate. Many of the English boroughs were small communities, three-quarters had fewer that 1,400 electors in 1832, so this 'organization of opinion', of elections and the electorate, could be carried out by a small, or very small, group of activists.

In such constituencies the relationship between electors, and between electors and the wider community, can be described in terms of social networks and the structure of an individual's network reflected their social identity, and could be used to establish their political identity. Such networks provided a mechanism through which votes and voters could be mobilized to provide electoral support when required. The lack of secrecy created a high level of politicization within the electoral community and this was maintained by the annual registration battles and, after 1835, by municipal elections in boroughs with reformed corporations. So the dynamics of electoral change combined with the particular social context of many English borough constituencies to produce a systematic organization of opinion.

But if electoral behaviour could be influenced by the structure and manipulation of social relationships in small borough electorates, what was the basis of voting and electoral activity in other types of constituency, in the county seats and larger boroughs? A network structure may have been general in many, or indeed all, communities but the interactions within such networks, the content of their linkages, would differ with the particular social context. So within county constituencies, the traditional hierarchical nature of many rural communities might be reflected in the use of social power as a mechanism to mobilize voters. In the larger boroughs, or the more industrialized constituencies, other social or group influences could be more important. However in all constituencies there would be regular, identifiable, turnover in the electorate and any electoral organization should be able to identify potential new voters, and could probably use social processes similar to those identified in Lancaster for electoral objectives.

This is partially confirmed by a series of printed canvassing lists for five elections in the Scottish county constituency of Linlithgowshire between 1838 and 1852.[1] The lists are structurally similar to those used by Jackson in Lancaster and are based on the register in force immediately before each election. They list individual electors by parish, town and, where appropriate, by street; the votes at the three previous elections in 1832, 1837 and 1838 are recorded, as is non-voting for those who were qualified but did not vote. The elector's qualification, whether they are a new voter, or are known to be a Conservative supporter, are noted too, as well as duplicate qualifications and movement within the constituency. The lists have blank columns for recording a canvassed opinion.

The 'Supplement to the List of electors', dated December 1840, illustrates how the lists were compiled. It records changes subsequent to the most recent register, the one in force before the election in question. So the 1840 list gives 'effect to the variations after appeal court 1840' and would have been used at the general election in July 1841. It is in two parts: 'I Disqualified names to be scored out of the printed list', and 'II New electors, or electors who have changed their residence, to be added to printed list'. There are also indications of how such a list was to be used: the canvasser in Bathgate should 'Commence at East End of the town, on the Glasgow Road'; in Carriden Parish: 'Commence at North Bank, on the road from Linlithgow', presumably 'walking' that part of the constituency in a similar manner to a census enumerator. The existence of these constituency wide printed lists suggests that they were produced by a county organization for distribution and use in the various parishes or localities. Linlithgowshire was a small constituency, electing only one Member of Parliament; according to Dod it had 730 electors in 1832, and 540 voted when the Conservative candidate won the 1838 by-election. There were no contests at any of the five subsequent elections between 1841 and 1852.

The lists confirm that the dynamics of electoral change were well understood, and that common techniques of voter identification, and perhaps even of electioneering and voter mobilization, could be used in different types of constituency, county as well as borough. Most English counties obviously presented problems of scale as the electorate would often be larger than in either the smaller boroughs or in Linlithgowshire, but such constituencies were not one community, they were a set of communities of varying size. As Moore notes, Cambridgeshire in 1835 was made up of 156 parishes with between 1 and 352 electors in each parish. Other county constituencies at the time were similar and were also composed of a set of communities of varying size.[2]

In large boroughs the candidates could also have fairly accurate information on their support in the electorate, and may have used similar canvassing techniques. More than 4,500 voted at the Leeds borough election of 1859 and a table in the published poll book suggests that both Liberal candidates polled to within one or one and a half per cent of their promises.[3] However the employment of similar techniques of election management does not necessarily imply that there was a similar basis to voting in these different types of constituency, the content of network linkages could differ and the increasing size of the electorate posed organizational problems as well, both in establishing the political identity of the now much larger number of new electors, and in canvassing the more extensive electorate.

After 1867 there was substantial growth in many borough electorates (see Table 7.1) and at the same time society was being transformed by wider, more general social and economic changes, and by political changes too. By the end of the nineteenth century, Britain was predominantly an urban and industrial society, one in which important social differences were expressed through an increasingly mature class system. Because of the restricted nature of the suffrage, the small size of many electoral communities, and the dynamics of open voting, electoral behaviour before 1867 could be relatively independent of the evolving system of social stratification. However, as the franchise widened and became more inclusive, and particularly after further reform in 1884/85, the electoral community became increasingly similar to the social community of which it had hitherto formed only a part. The introduction of secrecy in 1872 limited the overt hierarchical political influence of social superiors and allowed for greater community or peer group influence – although such changes were probably gradual and may have first started before the introduction of the ballot. It also made political opinions a private matter, rather than public knowledge. This not only depoliticized many social interactions, it eliminated the link between an electoral promise and the actual vote and so created greater uncertainty for candidates and constituency organizations.

The constituency party organizations that developed after 1832 continued to exist, even if in modified form, after the passing of the Ballot Act in 1872, and were one channel for the incorporation of the newly enfranchised. In many constituencies however their effectiveness was limited by the sheer scale of enfranchisement, one that required a more extensive organization than had been needed for a previously small borough electorate. The incorporation of the newly enfranchised electors after 1867 was helped by the existence of the more inclusive structure of political activity before reform, one in which opportunities for political participation existed outside the formal framework of voting in parliamentary elections. It was suggested that, as a consequence of the lack of electoral secrecy, the unenfranchised may have been as politicized as the electorate, indeed some non-electors were political actors, playing a role in the process of voter mobilization and the generation of political support. All of which contributed to the relatively smooth assimilation of the newly enfranchised after both the Second and Third Reform Acts, and the rapid transition between the 'non-class' electoral politics of the mid-nineteenth century and the class voting that subsequently characterizes mass electoral behaviour in Britain by the end of the nineteenth century. It made the electorate of the 1880s highly politicized 'when almost everywhere politics came to occupy a central position in community life' (Hanham, 1978, p. xiv).

It is to this period too that we can trace the recognizable outlines of a modern party system, although this develops after a number of further changes took place roughly simultaneously around 1885. First, the growth of national political campaigning, and national political competition, in contrast to the previously much more local political campaigns and constituency-based electoral competition; second, the development of national party organizations linking constituency parties to a central, national organization; third, the change in constituency structure from mostly two-member seats in which the elector had a range of voting options, to mostly one member seats, a change that channelled electors into voting for one party only and so reinforced a much more unambiguous partisan identification amongst electors.[4] However the growth of a national party system was complicated, and perhaps delayed, by a fourth factor, the change in the number of party groups represented in the House of Commons following the split in the parliamentary Liberal party over Irish Home rule.

With full enfranchisement class eventually became the most important influence on electoral behaviour in Britain although in the 1880s regional and denominational differences may have continued to influence voting.[5] These other factors interacted with, and constrained, the expression of the predominant class cleavage until the final major change in the suffrage, the Fourth Reform Bill of 1918.[6] After 1885 'electorates grew too big to canvass personally. Connections of patronage and power...[gave] way to making links with a mass electorate. Increasingly, too, local campaigning must be subordinated to national campaigning' (McLean, 2001, p. 101.) Electioneering had already changed following the introduction of secrecy and the growth of the electorate in 1867. But national election campaigns required national organization – and this developed more rapidly and more effectively in the Conservative party.[7]

The split between the Gladstonian Liberals and the Liberal Unionists in the mid-1880s delayed the development of a national party system, and reinforced the importance of local organization. The electoral base of the Liberal Unionists under Joseph Chamberlain was in Birmingham. The local organization there had its roots in the Birmingham caucus that was established to maximize Liberal representation under the minority representation clause of the Second Reform Bill.[8] As Cornford notes, it was the continuing effectiveness of their local organization that maintained the Liberal Unionist presence in parliament:

Perhaps the best example of a local elite...aided by a very efficient organisation...was the ability of Joseph Chamberlain and his friends to take Birmingham...out of the Liberal party, after they had led the Liberal victory there in 1885, and hold all seven seats for the unionist cause for the next thirty years. (Cornford, 1967, p. 423)

If the Liberal Unionist presence in the House of Commons depended on their local organization, this was less the case for the other two major parties. There was a crucial difference between the Conservatives and the (Gladstonian) Liberals in terms of national organization. Apart from the Liberal Unionists in Birmingham, lost to the party after 1885, the central Liberal organization was never as effective as that of the Conservatives. But such organization was increasingly the link between 'the party in office' and the 'party in the electorate', between the levels of organized opinion.

The activities of local parties between the First and Second Reform Bills resulted in a particular pattern of electoral politics and local electioneering. Open voting had important consequences for the work of local agents as it helped to create and maintain constituency organizations. Some aspects of this local organization changed after the introduction of secrecy. Other elements evolved when constituency electorates grew too large to 'organize' through a small group of activists, and changed further with the erosion of the particularistic links between individuals, electors and non-electors, that were the basis of electoral activity in the smaller borough constituencies of mid-Victorian England. While the earlier pattern of activity was important for local political organization, perhaps even until the restructuring of the constituencies in the mid-1880's, it was subsequently replaced by a different 'organization of opinion' as the party system evolved with the establishment of a more formal link between local and national party organizations, as the franchise broadened, as partisan identification grew, and as class became the primary influence on mass electoral behaviour.

Appendix 1
Poll Books and Nominal Record Linkage

A poll book is a list of the electors in a particular constituency at a particular election and shows how each elector cast his vote (or votes). Such lists can be found from the early seventeenth century. At first these were manuscript records, and took the form of a listing of names made at, or soon after, an election. As such they had a limited audience.[1] The first printed list showing the voting of electors dates from 1694, and such printed poll books are found with some frequency after 1700.[2] Plumb has argued that 'poll books are quite different [from lists of electors]. Usually they are written up after the election, from voting lists, and were made for the specific purpose of studying the way electors had voted' (Plumb, 1967, p. 53).[3] He suggests that the change from manuscript polling lists to printed poll books came with the growth in the size of the electorate in the counties and large boroughs in the 1690s, and the need for candidates to develop and extend techniques of political persuasion and control: 'The first books were handed about in manuscript, but later they were printed…and…sold at the booksellers. They provided a basis for canvassing and for exerting every possible sort of pressure on voters' (Plumb, 1967, p. 53).

By the time of the First Reform Bill in 1832 poll books were published for many elections, although they were not produced in every constituency or for every contest.[4] Vincent suggests that there was a general market in political information and that recognizing the possibilities, 'jobbing printers who usually published poll books…were looking around for a small profit' (Vincent, 1967, p. 1). The main market for such political information would be local and probably confined to the constituency in question. So most poll books were locally published – and would have contributed to the politicization of the community in question. And, as Plumb suggests, the information on past electoral behaviour, the possibility of linking a prior political promise to actual political performance, was important for the management of elections and the organization of opinion.

Vincent argues that 'poll books are texts which emerge *ex nihilo*, bearing within them ... certain kinds of pragmatic verification' and, 'one cannot, so to say, discern by internal evidence a historic election standing behind what is reported to us' (Vincent, 1967, pp. 3–4). But the origin of poll books varied and this variation reveals further details of the electoral practices of the time.

By 1832 there were official poll books, the manuscript record taken during the election, from which the official returns were made. Following the election these were sent to the Crown Office in London. These 'official' poll books were sometimes used as the basis for the 'unofficial' poll books published by local printers.[5] Most of the manuscript official poll books were intentionally destroyed in 1893 although a very few poll books were printed as part of the record of a parliamentary election enquiry.[6]

How reliable is the information in poll books given that most were unofficial publications? There are often minor discrepancies between the official returns and the figures in a published poll book.[7] However when several poll books were published for the same election, collation of the different editions usually shows almost total agreement.[8] Such differences, where they exist, are more frequent between elements of the secondary, non-electoral information given in many poll books. Occupational synonyms are often found where occupation is listed, and, although there may be differences in the address for electors with multiple qualifications, there are very few disagreements over the actual voting behaviour of electors.[9] This suggests that there was indeed a 'historical election' behind a printed poll book, and that the electoral information in poll books is, in general, reliable despite the 'non-official' nature of the source.

The internal organization of poll books varies, as does the relationship between poll books and other systematically recorded local data. Some poll books are copies of the official electoral register with the voting added for later publication.[10] Others are derived from the checklists of voters made by one or other of the competing parties at the time of the election, although these too may have used the electoral register as a basis.[11] The registration procedures were revised after recommendations of a House of Commons committee in 1826, and again by the Peel administration in 1843.[12] The register was revised annually with the revision subject to appeal and partisan contestation, and is an authoritative list of those entitled to vote in a constituency. The accuracy of the voting behaviour in poll books would have been reinforced by the 'full information' characteristics of the environment of open voting. However the accuracy of the other non-electoral information in poll books – occupation or address – is less readily confirmed.

Some poll books are only lists of electors and give no information other than the vote. However, by 1832 many give additional personal information, the most common being some location or an address for each elector. This occurs as the hundred, village or township, parish, street address or building. The first three are more common in county polls, the others in borough ones. The use of house numbers in street addresses becomes more common after the coming of the penny post in 1840. Other details are sometimes recorded – for example, the electoral ward or the polling district – but these shade over into considerations of the nature of the elector's qualification. In borough constituencies the Freemen voters are often listed separately to the £10 householders, and after 1867 those lodgers who qualify to vote may be listed separately too. In county constituencies the distinctions used are more numerous. The Northumberland (South) poll book for 1832 distinguishes between annuity, copyhold, freehold, leasehold, occupier, moiety, mortgagee or share as a basic distinction. This is then applied to various types of property such as a house, a mill, land, messuage, a farm, a coal mine, a cottage, a house for three lives, toll house, tenement, warehouse and so on.

Another commonly added item of social information is that of the 'occupation' or 'calling' of an elector. There are considerable difficulties in using this information, as the occupational data by itself is too inexact. What, for example, is meant by the categorization of an elector as a 'butcher'? Is he a master butcher, self-employed or employing others? Or is he an individual working in another's shop? There is also a much larger problem, our incomplete knowledge of the outlines of the system of social stratification between 1832 and 1868, and of the regional variations that occurred as well.[13] For the analysis of electoral data from poll books, the main value of occupational information is as a personal identifier. It is an attribute attached to an elector that can help us either to differentiate between electors of the same name, or to identify individuals as the same person at different elections. Occupation and address are the most common social information found in poll books, other information such as a title or an indication of kinship may be given, but some information, such as religious denomination, is rarely recorded.[14]

Nominal record linkage (NRL)

Most poll books contain voting data for one election only. A few list the behaviour of the electorate at two or more elections – the Bath poll book for 1837 also gives voting behaviour at both the 1832 and 1835 elections. But this is uncommon and if we wish to study electoral behaviour, or the physical change in the electorate over time, we need to link or merge information from two or more poll books. This is the general historical problem of record linkage: 'the bringing together of information concerning a particular historical individual derived from independent sources' (Winchester, 1971, p. 124).[15] With poll books for two successive elections, we need to identify an entry in each poll book as referring to the same elector, and then link their votes at the two elections to study their behaviour over time.

Taken together constituency poll books for two successive elections at times t_1 and t_2 contain information on three sets of electors: (1) those who voted at t_1 but not t_2; (2) those who voted at t_2 but not t_1; (3) those who voted at both t_1 and t_2.[16] The three sets can be identified by linking individuals common to both poll books, that is by identifying those electors who voted both at t_1 and t_2 through a comparison of the additional information on address or occupation that is available in the two separate poll books.

We have noted that, as well as the voting data, a poll book may list other information for each elector. So if we represent an elector's surname by N, his Christian name(s) by C^1, C^2, C^3...(for first, second, third...Christian name[17]); occupation by o, address by a, other individual information by x, and the vote as V, the poll book entries are of the general form N, C^1, C^2, C^3..., o, a, x, V.

Many poll books are arranged alphabetically by surname, so they are an ordered list of the form:

N^1	C^1	o^1	a^1	.	V
N^1	C^2	o^2	a^2		V
N^1	C^3	o^3	a^1		V
–	–	–	–		
–	–	–	–		
N^n	C^x	o^y	a^z	x^w	V

The surname and Christian name, N and C, are the primary or defining criteria for an elector; o, a and x – occupation, address and other information, are secondary or qualifying criteria. In addition there is voting information V but, as we are interested in linking this behaviour over time, the electoral data cannot be used to identify electors common to more than one poll book.

Record linkage is the comparison of two ordered lists of electors, usually from different points in time, and the identification of elements that the two data sets have in common. The assumption made in the linkage of electors is that an individual does not change his surname or his Christian name but he may change either his occupation or his address, but not both, over the period between elections.[18] So we can identify an elector N^1, C^1, o^1, a^1 at time t_1 as the same elector as either N^1, C^1, o^2, a^1, or elector N^1, C^1, o^1, a^2 at time t_2, but not an elector N^1, C^1, o^2, a^2. In the cases of record linkage reported in this study it is assumed that, in truly linked pairs of electoral entries, at most one of the secondary criteria will change between t_1 and t_2.[19]

Once an individual elector at two different points in time has been identified as the same historical person, the electoral data can be linked. This will give information both on the behaviour of electors over time, $V_1 \rightarrow V_2$, and on the physical change and turnover in the electorate. It will enable us to identify the new electors at t_2 as well as those who left the electorate between t_1 and t_2.

Poll books are printed records, based on essentially contested and visible official information, and they refer to a restricted stratum of the community. So we would expect a relatively high degree of accuracy in the information they contain. Indeed, when two different poll books for the same election have been compared, the level of agreement between them on all criteria, and on the electoral information that they contain, has been found to be very high. With printed records, and a short time interval between data sets, linkage is often unambiguous.[20]

For a series of elections, such as those for Bedford between 1832 and 1868, record linkage was effected serially over pairs of successive elections – 1835 was linked to 1837, 1837 was linked to 1841…and so on, to give the equivalent of a multi-wave panel with renewal.[21] But the last two poll books in the series, those for 1865 and 1868, do not list occupation. So in this case total agreement on all criteria was used to identify truly linked electoral entries in successive poll books and the effect of this may have been to reduce the number of electors identified as common to the two polls.

Appendix 2
Votes and Ballots

Between 1832 and 1867 most constituencies in the United Kingdom returned more than one member – there were 240 two-member, 7 three-member, 1 four-member seats and only 153 single member ones. In every constituency the elector had as many votes as there were seats being contested, the only limitation was that he could give no more than one vote to a candidate.[1] This created strategic opportunities for both parties and electors and means that we cannot derive the pattern of individual voting from the final candidate vote totals alone.[2]

Suppose that two parties each put up two candidates in a two-member seat. Call these parties A and B with the candidates for each party differentiated by subscripts 1 and 2. So there are four candidates A_1, A_2, B_1, and B_2. If one candidate from one party is opposed by two from the other party, then the candidates can be represented as A_1, A_2, and B_1, and similarly for other combinations of candidates.

Apart from non-voting there were a variety of ballots that the individual elector could give. In a two-member constituency, he might use only one of his two votes and 'plump' for a specific candidate. Or he could use both votes and support two of the candidates who were contesting the seat. Such double votes could be either for candidates of the same party, or he could vote across party lines for candidates from different parties and give a 'split' vote. In a two-member seat with four candidates – two from each 'party' – there were four possible plumpers and six possible double votes, a total of ten different types of vote available to an elector. Only two of these double votes would be consistent in party terms.

In a three-candidate contest with one candidate from one party facing two candidates from the other party, there are three possible single votes and three possible double votes; only one double vote is consistent in party terms.

	4-candidate contest					3-candidate contest		
	First vote:					First vote:		
	A_1	A_2	B_1	B_2		A_1	A_2	B_1
A_1	a_1	a_1a_2	a_1b_1	a_1b_2	A_1	a_1	a_1a_2	a_1b_1
Second A_2		a_2	a_2b_1	a_2b_2	A_2		a_2	a_2b_1
vote B_1			b_1	b_1b_2	B_1			b_1
B_2				b_2				b_2

These possibilities can be summarized in two matrices in which the individual votes are represented by the lower case letter for the party in question with appropriate subscripts.

Using this notation, the double votes a_1a_2, b_1b_2, are 'party' votes, all other votes a_xb_y are cross party or 'split' votes. Cox usefully calls a matrix of this type 'a ballot count', and the sum of the individual entries, or ballots, gives the total number of electors voting at a particular election.[3] The vote total for each candidate is the sum of each ballot in which the candidate appears – the total for A_1 in a four-candidate election is $a_1 + a_1a_2 + a_1b_1 + a_1b_2$; for A_2 it is $a_2 + a_1a_2 + a_2b_1 + a_2b_2$ and so on for the other candidates. Similarly in a three-candidate election with candidates A_1, A_2, and B_1, the total vote for A_1 will be $a_1 + a_1a_2 + a_1b_1$, and so on.

One statistic that can be calculated from a ballot count is the extent of split voting – the percentage of electors who cast their votes for candidates of different parties.[4] If the total number of ballots cast in any election is N, then the extent of split or cross voting, SV, is defined as [Σ $L_{1,2}T_{1,2}$]/N, that is, the proportion of all the electors who gave ballots for two candidates from different parties. This is important as an indicator of the level of party discipline amongst electors, the extent to which they voted in strictly partisan terms. We assume that apart from the 'split-voters', all other electors gave party votes – including those electors who 'plumped' and gave a single vote when there were two individuals standing for the party of the candidate that they supported.

This may not be inaccurate. An analysis of the voting at the Ripon election of 1832 shows that 167 electors voted for the two Liberal candidates, 158 for both Tories, two cast ballots across party lines and three plumped for a Tory candidate. So out of the 330 who voted, less than 1 per cent gave a split vote. The electorate voted overwhelmingly along party lines.[5]

However at the North Staffordshire election of 1837, the behaviour of the electorate was very different, see Table A2.1 below.

Table A2.1 Voting at North Staffordshire, 1837[6]

	T_1	L_1	L_2
T_1	2265	326	1628
L_1		2237	616
L_2			110

At this election some 27 per cent of electors voted across party lines, those voting L_1T and L_2T; 33 per cent gave a Liberal plumper, 2237 for L_1 and 110 for L_2; and only 616 or 9 per cent voted for both Liberals. In this context, where most votes are not cast along party lines, is a plumper a 'party' vote in the same sense as a double vote L_1L_2? Or is a plumper really a double vote of the type L-NV with some electors using the multiple ballot to express a preference between two candidates of the same party, and indicating support for only one of them.[7] Cox suggests that this is a distinctive use of the vote, and he labels it 'non partisan plumping' (NPP): 'a plumper is non-partisan if the person casting it could have used his other vote to support another candidate of the same party but did not, indicating the use of criteria other than the party label' (Cox, 1987, p. 97). But it is still a distinctive type of partisan behaviour and expresses a preference for only one of the two candidates of a particular party, so in this analysis it has been labelled 'preferential plumping' (PP).[8] Both the level of split voting (SV) and the extent of preferential plumping (PP) indicate a breakdown in party discipline within a constituency electorate and a failure to maximize party support.

Appendix 3
Measuring Electoral Change

Electoral change has two separate components: the partisan behaviour of individual electors and the physical turnover in the electorate. Between 1832 and 1868 both were important in influencing constituency election results, and to explain electoral change we need to identify and map both components. Nominal Record Linkage (NRL) can be used to link poll books and identify electors common to a constituency electorate at two successive elections at times t_1 and t_2. Electors who participated in both elections can have their voting behaviour linked and the data can then be used to map individual and collective electoral change. This process identifies electors qualified only at t_1 or only at t_2, and so we can also measure the physical turnover in the electorate. Such a process and analysis can be extended over a longer-time period by linking a series of poll books for successive elections.

Mapping partisan behaviour over time

Suppose that at the elections in a two-member constituency there were three possible votes for candidates from two different parties, Tory (T), Liberal (L), and a split or cross vote (X) as well as non-voting (NV). Those who were electors at both t_1 and t_2 could have followed several courses of action over the two elections. They may have voted or not voted, supported one party twice, changed their vote between the two parties, moved between voting for a party and splitting their votes between the two parties and so on. Each pair of actions has partisan consequence, and the universe of possible combinations of individual electoral choice, the pathways of individual voting behaviour and electoral change between t_1 and t_2 can be set out in a table in which each cell represents a particular pair of voting actions, see Table A3.1. In such

Table A3.1 A transition table for two elections

		Election t_2			
		L	T	X	NV
Election t_1	L	*			
	T		*		
	X			*	
	NV				*

a transition table the row entries refer to voting at the first election, the columns to electoral behaviour at the second one.[1] By placing each linked elector in the cell representing his pattern of voting over the two elections, we can summarize electoral behaviour and identify partisan change between the two elections.

Note that Table A3.1 refers only to those electors who participated in both of the elections. A full transition table for two successive elections will also include the two sets of electors who voted in only one of the elections, as in Table 4.5 for the voting at the Lancaster elections of 1847 and 1848. The cohort of new voters at the second election form an additional row at the bottom of the table, those electors who left the electorate after the first election are in a column placed to the right of the non-voters at the second election. Such a transition table allows us to distinguish between the aggregate support for a party, the row and column totals for the elections at t_1 and t_2, and the pathways of individual voting behaviour – the cell entries in the table.

The cell entries summarize the behaviour of individual electors and their pattern of stability and change. We can also use the table to derive a measure of overall electoral stability between the two elections. In Table A3.1 the starred cells contain those electors who voted the same way at both elections, T at t_1 and t_2, L at t_1 and t_2, X at t_1 and t_2 and NV at t_1 and t_2.[2] The proportion of all electors at the two elections who voted for the same 'party' on both occasions, the sum of electors in the 'starred' cells as a proportion of the electors who voted at both elections, is an indication of overall partisan stability, a summary of the aggregate voting behaviour for those electors who were qualified for both elections. Such an index varies between 0 and 1, the higher the index then the greater the proportion of voters who were consistent in their voting behaviour over the two elections. Its variation over the successive pairs of elections in Bedford gave an indication of aggregate partisan stability and change between pairs of elections, see Table 5.9.

In Table A3.1 the transition table has been simplified and is based on only three types of vote – T, L or X. It is of course possible to expand the table and use the full range of ballots available in a two-member seat to define the two dimensions, as is done in Table 4.5. However the reduced form of Table A3.1 is useful for comparison across a series of elections, as in Table 5.10 for the Bedford elections between 1832 and 1868.[3]

If we extend linkage to a series of elections rather than just two, we could use multi-dimensional transition tables to study long-term electoral change. However higher dimension tables become cumbersome to present, and difficult to analyse. To overcome this problem Drake suggested the use of 'psephological trees' to study electoral change over more than two elections – a branching tree representation of successive electoral choices – but this also lacks analytical clarity.[4] Longer-time series of three or more elections, each with several voting options, can rapidly generate a very large number of individual electoral pathways, many of which will contain few electors. It is the dominant pathways that are of particular interest, those that occur frequently within the total range of possible electoral behaviour over time.[5]

The analysis in Chapter 5 attempted to identify dominant patterns of partisan choice in Bedford between 1832 and 1868. Two types of elector were defined – consistent or party voters, and independent voters – a classification that allowed electors some flexibility in the use of the strategic possibilities of the multiple vote.[6] The analysis showed that this simplification reflected the voting behaviour of most electors. However they sometimes used the options available with the multiple vote to qualify their partisan support. This longer-term analysis of electoral change complemented the more detailed study of short-term change over two elections in Lancaster.

Change in the electorate and electoral turnover

The NRL disaggregates the joint electorate at any two elections at t_1 and t_2 into three disjoint subsets, see Figure A3.1.

The turnover in the electorate at Lancaster and Bedford was shown as a flow diagram, in which the physical change between elections was clearly identified, see Figures 4.1 and 5.2.

But the Bedford analysis went further. The electorate over the period between 1832 and 1868 was disaggregated into ten separate electoral cohorts according to their first qualification as an elector. $C_{(t)}$, the cohort at time (t), comprised those electors who were new voters entering the electorate for the first time at that election.[7] The total electorate at t comprises

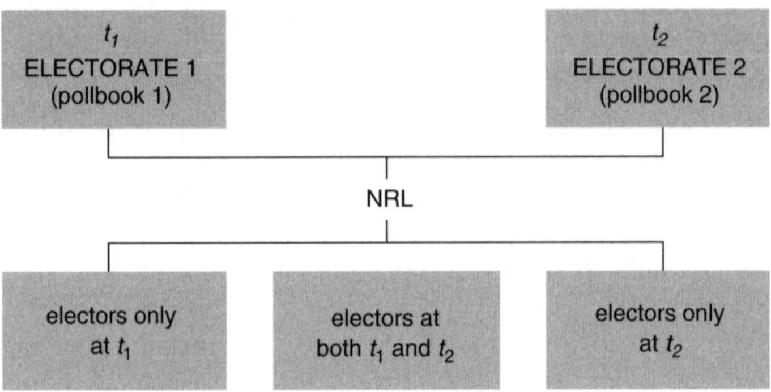

Figure A3.1 Identifying sets of electors by Nominal Record Linkage
Source: Drake and Mitchell, 1982.

the cohort of new voters, $C_{(t)}$, and the remaining electors from the previous cohorts of new voters at elections at (t–1), (t–2)…, that is $E_t = C_{(t)} + C_{(t-1)} + C_{(t-2)} + C_{(t-3)}…C_{(t-n)}$. Disaggregating the electorate into component cohorts reveals similarities across the cohorts, and any underlying pattern of change in the numbers of electors over time. The composition of the Bedford electorate during the inter-reform period, and the change in its constituent cohorts, is shown in Table 5.4.

The change in the 1832 cohort was plotted in Figure 5.3, and exhibits a characteristic pattern of decay over time. The other Bedford electoral cohorts exhibit a similar pattern, one also found in studies of change in groups of legislators.[8] But to compare the cohorts we need to derive summary statistics for this data.

The decline in the number of electors in the cohort over time, its decay, is continuous. If we assume that the underlying process is exponential, then we can model it by a simple equation. Suppose that the number of electors at time t_o is E_o. For any subsequent time $t > t_o$, let E_t be the number of electors remaining in the original cohort. $E_t < E_o$, the survival rate is necessarily negative as the cohort decreases in size over time. If we assume that the rate of change is constant and can be expressed by the differential equation $dE/dt = -ct$, where E is the number of electors still in the electorate at time t and c is a constant for each cohort, then under these assumptions, for any t,

$$E_t = E_o e^{-ct}$$

Where e is the exponential constant 2.718 and c is a constant for each cohort.[9] Since the logarithmic function is the inverse of the exponential

Table A3.2 Half-life and expectation
for Bedford electoral cohorts 1832–57[10]

Cohort	Half-life	Expectation
1832	11.4	16.4
1835	10.4	14.11
1837	11.9	17.0
1841	13.5	19.5
1847	10.8	15.5
1852	10.2	14.7
1857	10.4	14.11

function, a plot of the logarithmic transformation of the cohort data against time, gives points on a straight line with slope $-c$. The constant c can be estimated from this transformed data by least squares linear regression. The derived value of c can then be used to calculate the expectation for each distribution ($1/c$), the counterpart of the mean in discrete statistics.

For the first seven cohorts of Bedford electors between 1832 and 1857, the expectation varied between 122 and 161 months. Leaving aside the 1841 cohort, for the remaining six cohorts it varied in a fairly narrow range of between 122 and 141 months.

The other measure calculated for each cohort is the half-life, $0.693/c$, the equivalent of the median in discrete statistics, see Table 5.5. The half-life of the 1832 cohort was 11 years and 4 months; so after this period half of the cohort should have ceased to be electors, after a further 11 years and 4 months a further half of the surviving electors should have left, and so on, see Table A3.2.

Notes

1 Introduction – Explaining Open Voting
in England 1832–68

1. The categories employed in the contemporary analysis of elections in Britain largely derive from Butler and Stokes, 1969.
2. See Denver, 2007, pp. 21–3; 61–3 for a discussion of contemporary ideas about partisan identification and electoral behaviour.
3. Davis, 1972.
4. Foster, 1974; Vincent, 1966, also discusses the role of class; Foster and Vincent employ slightly different conceptions of class both from each other and from most current usage.
5. Moore, 1975; Olney, 1973.
6. Joyce, 1975.
7. For example, Nossiter, 1975, pp. 5–7.
8. The overall argument is set out in a series of works; see Moore, 1961, 1966, 1967, 1969, 1974 and 1975.
9. His analysis has not found wide acceptance, for a recent critique see Salmon, 2002, pp. 120–23.
10. The spirit of the Act was ignored in a decision of the Court of Common Please in 1843 that largely nullified this provision; see Moore, 1974, p. 101.
11. Yorkshire was divided into three constituencies; seven counties remained as one constituency with three seats; four remained one constituency with two seats; the Isle of Wight returned one member.
12. Moore, 1967, pp. 22–38.
13. Mills notes that patterns or rural land ownership in Lincolnshire were often quite dispersed, see Mills, 1980. The analysis also assumes that electors identified as voting in a particular parish actually lived there. This was not necessarily the case as non-resident voters are common in county constituencies during this period.
14. West Kent was unusual for a county constituency with only one uncontested election between 1832 and 1868, that in 1841, see Table 3.2. Poll books were published for all of these except 1832. The two Kent constituencies were re-divided to form three in 1867.
15. Mitchell, 1976a, pp. 239–52 gives a more detailed analysis of electoral change in these four communities.
16. On political tenancies see Hanham, 1959, and Olney, 1973.
17. The modern conception of deference in politics derives from Bagehot; for an extensive discussion see Newby, 1975.
18. Hanham, 1959, p. 13.
19. Cooper, 1988 discusses the political activities of landlords in Grimsby after the First Reform Bill; on Cambridge see Mitchell and Cornford, 1977.
20. See Neale, 1972, Chapter 2.

21. Moore does not consider the role of the non-electors, perhaps because he sees influence as mobilized from 'above' in deference communities.
22. For non-conformity and Liberalism see Vincent, 1966, Part 2; Vincent, 1967 has brief comments on the voting behaviour of clergymen as shown in poll books.
23. 'Thus, however often and however confidently the relationship between religion and politics has been asserted, it has seldom been demonstrated, at least in part because of the constraints imposed by the availability of data' Phillips, 1992, p. 278. Phillips does however assert it for a few specific groups – 'dissenting ministers and Roman Catholic priests were...remarkably uniform in their preference for Whig/Liberal/reforming candidates...' (Ibid., p. 278); and 'the deep rift between Anglican clergyman and the rest was immediately visible...' (Ibid., p. 279).
24. But, for example, the report in the *Lancaster Gazette* on the results of the 1847 election claims to show the voting of various religious denominations in this borough constituency, see Table 4.4.
25. The electors at the Newry election of 1868 had a choice between a Liberal and a Tory candidate; the poll book gives the religious affiliation of the electors, and their behaviour can be summarized as follows:

		Religion	
		Protestant	Catholic
	Liberal	44	341
Vote	Tory	361	11

Source: Newry poll book 1868.

The correlation coefficient is +0.86, indicating a strong connection between religious affiliation and voting behaviour at this election.
26. See also Phillips and Wetherell, 1991.
27. After 1804, to prevent bribery, 'the borough boundaries were extended beyond those of the parish of Aylesbury, and the 40 shilling freeholders of the three hundreds of Aylesbury were also given the vote', Davis, 1972, p. 22; the enlarged constituency covered about one-fifth of the whole county. Davis, 1972, pp. 48–49.
28. See also Davis, 1974, 1976a and 1976b.
29. This is a slightly weaker condition than the one used later, in Chapter 5; party loyalty would be slightly lower under the criteria used to analyse voting in Bedford; see Appendix 2 on the variety of ballots available.
30. Nossiter, 1975, see also Nossiter, 1970a and 1970b.
31. Baer, 1977 also maps the influence of employers in London during this period.
32. On corruption generally see Hanham, 1959, chapter 13; Gash, 1953, chapter 7; O'Leary, 1962; Gwyn, 1962.

33. From Charles Dickens, Pickwick Papers, chapter 13.
34. There is a description of the system of bribery at Sudbury in Gash, 1953, pp. 159–64.
35. We would expect to find other aspects of market behaviour. In a close election, with a fixed supply of votes, the price should increase as polling becomes closer and the price of a vote might fall very near the close of the poll when it was clear who was going to win. Not surprisingly evidence of such 'rational corruption' is hard to find!
36. Hanham gives a useful list of contemporary election inquiries, Hanham, 1972, pp. lxxxi–cxliv.
37. Ostrogorski , 1902; see Trinder, 1967 on the pressure felt by MPs for 'charitable' contributions and Hoppen's comments on similar activity in Irish constituencies, Hoppen, 1984.
38. The details of the Peterborough election are based on the evidence given to the House of Commons Committee which is printed in Parliamentary Papers, 1852–53 XVII, and the poll books for the general election of 1852 (July) and the by-elections in December 1852 and June 1853; see also Bromond, 1993.
39. Dod, 1853, p. 249; Hanham lists Earl Fitzwilliam as a patron returning two members for Peterborough, see Hanham, 1972, p. xxxv.
40. See also the accounts cited earlier – Davis, 1972, p. 98; Olney, 1973, p. 44; Nossiter, 1975, p. 158 and Joyce, 1975.

2 Elections and Party Organization in Victorian England

1. These distinctions were first made by Key; the formulation used here is derived from Sorauf; Cox gives a similar characterization of the British party system in the late nineteenth century; see Key, 1964; Sorauf, 1964 and 1967; Cox, 1987, pp. 122–23.
2. Cox, 1987 gives one account of the development of party voting in England after 1832.
3. For a definition of a 'political tendency' see Rose, 1964; Rose's analysis is of party politics in the modern era but his distinctions between party, faction and tendency are just as applicable to this earlier period; on the development of the party system see Mitchell, 1976a, pp. 2–97.
4. W.S.Gilbert in 'Iolanthe', 1882.
5. On the effect of the Municipal Corporations Act in creating another level of electoral competition and the relationship between municipal and parliamentary politics, see Fraser, 1976 and Phillips and Wetherell, 1994; on the annual registration battles see Prest, 1977, Cornford and Mitchell, 1978 and Salmon, 2002, pp. 38–42.
6. Mitchell, 1976b discusses some of the strategic possibilities created by elections in multi-member seats; for a more detailed analysis of the calculus of voting see Cox, 1984; for a nineteenth-century statement of electoral strategy see Cox and Grady, 1868.
7. For discussions of split voting see Mitchell, 1976a, pp. 116–23 and Cox, 1987, pp. 95–112, as well as Phillips and Wetherell, 1995, pp. 416–24, and Appendix 2.

8. Note that these figures, and those in Table 1.2, refer to England and Wales; in Scotland about one in eight adult males had the vote, in Ireland about one in twenty; Butler and Cornford, 1969, p. 330. Salmon, 2002 has a detailed discussion of the increase in the electorate after 1832.

9. For an alternative account of enfranchisement in Britain see Colomer, 2001, pp. 47–50 and his table 2.1.

10. Sources for Table 1.2 – Butler and Cornford, 1969; Deane and Mitchell, 1962 and Salmon, 2002. The figures for the electorate between 1832 and 1868 should be treated with caution due to the possibility of the double counting of electors with multiple qualifications.

11. See Salmon, 2002, appendix 2, pp. 253–55 for a fuller statement of voting qualifications in England and Wales.

12. The outline of many of these changes can be gauged from the historical statistics in Deane and Mitchell, 1962; Perkin, 1969 gives one interpretation of the development of the modern-class system in the nineteenth century; the growing nationalization of electoral response is discussed by Stokes, 1967 and Nossiter, 1970a.

13. See Mitchell, 1982b.

14. On the effects of secrecy, see Rokkan, 1961.

15. Quoted in Hanham, 1972, p. xxxii.

16. Hanham maps constituencies by electorate and population, see Hanham, 1972, pp. xxii–xxvii; Vincent suggests 'the medium-sized constituency…normally a market, county, or cathedral town…. was in any case the central element in the English electoral system' Vincent, 1967, p. 4.

17. For a recent study of the role of local and national political organizations in the period between 1832 and 1841, see Salmon, 2002 particularly parts I and III.

18. Salmon provides a detailed study of the basis of the electoral register after 1832, and discusses the growth in the electorate between 1832 and 1841, Salmon, 2002, pp. 19–42, 58–77 and 238–48; the changes in the number of registered electors in the decade after 1832 are given in Salmon, 2002, appendix 3, pp. 257–266. The official poll books were all destroyed in a fire and existing pollbooks are, with a very few exceptions, unofficial publications usually produced by local printers, see Appendix 1.

20. In a two-member seat an elector could cast one, two – or no – votes. As a result the relationship between individual votes (ballots) and final candidate vote totals could be less than obvious; for a discussion of ballots and votes see Appendix 2.

21. See Winchester, 1973a.

22. For more information on poll books see Appendix 1; the most complete reference work on poll books is Sims, 1984.

23. For aspects of the debate over class analysis see Vincent, 1966; 1967; Neale, 1972; Foster, 1974; Phillips, 1992.

24. On Nominal Record Linkage see Appendix 1, Wrigley, 1973 and Elklit, 1985b; 1988 and Elklit and Skytte, 1980.

25. See Appendix 3; for a discussion of transition tables and electoral change in this period see Mitchell, 1982a; on panels see Phillips, 1984, pp. ix–xii; a few poll books have voting data for more than one election.

26. It also confirms the long-term stability in partisan behaviour found in other frequently contested constituencies, see Mitchell and Cornford, 1977; Phillips and Wetherell, 1991.
27. Except at the elections before and after the Second Reform Bill.
28. See Colomer, 2001, p. 48.
29. Accepting some financial payment was one way to offset such costs.
30. Mitchell, 1969b as quoted in Thompson et al., 1991, p. 176. This study looks at only the political and electoral consequences that follow from the social situation of the individual voter, it ignores aspects of inter-personal relationships that could be used to account for other social transactions.

3 Some Electoral Consequences of the Great Reform Bill

1. Mrs Arbuthnot, quoted in Cannon, 1973, p. 20.
2. Brock, 1973 is an account of the passage of the 1832 Act; Seymour, 1915 discusses the effects of franchise and other changes brought in by the first three reform bills; Butler, 1961 covers changes after the Fourth Reform Bill; Moore, 1961 is a revisionist account of the 1832 bill that emphasizes the redistribution of seats that accompanied Reform; Prest, 1977, Cornford and Mitchell, 1978 and Salmon, 2002 suggest the importance of both the provisions for electoral registration and the Municipal Corporations Act of 1835; Powell, 1973 provides an alternative interpretation of the Reform Act within the context of democratization.
3. The vote on the increased grant to the Catholic institution at Maynooth in 1845 was opposed by those who saw a danger to the established church, those, such as Dissenters, who disliked Rome, as well as those opposed to the principle of state financial help for religion.
4. Salmon suggests that Gash may have overemphasized the continuities between pre- and post-reform systems, see Salmon, 2002.
5. Phillips, 1992 also discusses the continuities between pre- and post-Reform systems.
6. See Hanham, 1972, pp. xxxiv–xxxvi; another list of post-Reform nomination boroughs is in Gash, 1953, appendix D, pp. 438–9; family boroughs are discussed Ibid., pp. 193–201.
7. Salmon, 2002, table 1, p. 23; see also the discussion in Cannon, 1973, pp. 290–92; O'Gorman suggests figures of 440,000 and 656,000, see O'Gorman, 1993 and Beales, 1992.
8. The borough electorates in both Lancaster and Colchester were reduced by reform. In Lancaster the electorate decreased from 'some 4000 to hardly more than 1000', Cannon, 1973, p. 257; see also Chapter 3. What is perhaps surprising is that this did not happen in more seats given the conservative aims of the act:

    > what was intended by the cabinet was no more than a pruning, purification and enlargement of the existing electoral structure. The new franchise qualifications in both county and borough were in all cases higher than the lowest of the existing qualifications … it was a rationalization of the old untidy electoral machinery rather than a downward extension. (Gash, 1986, p. 57).

9. Cambridge had 1372 electors after Reform in 1832 and 122 of them were still in the electorate in 1868. The decline in numbers was fairly rapid, by 1840 the Reform cohort of electors made up less than half of the electorate, see Mitchell and Cornford, 1977, p. 266, table 1. For more on electoral turnover in borough electorates, see Chapters 4 and 5. For the increase in the electorate in 1867, 1885 and 1918, see Table 2.2.
    Salmon argues that the initial post-reform figures were artificially low and that registration activity helped to produce a growth in the registered electorate after 1835, see Salmon, 2002.
10. On urban penetration of the counties before 1832, see Cannon, 1973, appendix 5, pp. 293–98.
11. The debate about the significance of uncontested seats can be followed in Gash, 1953, p. 440; Lloyd, 1965; Aydelotte, 1971; Moore, 1974; see also Dunbabin, 1966. The figures in some of these analyses differ due to confusion between uncontested constituencies and uncontested seats.
12. Although the number of uncontested seats is not significant after 1945 this does not mean that all the major parties contested all the seats at every general election after that date. Only in 1964 did the Conservative party put up candidates in all 630 seats; at that election the Labour party contested 628 seats, see Butler and Cornford, 1969, p. 360.
13. The growth and activity of party organization between 1832 and 1841, at both local and national levels, is the major theme of Salmon's study of the working of the post-Reform system, see Salmon, 2002.
14. Gash, 1982 has a useful discussion of the Conservative party in parliament after 1832. A more general discussion of the role of party during this period can be found in Beales, 1967. Gash, 1983 covers the electoral organization of the party after 1832; see also Salmon, 2002, pp. 43–74. For the period following 1868 see Feuchtwanger, 1968; Vincent, 1967; Adelman, 1970; Hanham, 1959, part 3 and Hanham, 1961. Cox, 1987 provides one explanation of the development of a link between the party in parliament and the party in the electorate; Mitchell, 1976a, pp. 1–96 gives an overview of the development of the party system between 1832 and 1868; the linkages to municipal politics are explored in Fraser, 1976; Cornford and Mitchell, 1978; Phillips and Weatherell, 1991; 1994 and Salmon, 2002.
15. After 1832 both a national party organizer and a national party organization can be identified, particularly for the Conservative party; Gash comments that 'well before the general election of 1841, the [Conservative] party possessed a widespread if loose connection of local organisation throughout England', (Gash, 1983, p. 144). Of the individual party organizers Parkes, Bonham and Coppock all have entries in the Dictionary of National Biography, and Parkes is extensively discussed both in Gash, 1953 and in 'Bonham and the Conservative party 1830–1857', pp. 118–35 in Gash, 1986; see also Salmon, 2002, pp. 44–68 on the linkage between local and national organization in the period between 1832 and 1841. On party organization more generally see Panebianco, 1988 and Katz and Mair, 1994.
16. The distinction between borough and county seats survived until the changes that followed the Third Reform Act 1884/85; university seats formed a third category of seat until 1948. Borough seats were largely urban but county seats could include some urban parishes, or even whole industrial

    areas, as in County Durham, see Gash, 1953, appendix B – The Enlargement of the Boroughs in 1832, pp. 432–33.

17. For most constituencies there were ten general elections between 1832 and 1868. However seats disfranchised in 1867 were only contested at nine general elections, so the basis of the figures differs for a small number of seats. The effect is to make medians and averages lower than they otherwise might have been. Similarly the 1868 election results have not been used for the counties that were divided or redistricted in 1867. In Scotland those counties that were divided in 1867 have only nine elections. Of the two Scottish counties that were combined in 1867 one has ten results, the other nine. Details of all the elections are taken from McCalmont, 1971. Some of the differences between England and Wales on the one hand, and Scotland and Ireland may stem from the differences in the extent of enfranchisement, see Chapter 2 note 8.

18. For a discussion of class in this period see Perkin, 1969; Neale, 1972; and Phillips, 1992.

19. Hanham suggests the importance of borough seats in this period, particularly the smaller boroughs – 'the whole balance of the electoral system was so tilted that it gave disproportionate emphasis to the smaller towns' (Hanham, 1972, pp. xxiii), see also Vincent, 1967.

20. The distinction between centre and periphery, and their relationship during the processes of nation building and political mobilization in a European context, receive particular attention in the work of Rokkan; see especially Rokkan, 1970, part I; Flora, 1999, pp. 116–18 and pp. 122–26; a pioneering analysis of centre and periphery in Norway can be found in Rokkan and Valen, 1962, reprinted as pp. 181–225 in Rokkan (1970).

21. There is an extensive literature on the role of deference in English politics from the eighteenth century onwards, and the concept is central to Moore's analysis of electoral behaviour in this period, see the discussion of Moore in Chapter 1; for a discussion of the eighteenth and early nineteenth centuries see O'Gorman, 1989, pp. 225–44; Kavanagh, 1971 provides a critique of the use of deference in the analysis of modern British politics.

22. The figures for the constituency population in 1831 and electorate in 1832 are taken from McCalmont, 1971. The figures for the electorate are subject to the vagaries of registration and the problem of electors with multiple qualifications.

23. But see the comment about Aylesbury in Chapter 1 note 27.

24. Cox also examined the link between constituency size and the parliamentary activity of MPs, see Cox, 1987, pp. 56–60. Interestingly he concludes, 'the politics of large places...required a different kind of campaigning ...' (Ibid.). In the larger seats the proportion of adult males enfranchised varied too. In 1832 Taylor found that it ranged between 2.2 per cent in Halifax to 88.2 per cent in Preston; by 1861 it fell between 11.2 per cent in Stockport to 51.6 per cent in Coventry, see Taylor, 1997, table 2.1, p. 57.

25. For example Moore's analysis of Cambridgeshire in 1835 showed that it was made up of 156 parishes and that these contained between 1 and 352 electors each, see Moore, 1975, Table 7, pp. 65–79.

26. To give just one example, Droitwich was contested at only two general elections between 1832 and 1868 and at the election of 1835 over 90 per cent of the electorate cast a vote, see Smith, 1844–50, Volume 2, p. 130.

4   Organizing the Vote in Lancaster

1. See also Salmon, 2002, pp. 20–22, 27–37.
2. On the Registration Act of 1843, see Prest 1977; on the politicization of the registration, Salmon, 2002, pp. 38–42.
3. The figure for the 1818 election is from Smith, 1844–50, Volume 1, p. 179; Cannon suggests that the Lancaster electorate was reduced from about 4,000 to hardly more than 1,000, see Cannon, 1973, p. 257; contemporary poll books give a slightly lower figure but Reform certainly reduced the electorate considerably.
4. See also Seymour, 1915, pp. 389–90.
5. He was MP from 1824 to 1852, defeated in the 1852 election he was re-elected at a by-election and was again an MP from 1853 to 1857.
6. Poll books exist for all general elections in Lancaster between 1837 and 1865; in addition there are poll books for by-elections in 1848, 1853 and 1864; see Sims, 1984, pp. 105–106.
7. Quoted in Mitchell and Cornford, 1977, p. 262. They discuss the impact of the Corn Law issue on Cambridge electors in detail and show its effect on voting in the borough during the mid-1840s, see Mitchell and Cornford, 1977, pp. 261–62.
8. For an alternative analysis that suggests that more than attitudes over the Corn Laws were involved in the politics surrounding the election of 1847, see McLean 2001, especially Chapter 2.
9. Connacher classifies Greene as a Peelite on the basis of his voting during the parliament of 1841–7, Connacher, 1972, pp. 220–35.
10. In Lancaster each elector had two votes at the general election – a plumper is a single vote given to one candidate with the second vote not used, see Appendix 2.
11. The heterogeneous nature of the Conservative parliamentary party between 1841 and 1847 is outlined in Connacher, 1972, pp. 11–12; see also Aydelotte 1972.
12. On the Liberal party, see Vincent 1966; for the Conservatives, Stewart 1978.
13. The figures are from Bean 1890; on party voting see Mitchell, 1976a, pp. 108–30, Cox, 1987, pp. 91–112, and Appendix 2.
14. This is the analysis of votes from the Lancaster poll book of 1848. The figures differ slightly both from those given in Bean 1890 and from the figures in the *Lancaster Gazette* of July 31, 1847. In Table 4.3 each cell represents the number of votes given for the particular combination of row and column co-ordinates – for example, 328 electors gave a double vote for Greene and Salisbury. The diagonal entries are the single votes or plumpers – 254 electors voted for Gregson only. Note: the entries below the diagonal are omitted, as they are identical to those above.
15. See also Cox, 1987, pp. 91–112; Phillips and Wetherell, 1995, pp. 414–24.
16. Socinians were a non-conformist sect that denied the divinity of Christ – Socinianism is related to modern Unitarianism; there is no analysis of voting by the majority of Anglican voters.
17. The same paper also lists the 33 electors who were struck off – 23 Liberal voters and 10 Tory.

18. This is done using Nominal Record Linkage (NRL), a systematic technique for bringing together information on individuals from several sources. See Appendix 1 for a discussion of NRL. Its use in electoral analysis is discussed in Mitchell and Cornford, 1977; Mitchell, 1982a; Elklit, 1985a; Elklit, 1985b; Elklit, 1988, and Elklit and Skytte, 1980.

19. The blank cell in this row represents the new voters in 1847 who left the electorate before the 1848 election. We have no other information on these electors, as they are not listed in either poll book, but see note 32.

20. The data in Table 4.5 comes from the linkage of poll books for 1847 and 1848. There is a difference between this data and the official returns. About eighteen votes for Gregson and two for Greene appear to have been omitted and so the vote totals in Table 4.5 do not match the declared official figures for the two elections. Indeed the totals reverse the official results of the 1848 poll. This is a not uncommon level of disagreement between different sources for nineteenth-century electoral data, in this case it is less than 2% overall, see also Cox, 1987, p. 96. Appendix 3 has a further discussion of transition tables. The * indicates a cell for which we have no data – the new voters who left the electorate before the 1848 election.

21. In either case it shows electors using the multiple vote to express distinct preferences between candidates, see the discussion of preferential plumping in Appendix 2.

22. Cooper 1988 is an extensive investigation of the politics of the Freemen in the borough constituency of Grimsby in the period before and after Reform.

23. The population of Lancaster increased from 12,613 in 1832 to 16,168 by 1851, (Dod, 1853, p. 174).

24. Hanham 1961 discusses local organization; Hanham, 1972, pp. xlii–lxix includes extracts from a contemporary handbook on the local organization of an election campaign by Cox and Grady 1868; some of the text is reprinted in Cox and Grady 1974; see also Salmon 2002.

25. Table 4.5 shows that 114 electors left the electorate between the two polls – 21 Liberal voters, 43 Tories, 23 split voters and 27 non-voters. Calculating chi-square with three degrees of freedom we find that at 73.18 it is highly significant. This suggests that the distribution of partisan preferences amongst those who left the electorate after the 1847 election was different to those who remained. The main problem is the number of split voters and non-voters who left. We can say nothing about how the split voters might have behaved but the non-voters of 1847 favoured the Tory candidate by almost 2:1 in 1848. Although the Liberals had an advantage amongst the new voters, the overall pattern of voting in this group is not significantly different in 1848 from that of the electorate as a whole.

26. For comments on electoral management before 1832 see O'Gorman, 1989 and Phillips, 1982a; 1982b; Cooper, 1988 is a local study that examines a constituency before and after 1832; on the effects of municipal reform, see Fraser 1976.

27. These notebooks are in the possession of the author.

28. See Cox and Grady, 1868; 1974; all the ward notebooks reflect the general management principles that they recommend, see also Cox and Grady as quoted in Hanham, 1972, pp. iv and lix, and Salmon, 2002.

29. This is also found in other surviving canvasses. Salmon quotes entries from one for the Newark election of 1841 – 'wife says he will vote' and 'wife

promised'. Disraeli even suggested that 'if men have the vote, the women have the influence'; see Salmon, 2002, p. 97.

30. The coverage of the surviving notebooks varies both for period and area; for 1847–48 there are books for Districts 1, 4 and 5; for 1849–50 – District 3; for 1850 – District 1 and for 1850–51 Districts 1 and 3. The annual revision of the register took place in the autumn and was followed by the publication of the register. At this time the register ran from the 1st of November one-year to the 31st of October the following year. All of these notebooks were pre-printed, confirming the routinization of local electoral activity – 'one effect of this [the provisions of the 1832 Act] was that printed pre-election books, containing step-by-step instructions and blank response columns... became increasingly common after 1832', Salmon, 2002, p. 98.

31. See Wrigley, 1966; walk lists are still used in local campaigning.

32. These two could be electors who qualified to vote after the 1847 election but who had left the electorate before 1848, see note 19.

33. There is a growing literature on modern political marketing and campaigning; Shea 1996 discusses the use of voter targeting in US elections today; the earlier analyses in Meadow 1985 and Swerdlow 1988 suggest that the use of social information to target individuals and groups of voters has much in common with the methods used in the nineteenth century.

34. Cooper 1988 gives a detailed account of landlord influence in Grimsby around 1832.

35. The level of accuracy in the Lancaster canvassing is very similar to that achieved in Bedford in 1835, see Table 5.20; canvassing is discussed further in Chapter 6.

5 Electoral Change in Bedford 1832–68

1. In this nineteenth-century context a constituency electoral cohort is defined by the first potential participation at a parliamentary election. Some electors could have voted previously in another constituency; they could possess multiple qualifications for a borough and the surrounding county. After 1835 they may have qualified as an elector in municipal elections as well. Modern usage, under universal suffrage, normally defines a cohort by age, see Butler and Stokes, 1969, p. 50.

2. Figures from Cambridge poll book data; see Mitchell and Cornford, 1977, p. 272.

3. Note that there are differences between the aggregate data from McCalmont and the figures in the Bedford poll books. The ballot data and the individual level data are from the Bedford poll books. There is no published poll book for the 1832 election and data for that election is derived from Smith 1842 and from a canvass book for 1835; see also note 9 and Appendix 1.

4. Some of the problems of using Nominal Record Linkage over a series of elections and poll books are discussed in Mitchell, 1976a, pp. 398–412.

5. The 'three quarters of borough constituencies...[with]...less than 1400 electors' identified in Table 3.3.

6. Copies of the Bedford poll books are in the Bedford Record Office and at Bedford Town Hall; there is no poll book for the 1832 election. However

there is a printed register for 1835 with manuscript additions giving both the promise and the vote for the 1835 election, as well as the vote given in 1832 for those electors who took part in the earlier election. This leaves the number of those who voted only at the election of 1832 unknown. Smith, 1842, gives the number of single votes (plumpers) for each candidate in 1832, so the full ballot breakdown can be reconstructed. We know the voting behaviour of those who were still electors in 1835, but information on the non-voters in 1832 is lacking, as is the voting of those who voted in 1832 but left the electorate before the 1835 election; see also note 9.

7. See Mitchell, 1982a, pp. 96–97.

8. There is no way of identifying the electors who were qualified to vote before 1832; the two candidates in the 1831 election were returned unopposed and no list of pre-Reform electors has been traced.

9. Note the difference between the 1832 figures in Figure 5.2 and in Table 5.1. We do not know the number of non-voters at the 1832 election. The ballot data suggests that 961 electors voted; both Dod 1853 and Smith 1842 give the electorate as 1572. This is almost certainly inaccurate given the voting figures in 1832 and those we have for 1835. It would suggest 611 non-voters, some 40 per cent of the electorate. (The high figure may result from duplicate qualifications.) There was an average non-voting rate of 6.6 per cent for the other elections between 1835 and 1868. Using this figure for 1832 suggests an electorate of 1,029. The 1832 cohort data used in Figure 5.2, Table 5.4 et seq, refers only to identified individuals who voted in 1832. A few 1832 non-voters who voted at later elections will be recorded as members of later cohorts. Those who left the electorate between 1832 and 1835 are omitted completely. This introduces a small element of possible inaccuracy into the data. A check was also made to see if the electors who left at time (t) were re-registered as voters at the later elections (t+2), (t+3) etc.

10. In the 1960s turnover was estimated at between 1 per cent and 2 per cent of the electorate, see Butler and Stokes, 1969. The nineteenth century and contemporary situations are not strictly comparable. Migration between constituencies need not today produce disfranchisement in the same way that it did in the mid-nineteenth century, and turnover in a partially enfranchised electorate may have been greater than in a fully enfranchised one.

11. '…it was the recruitment of "new" voters on to the registers that was ultimately to prove fundamental to the electoral performance of the parties after 1832' (Salmon, 2002, p. 77).

12. But see Salmon, 2002 especially pp. 218–21.

13. For a discussion of the problems raised by migration see Wrigley, 1972; for the United States, Bourke and DeBats were able to trace the migration patterns of some of the voters of Washington County in Oregon during the 1850s, also under conditions of open voting, see Bourke and DeBats, 1995.

14. Although some electors in the 1832 cohort may have voted in earlier elections, it includes the Reform Generation; for a general discussion of political generations see Rintala, 1966 and 1968; cf. Mitchell and Cornford, 1977 on the Cambridge electorate.

15. This could be the result of party activity increasing the number of new electors registered.
16. The other cohorts exhibit the same pattern of change and decay over time, see Appendix 3 for a discussion of the calculation of the half-life and other summary measures for this continuous data.
17. As in the case of Lancaster discussed in Chapter 4; for another example, in Bridgnorth, see Drake and Mitchell, 1982, p. 97.
18. See the discussion of ballots and votes in Appendix 2.
19. Cox and Grady, 1868 give a nineteenth-century discussion of strategic possibilities; see also Mitchell, 1976b.
20. See Cox, 1987, pp. 95–97 for a discussion of preferential plumping where an elector gave a single vote for one party candidate when there were two candidates of the same party standing in an election in a two-member constituency; Cox labels this type of voting 'non-partisan plumping'.
21. Mitchell and Cornford discuss the electors in Cambridge who changed between the parties over the Corn Law issue, see Mitchell and Cornford, 1977, pp. 260–62.
22. For a further discussion of party voting after 1832 see Mitchell, 1976a, pp. 117–24 and 128–52, and Cox, 1987, pp. 97–112.
23. Bedford here is different to other boroughs – 'Tory voters were generally less likely to change their colours in a subsequent election than Liberal ones, although the variation was often marginal' (Salmon, 2002, p. 77).
24. See Mitchell, 1976a, pp. 117–21 and Cox, 1987, p. 103, table 9.4.
25. The differences in the data of Tables 5.4, 5.6, and 5.8 reflect differences in the data sources. The data in Table 5.8 are from the poll books; the figures in Tables 5.4 and 5.6 are from linked poll book data and may include voters who were disqualified at one or more elections.
26. For transition tables, see Mitchell, 1982a, pp. 98–102; Appendix 3 has a fuller discussion of the measurement of aggregate vote stability.
27. See Mitchell and Cornford, 1977; The Cambridge series included eight by-elections, so the pairs of elections fell closer together than did those for the general elections in Bedford.
28. Denmark used open voting until 1901, see Elklit and Mitchell, 1983; the Fredericia data is in Elklit, 1988, tables 8.5–8.7, pp. 243–47, stability was less than 50 per cent between three pairs of successive elections; for Sweden, Lewin estimated the 'flow of the vote' at successive pairs of elections between 1887 and 1964: ' our estimates of the flow of the vote between the parties indicates that the voters behaviour is characterised by a high degree of stability' (Lewin, Jansson and Sorbom, 1972, pp. 236–56). Because of the nature of the data used, and the method of estimation, it is difficult to make an exact comparison with poll book data.
29. See also Heath et al., 1991, tables 2.10–2.14 on pp. 26–28; McLean recalculates modern vote stability from the Butler and Stokes data to suggest a higher level of stability – 1959–63 89.7%; 1963–64 85.8% and 1964–66 90%, see McLean, 1992, p. 510; the original discussion is in Butler and Stokes, 1969, pp. 285–292; their discussion of transition tables, Ibid., p. 277.

    Norris 1995 gives slightly different figures. She estimates the level of stable votes at recent elections as: 1964, 64%; 1966, 74%; 1970, 66%; 1974, 58%; 1979, 62%; 1983, 64%; 1987, 69%; 1992, 62%. See Norris, 1995, p. 113.

30. See also the discussion of the influence of the social context of voting behaviour in Chapter 6.

31. Source: 1835 canvass book; linked Bedford individual level electoral data from poll books. Note that all the tables in 5.10 have been standardized – all rows sum to 100 per cent – although there may be rounding errors. The totals column gives the contribution of each row to the total of electors involved, e.g. Table 5.10(b) refers to all the electors qualified for the elections of 1835 and 1837; some 83 per cent of those voting Liberal in 1835 also voted Liberal in 1837, 6 per cent voted Tory, 8 per cent gave a split vote, and 3 per cent did not vote in 1837. The 1835 Liberal voters comprised 41% of all those who voted at both elections, and so on.

32. The table does not include the Tory electors from 1847 who voted Liberal in 1852, or did not vote, so the percentage figures differ slightly from those in Table 5.10(e).

33. The classification of elections as 'deviating', 'realigning' and 'maintaining' comes from Campbell, 1966 and is a development of ideas in Key, 1955; Pomper, 1967 adds a fourth type – 'converting'; all three articles are reprinted in Clubb and Allen, 1971. But it is probably inappropriate to use these labels for electoral change in a single constituency in the period before mass enfranchisement.

34. McLean suggests that 'a party oriented electorate was emerging, whose members voted in a Downsian way for the party which maximised their expected utility. When…voters lost their cues as to which party (or candidate) stood for what, hence the surge in split voting …' (McLean, 1992, p. 308).

    This may well apply over a major issue such as the Corn Laws – but free trade does not appear to have been a significant issue in Bedford during the 1852 election, the problems seem to have been caused by a mixture of local issues and personalities. Stuart, the Conservative candidate had been one of Bedford MPs since 1841; Anstey, the losing Liberal candidate, was an 'outsider' and had previously been MP for Youghal; Whitbread, the second Liberal, who was elected, was a prominent employer and a member of an influential local family. He was persuaded to stand rather late in the day and seems to have been sponsored by the local Financial Reform Association. According to reports of the election in the Bedford Times during May and June 1852, local issues were prominently discussed, particularly the question of the appointment of the Trustees of a local charity. The only 'national' issue raised was that concerning the funding of Maynooth, on which the two Liberals appear to have differed significantly.

35. This and other consequences of the Second Reform Bill are discussed in more detail in Chapter 7.

36. The canvas book is in Bedford Town Hall; there are slight differences in the figures between Tables 5.19 – from a poll book – and Table 5.20 from the canvass book.

37. Under the minority representation clause the elector in a three-member seat had only two votes; on the implications of the clause for party organization in such seats, see Mitchell, 1976b; on the Birmingham caucus, Tholfsen, 1959.

6 The Voter and the Electoral Community

1. See Cox, 1987 for one account of the growth of party voting in the late-nineteenth century; Phillips and Wetherell suggest that ' the politicisation ... stemming from the Great Reform Act converted voters into partisans ...' (Phillips and Wetherell, 1991, p. 646); see also Phillips (1992).
2. The phrase is from Perkin, 1969, chapter 9.
3. The title of an influential book by Laslett, 1965.
4. Nossiter, for example, argues that industrialization may at first have increased the differentiation of constituencies in Britain both socially and geographically, see Nossiter, 1975.
5. See Cornford, 1963 and Clarke, 1971 for aspects of this transformation.
6. For the extent of enfranchisement see Table 2.1 and Butler and Cornford, 1969; Mitchell, 1982b discusses electoral stratification.
7. Cf. Vernon, 1993.
8. Prest, 1977 is a standard work on the politics of registration in this period, see also Salmon, 2002.
9. Comment at the time noted 'a national pattern of Whig decline and relentless Conservative advance'; see Brett, 1996a, p. 112.
10. See Chapter 4; Mitchell and Cornford, 1977 and Cornford and Mitchell, 1978 examine the relationship of registration to electoral politics in Cambridge in the period after 1832.
11. Salmon comments that 'extant registration accounts suggest that Tory registration campaigns were usually better funded than those of the Liberals', Salmon, 2002, p. 73.
12. Fraser, 1976, see also the comments in Salmon, 2002 especially pp. 221–24.
13. Cambridge Advertiser, quoted in Mitchell and Cornford, 1977, p. 255.
14. See the references to local politics in Josiah Chater's diary, Porter, 1975.
15. 'The Municipal Corporations Act managed to create partisans who responded to the national political world even at local elections' Phillips and Weatherell, 1994, pp. 82–83.
16. Lee, 1963 provides an account of the early stages of county government in Cheshire.
17. Some idea of the variety of the small particularistic rewards can be gauged from the diary of H.W. Tancred, the MP for Banbury, see Trinder, 1967.
18. Some of the rewards of municipal power were indeed on a small scale, such as the contract for cutting the hair in the local prison!
19. See Cornford and Mitchell, 1978.
20. Foster, 1974 discusses the use of threats in Oldham and elsewhere; Vincent, 1967 notes the use of 'black lists' and exclusive dealing; in Cambridge lists of those traders who supported the Tory candidates were published after the elections of 1835, 1837 and 1839.
21. On the connection between dissent and the Liberals, see Phillips, 1992.
22. Fraser, 1976 is a major study of municipal politics; Phillips and Wetherell, 1994 also examine the relationship between parliamentary and municipal politics in Shrewsbury after Reform. Note too the comments by Salmon 'one ... feature of municipal reform was that the newly-created municipal electorate often turned out to be much smaller than the parliamentary one', and

'contrary to studies that have assumed both a quantitative and a qualitative gulf between the municipal and the parliamentary electorate,..., the former franchise was a microcosm of the latter' (Salmon, 2002, pp. 218 and 221).

23. The existing poll books for municipal elections show that voting at these elections rapidly became similar to voting at parliamentary elections.

24. See Phillips and Wetherell, 1994 for an analysis of the overlap between parliamentary and municipal electorates. They conclude that 'the parliamentary voters may have contributed a majority [of the municipal electorate] but the additional 30 percent who did not qualify should have been sufficient to generate a municipal electorate with a social structure considerably different from that common to parliamentary electorates.' However, the evidence 'suggests that Shrewsbury's electors who were excluded from the parliamentary fold broadly resembled their counterparts who held both franchises. The socio-economic composition of those who held both franchises was indistinguishable statistically from those who held only the parliamentary franchise' (Phillips and Wetherell, 1994, p. 63).

25. The two levels of political activity were quickly linked: 'voters began to exhibit the same partisan choices in both national and local elections. Recent research on municipal polls in particular, has revealed that...the nationally oriented behaviour elicited in the election of MPs was quickly reproduced at a local level in the selection of new town councillors...voters behaved almost identically at both types of contest' (Salmon, 2002, p. 196).

26. See Vincent, 1967 and Mitchell, 1982b.

27. Boissevain, as quoted by Bott, 1971, pp. 317–18.

28. This section draws heavily on Mitchell, 1969b; see also Barnes, 1969.

29. The content of some of the links in Lancaster can be deduced from the entries in Table 4.8.

30. See also Mayer, 1962, 1963 and 1966.

31. An entry in a Lancaster notebook notes 'wife warm Liberal' for one elector, see Table 4.6.

32. The most accessible account of his views on electoral secrecy can be found in Rokkan, 1961; these are further explored in Mitchell, 1992; for an overview of Rokkan's work, see Flora, 1999; for other aspects of secrecy see Bertrand, Briquet and Pels, 2007.

33. Apart from the informal influence referred to above, some women participated more formally in the electoral process. In the period between 1832 and 1868, there were two women borough proprietors, see Gash, 1953, pp. 219–25. In Cambridge in the early 1840s one of the chief agents of bribery was a mysterious veiled lady, and Smith notes that one woman voted in Manchester in 1867 and several others voted at elections in 1868, see Smith, 1966, p. 205. Women were politically active in other ways too:

> the large number of Conservative volunteers also resulted from the general inclusion of women and wives at festivals and balls, and their specific recruitment into additional organisations.... It was not unusual for their assistance to be publicly acknowledged in an association's published list of subscribers and supporters...Female Liberal activists, by contrast, are conspicuously absent from the record...(Salmon, 2002, p. 64)

34. See Mitchell, 1982b.

35. For comments on how a local party should run an election campaign, including making its own checklists, see Cox and Grady, 1868.
36. 'Voting regularity emerges as a sign of membership in networks or chains of communication and connection ...' (Bourke and DeBats, 1995, p. 246).
37. See also the discussion of voting consistency in Buckingham see Table 1.3 and Davis, 1972; for Shrewsbury, Phillips and Wetherell, 1991 and 1994; the figures for Bedford are in Table 5.6.
38. A full discussion is in Mitchell and Cornford, 1977.
39. On the effects of political competition see Dahl, 1966 and 1971. In a canvass book for part of the North Devon constituency in 1857 only about 51 per cent of electors voted as they had promised. However, between 1832 and 1868, North Devon was contested only twice, possibly reflecting successful elite political management; for a further discussion of canvassing in rural areas see Eastwood, 1997, pp. 31–33.
40. Such information could also be gathered in some county constituencies, see the discussion of canvassing in Linlithgowshire in Chapter 8.
41. The quotation is from Mitchell, 1969b, p. 9; Mayer's analysis of politics in Dewas is in the three articles cited in note 30 supra; for politics in India see also Carter, 1975.
42. This outline of Mayer's analysis is drawn from Mitchell, 1969b, pp. 38–39.
43. Cf. Carter, 1975 on horizontal and vertical alliances in India; one would expect that in a small bounded community such horizontal linkages would almost certainly exist and also that the number of intermediate stages between the initiator of an action set and the terminal respondents would be small. In such small communities problems might well arise from competing linkage contents – cf. the idea of cross pressures in modern voting research.
44. The diary of H.W. Tancred as MP for Banbury throws light on the relationship between an MP and his agent, see Trinder, 1967; Gash discusses the work of national agents in this period, see Gash, 1982, and 1983.
45. In his discussion of London, Baer notes that 'there is increasing evidence from nineteenth century Britain that the social networks of traditional society could survive the vagaries of industrialisation', (Baer, 1977, p. 238).
46. See Vincent, 1967.
47. For another account that also stresses the role of social networks and organization in electoral politics, see Baer, 1977.

7 After the Second Reform Bill

1. 'The 1870's saw the formation of parties different in nature because different in their essential institutional function....' (Hawkins, 1989, pp. 638–9).
2. On the consequences of the Third Reform Act see Cornford, 1963 and Clarke, 1971; the political background to the passage of the Act is discussed in Jones, 1972 and Hayes, 1982.
3. On the regulation of corruption see O'Leary, 1962 and Gwyn, 1962.
4. Stokes, 1967 is a succinct summary of the nationalization of electoral response at the end of the nineteenth century.
5. See Smith, 1966 and Cowling, 1967 for details of the background to the Act.

6. These are the increases in England based on the figures in Smith, 1966, p. 236.
7. 'Though fifty-two seats (mainly in small two-member boroughs) were abolished, only seventeen of these involved the disfranchisement of whole constituencies' (Hoppen, 1998, p. 252) who also discusses the pattern, and the effects, of the redistribution of seats in 1867; the minority representation clause applied in all three-member seats; the elector had only two votes in these constituencies. In Birmingham the clause was a major factor in the role of the Birmingham Caucus, and so in the rise and effectiveness of constituency organization, see Tholfsen, 1959; some of the strategic implications of the clause are explored in Mitchell, 1976b.
8. The same pattern is found in Cambridge, see Mitchell and Cornford, 1977.
9. See Berelson, Lazarsfeld and McPhee, 1954.
10. Source: PP 1865–6 LVII and 1868–9 L; the regions are those defined by Pelling (1967).
11. On the alterations to the counties see Cowling, 1967, appendix II pp. 344–5.
12. Pelling, 1967 provides a discussion of the regional variations in British politics between 1885 and 1910.
13. For the full results, see McCalmont, 1971 and the discussion in Smith, 1966.
14. In this table the measure of party voting used is a strict one, single votes or preferential plumpers have been excluded where there were two candidates of a party standing.
15. Mitchell and Cornford, 1977 provide similar data for Cambridge; vote stability decreased in 'deviating' elections such as that in Bedford in 1852, and in many constituencies in 1847; see Cox, 1987.
16. There were probably local factors at work, see the discussion of Bedford elections in Chapter 5, but note that this is a relatively low level of split voting for a Bedford election in the period 1832–68, see Table 5.8.
17. Mitchell and Cornford, 1977.
18. See Table 5.3.
19. Quoted in Moore, 1967, p. 44.
20. The Act 'had created more working-class constituencies in the cities but it had provided no simple and cheap way of electioneering in them' (Hanham, 1978, p. xx).
21. Foster, 1974 argues that this was also the case for industrial boroughs such as Oldham for the period just after the First Reform Bill.
22. See Perkin, 1969; Hoppen, 1998, pp. 254–71.
23. The literature on class and voting in Britain in the modern era is very extensive. For a discussion that brings out some of the complexities in the period between 1945 and 1970, see Rose, 1974; analysis for the period after 1970 has tended to qualify the role of class – a process that starts with Butler and Stokes 1969; for an overview, see Evans, 1999.
24. On the role of class more generally in this period, see Neale, 1972 and 1981.
25. In Figures 7.1 and 7.2 the stratified pyramid is a highly conventionalized representation of the social stratification of English society during this period. The horizontal lines represent class divisions although the number of divisions – classes – is arbitrary, as is their relative size; for a similar analysis see Chodak, 1964.

26. Some large and open constituencies had an extensive electorate before 1832 – for example, Lancaster and Preston. The 'new' franchise after 1832 may well have reduced the number of electors by eliminating those who did not reach the property qualification.
27. See Vincent, 1967, p. 25.
28. Perkin, 1969, p. 176.
29. Foster, 1974; see also the discussion of class explanations of open voting in Chapter 1.
30. 'According to an official inquiry a majority of voters in eight boroughs supported themselves by daily manual labour, usually as non-industrial artisans and the like', (Hoppen, 1998, p. 240) quoting from Returns PP, 1866, volume LVII.
31. There has been little analysis of the relationship between electorates at the two levels although Phillips and Wetherell, 1994 conclude that 30 per cent of the municipal electorate in Shrewsbury did not qualify for the parliamentary franchise; see also Salmon, 2002.
32. Fraser, 1976; Foster, 1974.
33. Hollis, 1974 is an introduction to 'pressure from without'; for the world of 'causes' and pressure groups in this period; see Hamer, 1977.
34. Although it mainly covers the period before 1832, Tilly, 1995 is a study of some of these other channels of political communication, see also Thompson, 1963 and Rude, 1964; Steinberg, 1999 provides some local studies.
35. Vincent, 1966 compares electoral politics to public play; see also Vernon, 1993.
36. Quoted in Joyce, 1975, p. 526.
37. The elections of 1874 and 1880 were very corrupt, see Hanham, 1959; Hoppen suggests that the introduction of secrecy made little or no difference in the larger cities, see Hoppen, 1998, p. 259.
38. There is an extensive literature on 'working class Tories', in particular McKenzie and Silver, 1968 and Nordlinger, 1967; in some areas working-class support for the Tories was established quite early, see Clarke 1971.
39. See Rokkan, 1970 p. 36.
40. For the 1880s Cornford suggests that 'beside their political functions, the local associations by their informal activities, reinforced the slowly dissolving social ties that were the strength of traditional Toryism', (Cornford, 1964, p. 424); this creation of secondary organizations did not go as far as it did in Germany where the network of secondary party organizations produced 'negative' community integration, see Roth, 1963.
41. The question of religion and voting behaviour in England up to 1918 is problematic; on the role of the Quakers in Darlington, see Nossiter, 1975; Wald goes further and suggests 'religion was the major factor in elections from 1885 to 1910', (Wald, 1983, p. 161); but see the methodological comments on Wald's analysis in Phillips, 1984, p. xv; Mathew, McKibbin and Kay, 1976 examine some of the effects of the further expansion of the suffrage in 1918.
42. See also Cornford, 1963.
43. This includes the final full incorporation of the working class into the electorate after 1918 and the later enfranchisement of women.

8   The Organization of Opinion

1. There are copies of all five printed lists in the National Library of Scotland: 'List of the electors of the County of Linlithgow arranged according to the order of their residence, corrected after Appeal Court, 1838; 1844, 1846, 1851'; and 'Supplement to List of the electors of the county of Linlithgow; to enable the holders of the list printed after the appeals courts 1838 to give effect to the variations after appeal court 1840. Corrected up to 12th December 1840'.
2. On Cambridgeshire see Moore, 1975, pp. 65–79, table 7.
3. The problem for the Liberals seems to have been that some of their 'promises', as well as many electors recorded as 'Doubtful', subsequently polled for the Tory candidate; see the Leeds poll book for 1859.
4. See Appendix 2 for a detailed discussion of voting in two member constituencies.
5. McLean argues that a second, centre-periphery dimension was also important in British politics in this period, see McLean, 2001, pp. 99–104; see Mitchell, 1976a, pp. 9–21 for another analysis of the dimensionality of the nineteenth-century party system. The importance of the class cleavage is stressed in several accounts of electoral politics after 1885; for one example see Clarke, 1971.
6. The electorate grew from 7.7 million in December 1910 to 21.4 million after 1918, see Butler and Cornford, 1969.
7. On the Conservative adoption of mass organisation, see Cornford 1964 and 1967.
8. Birmingham became a three-member constituency after 1867 but the individual elector had only two votes. By organizing the behaviour of its supporters, the local organization helped the Liberals to win all three seats, see Mitchell, 1976b, pp. 25–28.

Appendix 1   Poll Books and Nominal Record Linkage

1. For early polling lists, see Hirst, 1975.
2. See Speck, 1970 and Sims, 1984.
3. Baskerville, Adman and Beedham, 1991 suggest that manuscript county poll books served quite specific organizational purposes in early eighteenth-century elections.
4. For a list of known poll books see Sims, 1984. Printed poll books can also be found for some non-parliamentary elections; for municipal elections after 1835 and for other elected public offices such as sheriff or coroner.
5. The publisher of the South Derbyshire poll book for 1865 thanks the authorities for their help, as does that of the Dover poll book for 1868.
6. See Drake, 1973 on the destruction of the official poll books; some do survive, those for the West Suffolk elections of 1832 and 1835 are in the West Suffolk Record Office; the Committee reports into the Stafford Borough election of 1832 and the Roxburghshire election of 1837 both contain a poll book.

7. As in the figures for the Lancaster elections of 1847 and 1848 in Chapter 4; the existence of minor disagreements between sources is also noted by Cox, 1987, p. 97; for a discussion of the different errors in manuscript poll books, see Baskerville, Adman and Beedham, 1991, pp. 390 et seq.

8. See the comments on the series of Cambridge poll books for elections between 1832 and 1868 in Mitchell and Cornford, 1977.

9. Of course two poll books could both derive from a common erroneous source; over sixteen elections in Cambridge between 1832 and 1868, disagreements in electoral data occurred in less than 0.2% of the cases involved; for more details see Mitchell and Cornford, 1977.

10. For example the Norwich poll book for 1835. The register was not necessarily a neutral document but at least it had an official imprimatur and status. The annual and contested nature of registration in the boroughs may also have increased the accuracy of the personal information contained in electoral registers.

11. For details of record keeping practices at elections see Cox and Grady, 1868; the Dublin poll book for 1868 is derived from the Liberal checklists, that for 1859 from the Conservatives ones; the poll book for the Derbyshire South election in 1868 is announced as being based on the lists of both parties.

12. See Prest, 1977 for further details.

13. For a further discussion of some of the difficulties over using this information and over the nature of social stratification in the period between 1832 and 1868, see Neale, 1972.

14. One of the rare poll books that give denomination is that for Newry in 1868; when occupations are listed, ministers are sometimes qualified as Anglican or dissenting. See Sims (1984) for an indication of the other information available in particular poll books.

15. On poll books and NRL see also Phillips, 1984, pp. ix–xii.

16. It will be assumed that each poll book is a complete enumeration of the electors in the constituency and that it lists the non-voters as well as those who voted; some poll books published after 1832 do not list non-voters.

17. Most electors had only one Christian name; those with two Christian names made up less than 15 per cent of the electorate in Cambridge; those with three are very uncommon. The possession of more than one Christian name becomes more common towards the end of the 1832–68 period.

18. Since we are mainly using data from general elections, the maximum gap between two successive elections is the six years between 1841 and 1847, and again between 1859 and 1865. The shortest period between elections is the two years between 1835 and 1837, and again between 1857 and 1859.

19. Previous linkage studies of social data where the separate records have a ten-year gap have also assumed agreement in name and one of a larger set of secondary criteria, see Anderson, 1971 and Winchester, 1971. Other studies of electoral behaviour based on NRL include Mitchell and Cornford, 1977, Elklit, 1988 and Phillips, 1992; see also Elklit, 1985b; Elklit and Skytte, 1980, Mitchell, 1982a and Phillips, 1984.

20. For a more detailed discussion of the problems of linkage see Mitchell, 1976a, pp. 401–12, Mitchell and Cornford, 1977 and Mitchell, 1982a. This discussion of NRL is based on the use of printed records, other distinct and separate problems occur with manuscript data.

21. Note the assumptions behind the linkage process make it non-transitive and this may introduce other technical problems with a series of poll books, see Mitchell, 1976a, pp. 405–12. In Bedford the electors who left the electorate at time (t) were also compared to the new electors at (t+2), (t+3), ..., to identify electors who were de-registered and later re-qualified.

Appendix 2   Votes and Ballots

1. The minority representation clause applied in seats with more than two MPs after 1867; in these seats the elector had one less vote than the number of MPs, that is only two votes in a three-member seat.
2. Mitchell, 1976b and Cox, 1984 cover some of the strategic aspects of elections in multi-member seats.
3. See Cox, 1987, p. 97; see also Mitchell, 1976a, pp. 114–15.
4. Cox, 1987, p. 96.
5. This breakdown of the vote is from Smith, 1844–50, Volume II, p. 166.
6. From Smith, 1844–50, Volume II, p. 40.
7. As at the Lancaster election of 1847.
8. Because the elector is showing a preference by not supporting one candidate, this type of voting has something in common with both negative and approval voting, see Brams, 1977, Brams and Fishburn 1983, Cox, 1984.

Appendix 3   Measuring Electoral Change

1. A transition table, such as Table A3.1, is a two-dimensional property space defined by two qualitative attributes, in this case voting at t_1 and t_2, see Barton, 1955. Such tables can be found in some poll books – the Stafford poll book for 1869 prints a table summarizing the pattern of voting in the constituency at the general election in 1868 and the by-election in 1869.
2. Under open voting we assume that non-voting, particularly non-voting at two or more successive elections, is a deliberate electoral choice. It was one way for an elector to avoid identification with either of the 'parties' or candidates who were seeking his electoral support. It also avoided potential conflicts in his personal network between the elector and others with different partisan loyalties. Similar reasons could also cause split-voting (X) at successive elections. Both types of behaviour represent an 'avoidance' of partisan behaviour in the sense of unequivocally voting for one party rather than another. However they can both represent a consistent electoral choice, hence their inclusion in the summary measure of partisan behaviour.
3. To help comparison those tables were standardized with the total of row entries as 100 per cent.
4. See Drake, 1971 and Mitchell, 1982a, pp. 106–107.
5. The behaviour of electors at the Bedford elections of 1847, 1852 and 1857 is summarized in Figure 5.4; note that over the three elections the number of electors who fall into the two major patterns of behaviour over time has already been reduced to less than 15 per cent of the 1857 electorate.
6. See Chapter 5, Section IV.

7. There are a few electors who leave the electorate through some form of disqualification and then rejoin at a later date, as well as the potential confusion of a father and son with the same name, address and qualification. Sometimes such pairs of electors are differentiated through suffixes such as 'senior' and 'junior', but this is not consistently the case. If one of an identical pair of electors subsequently leaves the electorate, is it necessarily the father through death? This and similar types of problem may well introduce minor errors in the process of personal identification that is the basis of NRL. So it is possible that a few electors in C_t may have been members of previous cohorts $C_{(t-2)}$ or earlier, see comments in Mitchell, 1976a, Mitchell and Cornford, 1977.
8. For an equivalent analysis and characterization of the turnover in the membership of the Canadian House of Commons, see Casstevens and Denham, 1970; this is generalized to other legislatures in Casstevens, 1978.
9. For a fuller exposition of this type of analysis, see Casstevens, 1977.
10. In years and months, from Mitchell, 1976a, p. 340.

Bibliography

Contemporary sources

Reference works

Bean, W.W. (1890) *The Parliamentary Representation of the Six Northern Counties* (Hull: printed for the author).

Cox, E.W. and Grady, S.G. (1868) *The New Law and Practice of Registrations and Elections*, 10th Edition (London: Law Times); extracts on *'Hints to solicitors for the conduct of elections'*, reprinted (1974) (Milton Keynes: Open University Press).

Dod, C.R. (1853) *Electoral Facts From 1832 to 1853 Impartially Stated, 2nd Edition*, with an intoduction by H.J. Hanham (reprinted Brighton: Harvester Press 1972).

McCalmont, F.H. (1971) *McCalmont's Parliamentary Poll Book British Election Results 1832–1918, 8th Edition*, with an introduction and additional material by J. Vincent and M. Stenton (Brighton: Harvester Press).

Powell, D., Rodwell, H. and Dew, E.L.E (1853) *Reports of the Decisions of Committees of the House of Commons in the Trial of Controverted Elections during the Fifteenth Parliament of the United Kingdom* (London: V and R Stevens and G.S. Norton).

Smith, H.S. (1842) *The Register of Parliamentary Contested Elections*, 2nd edition (London: Simpkin, Marshall).

Smith, H.S. (1844–50), *The Parliaments of England,* 3 Volumes (London: Simpkin, Marshall).

Poll books

Bedford: 1835, 1837, 1841, 1847, 1852, 1857, 1859, 1865, 1868.
Cambridge: 1832, 1834, 1835, 1837, 1839, 1840, 1841, 1843, 1845, 1847, 1865, 1868.
Canterbury: 1847 (Smithson).
Dover: 1868.
Gloucester: 1865, 1868.
Hereford: 1865, 1868.
Ipswich: 1865, 1868.
Lancaster: 1847, 1848.
Leeds: 1859.
Newry: 1868.
Norwich 1835.
Stafford Borough: 1869.
Sudbury: 1837.

Electoral registers, canvass books and other manuscript material

Bedford Electoral Register and Canvass Book 1835 [Bedford Town Hall].
North Devon (1857) Ilfracombe Polling District: Electoral Register, 1856 with ms canvass for the 1857 general election [collection: author].

Durham City Electoral Register 1868/canvass book [Guildhall Library].
Lancaster Electoral Management Notebooks [collection: author].
Canvass Book: St Ann's Ward 1841;
Mr. Jackson's Notebook [dated July 1843].
Ward notebooks: Ward 1 Town Hall 1847–48; 1850; 1850–51; Ward 3 Assembly Room 1850–51; Ward 4 Girl's National School 1847–48; 1849–50; Ward 5 St.Thomas School 1847–48.
List of the electors of the County of Linlithgow arranged according to the order of their residence, corrected after Appeal Court, 1838; 1844; 1846; 1851. (National Library of Scotland)
Supplement to List of the electors of the county of Linlithgow; to enable the holders of the list printed after appeal courts 1838 to give effect to the variations after appeal court 1840. corrected up to 12 December 1840 (National Library of Scotland).

Parliamentary papers

Committee report on Peterborough election – (1852–3), HC XVII.
Electoral Returns: Boroughs and Counties, 1865–66, HC 1866 [3626], lvii.
Electoral Returns (Cities and Boroughs) and Electoral Returns (Counties) pp. 109–117 in HC 1868–9 L.

Local Newspapers

Bedford Times
Cambridge Advertiser
Lancaster Gazette
Lancaster Guardian

Secondary sources

Adelman, P. (1970) *Disraeli, Gladstone and Later Victorian Politics* (London: Longman).
Allardt, E. and Littunen,Y. (eds) (1964) *Cleavages, Ideologies and Party Systems*, Transactions of the Westermarck Society, Volume X. (Helsinki: Academic Bookstore).
Allardt, E. and Rokkan, S. (eds) (1970) *Mass Politics Studies in Political Sociology* (Glencoe: Free Press).
Almond, G.A., Flanagan, S.C. and Mundt, R.J. (eds) (1973) *Crisis, Choice and Change* (Boston: Little Brown).
Anderson, M.L. (1971) *Family Structure in Nineteenth Century Lancashire* (Cambridge: Cambridge University Press).
Aydelotte, W.O. (1971) *Quantification in History* (Reading, Mass: Addison Wesley).
Aydelotte, W.O. (1972) 'The disintegration of the Conservative Party in the 1840s: A study of political attitudes', pp. 319–436 in Aydelotte, W.O., Bogue, A.G. and Fogel, R. (eds) *The Dimensions of Quantitative Research in History* (London: Oxford University Press).
Baer, M.B. (1977) 'Social structure, voting behaviour and political behaviour in Victorian London', *Albion*, vol. 9, no. 3, 227–41.

Barnes, J.A. (1968) 'Networks and the political process', pp. 107–30 in Swartz, M.J. (ed.) *Local Level Politics* (Chicago: Aldine).

Barnes, J.A. (1969) 'Networks and political process', pp. 51–76 in Mitchell, J. Clyde (ed.) *Social Networks in Urban Situations* (Manchester: Manchester University Press).

Barnes, J.A. (1972) *Social Networks* (Reading Mass: Addison-Wesley).

Barton, A.H. (1955) 'The concept of a property space', pp. 40–53 in Lazarsfeld and Rosenberg.

Baskerville, S.W., Adman, P. and Beedham, K.W (1991) 'Manuscript poll books and English county elections in the first age of party: A reconsideration of their provenance and purpose', *Archives*, XIX, 384–403.

Beales, D.E.D. (1967) 'Parliamentary parties and the "independent" Member 1800–1860', pp. 1–19, in Robson.

Beales, D.E.D (1992) 'The electorate before and after 1832: The right to vote, and the opportunity', *Parliamentary History*, xi, 139–150.

Berelson, B., Lazarsfeld, P.F., and McPhee, W. (1954) *Voting* (Chicago: Chicago University Press).

Bertrand, R., Briquet, J–L. and Pels, P. (eds) (2007) *Cultures of Voting the Hidden History of the Secret Ballot* (London: Hurst).

Boissevain, J. (1974) *Friends of Friends – Networks, Manipulators and Coalitions* (Oxford: Blackwells).

Bott, E. (1971) *Family and Social Network*, 2nd Edition (London: Tavistock).

Bourke, P. and DeBats, D. (1978) 'Identifiable voting in nineteenth century America: Towards a comparison of Britain and the United States before the secret ballot', *Perspectives in American History*, vol. 11, 259–88.

Bourke, P. and De Bats, D. (1995) *Washington County Politics and Community in Antelbellum America* (Baltimore: The John Hopkins University Press).

Brams, S.J. (1977) 'When is it advantageous to cast a negative vote?', pp. 564–72 in Henn, R. and Moeschlin, O. (eds) Mathematical economics and game theory: Essays in honour of Oskar Morgenstern, *Lecture notes in Economics and Mathematical Systems*, Volume 141 (Berlin: Springer Verlag).

Brams, S.J. and Fishburn, P., (1983) *Approval Voting* (Boston: Birkhauser).

Brett, P. (1996a) 'Party politics, constituency organization, and the power of the electoral register: National perspectives and the Bristol battleground 1832–1841', *Southern History*, 18, 87–116.

Brett,P. (1996b) 'Political dinners in early nineteenth-century Britain: Platform, meeting place and battle ground', *History*, lxxxi, 527–52.

Brock, M. (1973) *The Great Reform Act* (London: Hutchinson).

Bromond, T. (1993) 'A complete fool's paradise: The attack on the Fitzwilliam interest', *Parliamentary History*, vol. 12, 47–67.

Butler, D.E. (1961) *The Electoral System in Britain since 1918*, 2nd edition (Oxford: Clarendon Press).

Butler, D.E. and Cornford, J.P. (1969) 'United Kingdom', pp. 330–351 in Rokkan and Meyriat.

Butler, D.E. and Stokes, D. (1969) *Electoral Change in Britain* (London: Macmillan).

Campbell, A. (1966) 'A classification of presidential elections', pp. 63–77 in Campbell et al. (1966) *Elections and the Political Order* (New York: John Wiley).

Cannon, J. (1973) *Parliamentary Reform 1640–1832* (Cambridge: Cambridge University Press).

Carter, A. (1975) *Elite Politics in Rural India* (Cambridge: Cambridge University Press).

Casstevens, T.W. (1978) *Exponential Models of Legislative Turnover* (Newton: UMAP).

Casstevens, T.W. and Denham, W.A. (1970) 'Turnover and tenure in the Canadian House of Commons 1867–1968', *Canadian Journal of Political Science*, vol. III, no. 4, 655–61.

Chambers, W.N. (1967) 'Party development and the American mainstream', pp. 3–32 in Chambers and Burnham.

Chambers, W.N. and Burnham, W.D. (eds) (1967) *The American Party Systems: Stages of Development* (London: Oxford University Press).

Chodak, S. (1964) 'The societal functions of party systems in Sub-Saharan Africa', pp. 256–80 in Allardt and Littunen.

Clarke, P.F. (1971) *Lancashire and the New Liberals* (Cambridge: Cambridge University Press).

Clarke, P.F. (1972) 'The electoral sociology of modern Britain', *History*, 57, 31–55, February 1972.

Clubb, J.M. and Allen, H.W. (eds) (1971) *Electoral Change and Stability in American Political History* (New York: Free Press).

Colomer, J. (2001) *Political Institutions, Democracy and Social Choice* (Oxford: Oxford University Press).

Connacher, J.B. (1972) *The Peelites and the Party System* (Newton Abbott: David and Charles).

Cooper, C.J. (1988) Electoral Politics in Grimsby 1818–1835, unpublished PhD dissertation, The Open University.

Cornford, J.P. (1963) 'The transformation of conservatism in the late nineteenth century', *Victorian Studies*, vol. 7, 35–66.

Cornford, J.P. (1964) 'The adoption of mass organization by the Conservative Party' pp. 400–24 in Allardt and Littunen.

Cornford, J.P. (1967) 'The parliamentary foundations of the hotel Cecil', pp. 268–311 in Robson.

Cornford, J.P. and Mitchell, J.C. (1978) 'Constituency politics and party organisation in early Victorian England' paper given at the annual meeting of the European Consortium for Political Research, Grenoble 1978.

Cowling, M. (1967) *Disraeli, Gladstone and Revolution – The Passing of the Second Reform Bill* (Cambridge: Cambridge University Press).

Cox, G.W. (1984) 'Strategic electoral choice in multi-member districts: Approval voting in practice?' *American Journal of Political Science*, vol. 28, 722–38.

Cox, G.W. (1987) *The Efficient Secret: The Cabinet and the Development of Political Parties in Victorian England* (Cambridge: Cambridge University Press).

Dahl, R.A. (ed.) (1966) *Political Opposition in Western Democracies* (London: Yale University Press).

Dahl, R.A. (1971) *Polyarchy, Participation and Opposition* (London: Yale University Press).

Davis, R.W. (1972) *Political Change and Continuity, 1760–1885: A Buckinghamshire Study* (Newton Abbott: David and Charles).

Davis, R.W. (1974) 'The Whigs and the idea of electoral deference', *Durham University Journal*, n.s. 36, 1 (December 1974), 79–91.

Davis, R.W. (1976a) 'The mid-nineteenth century electoral structure', *Albion*, 8, 2 (Summer 1976), 142–53.

Davis, R.W. (1976b) 'Deference and the aristocracy in the time of the Great Reform Act', *American Historical Review*, 88, 3 (June 1976), 532–39.

Deane, P. and Mitchell, B.R. (1962) *Abstract of British Historical Statistics* (Cambridge: Cambridge University Press).

Denver, D. (2007), *Elections and Voting in Britain*, 2nd edition (Basingstoke: Palgrave).

Drake, M. (1971) 'The mid-Victorian voter', *Journal of Interdisciplinary History*, vol. 1, no. 3, 473–90.

Drake, M. (ed.) (1973) *Applied Historical Studies: An Introductory Reader* (London: Methuen).

Drake. M. and Mitchell, J.C. (1982) Units 6–7, pp. 14–82, *Introduction to Historical Psephology, D301 Second Series: Historical Sources and the Social Scientist* (Milton Keynes: Open University Press).

Dunbabin, J.P.D. (1966) 'Parliamentary elections in Great Britain 1868–1900', *English Historical Review*, vol. 81, 82–99.

Eastwood, D. (1997) 'Contesting the politics of deference: The rural electorate 1820–60', pp. 27–49 in Lawrence and Taylor.

Elklit, J. (1983) 'Mobilization and partisan division, open voting in Fredericia, Denmark', *Social Science History*, vol. 7, no. 3, 235–66.

Elklit, J. (1985a) 'Open voting in Prussia and Denmark, or the complexity of comparison, some post-Rokkanian reflections', *Historical Social Research*, no. 33, July 1985, 2–16.

Elklit, J. (1985b) 'Nominal record linkage and the study of non-secret voting: A Danish case', *Journal of Interdisciplinary History*, vol. XV, no. 3, 419–43.

Elklit, J. (1988) *Fra aaben til hemmelig afstemming* [From open to secret voting], (Aarhus: Politica).

Elklit, J. (2000) 'Open voting' pp. 191–193 in Rose, R. (ed) *International Encyclopaedia of Elections* (Washington DC: CQ Press).

Elklit, J. and Mitchell, J.C. (1983) 'Wahlen und massendemokratie in England und Danemark', pp. 351–76 in Busch, D. and Steinbach, P. (eds) *Vergleichende Europaische Wahlgeschicht* (Berlin: Verlag).

Elklit, J. and Skytte, J. (1980) *Find Person By Name* (FPN), Aarhus.

Evans, G. (ed.) (1999) *The End of Class Politics?* (Oxford: Oxford University Press).

Feuchtwanger, E.J. (1968) *Disraeli, Democracy and the Tory Party* (Oxford: Clarendon Press).

Flora, P. (ed.) (1999) *State Formation Nation-Building and Mass Politics in Europe. The Theory of Stein Rokkan* (Oxford: Oxford University Press).

Foster, J. (1974) *Class Struggle and the Industrial Revolution* (London: Weidenfeld and Nicholson).

Fraser, D. (1976) *Urban Politics in Victorian England: The Structure of Politics in Victorian Cities* (Leicester: Leicester University Press).

Gash, N. (1953) *Politics in the Age of Peel: A Study in the Technique of Parliamentary Representation* (London: Longmans).

Gash, N. (1965) *Reaction and Reconstruction in English Politics* (Oxford: Clarendon Press).

Gash, N. (1977) *Politics in the Age of Peel*, 2nd Edition (Hassocks: Harvester Press).

Gash, N. (1982) 'The organization of the Conservative Party 1832–1846 Part I: The parliamentary organization', *Parliamentary History I*, 137–59.

Gash, N. (1983) 'The organization of the Conservative Party 1832–1846 Part II: The electoral organization', *Parliamentary History II*, 131–52.

Gash, N. (1986) *Pillars of Government and Other Essays on State and Society 1770–c.1880* (London: Edward Arnold).

Gwyn, W.B. (1962) *Democracy and the Cost of Politics in Britain* (London: University of London Press).

Hamer, D.A. (1977) *The Politics of Electoral Pressure: A Study in the History of Victorian Reform Agitation* (Hassocks: Harvester Press).

Hanham, H.J. (1959) *Elections and Party Management: Politics in the Time of Disraeli and Gladstone* (London: Longmans).

Hanham, H.J. (1961) 'The first constituency party?', *Political Studies*, vol. 9, 188–89.

Hanham, H.J. (1968) *The Reformed Electoral System in Great Britain* (London: Historical Association).

Hanham, H.J. (1972) 'Introduction', pp. vii–cxliv in Dod (1972).

Hanham, H.J. (1978) 'Introduction', pp. ix–xxi in *Elections and Party Management: Politics in the Time of Disraeli and Gladstone*, 2nd edition (Hassocks: Harvester Press).

Hawkins, A. (1989) "Parliamentary Government" and Victorian Political Parties, c.1830–c.1880, English Historical Review, civ, pp. 638–69.

Hayes, W.A. (1982) *The Background and Passage of the Third Reform Act* (New York: Garland).

Heath, A.F. et al. (1991) *Understanding Political Change: The British Voter 1964–1987* (Oxford: Pergamon).

Heesom, A. (1988) ' "Legimate" versus "illegitimate" influences: Aristocratic electioneering in mid-Victorian Britain', *Parliamentary History*, vii, 282–305.

Hennock, E.P. (1971) 'The sociological premises of the first reform act: A critical note', *Victorian Studies*, vol. XIV, no. 3, 321–27.

Hirst, D.L. (1975) *The Representative of the People? Voters and Voting in England under the Early Stuarts* (Cambridge: Cambridge University Press).

Hogh, E. (1972) '*Vaelgeradfaerd i Danmark 1849–1901*' En Politisk Sociologisk Analyse (Copenhagen: Paludans Forlag).

Hollis, P. (ed.) (1974) *Pressure from Without* (London: Edward Arnold).

Hoppen, K.T (1984) *Elections, Politics and Society in Ireland 1832–1885* (Oxford: Clarendon Press).

Hoppen, K.T. (1985) 'The franchise and electoral politics in England and Ireland, 1832–1885', *History*, lxx, 202–17.

Hoppen, K.T. (1996) 'Roads to democracy : Electioneering and corruption in nineteenth-century England and Ireland', *History*, lxxxi, 553–71.

Hoppen, T. (1998) *The Mid-Victorian Generation, 1846–86* (Oxford: Clarendon Press).

Jones, A. (1972) *The Politics of Reform 1884* (Cambridge: Cambridge University Press).

Joyce, P. (1975) 'The factory politics of Lancashire in the late nineteenth century', *The Historical Journal*, vol. XVIII, no. 3, 525–54.

Katz, R S. and Mair, P. (eds) (1994) *How Parties Organize: Change and Adaptation in Party Organizations in Western Democracies* (London: Sage).

Kavanagh, D.A. (1971) 'The deferential English: A comparative critique', *Government and Opposition,* vol. 6, no. 3, 330–60.

Key, V.O. (1955) 'A theory of critical elections', *The Journal of Politics,* vol. 17, no. 1, 3–18, (also reprinted as pp. 27–44 in Clubb and Allen).

Key, V.O. (1964) *Politics, Parties and Pressure Groups, 5th edition* (New York, Crowell).

Laslett, P. (1965) *The World We Have Lost* (London: Methuen).

Lawrence, J. (1998) *Speaking for the People: Party, Language and Popular Politics in England, 1867–1914* (Cambridge: Cambridge University Press).

Lawrence, J. and Taylor, M. (eds) (1997) *Party, State and Society – Electoral Behaviour in Britain since 1820* (Aldershot: Scolar Press).

Lazarsfeld, P.F, Berelson, B. and Gaudet, H. (1944) *The People's Choice* (New York, Duell).

Lazarsfeld, P.F. and Rosenberg, M (1955) *The Language of Social Research: A Reader in the Methodology of Social Science* (Glencoe: Free Press).

Lee, J.M. (1963) *Social Leaders and Public Persons: A Study of County Government in Cheshire since 1888* (Oxford: Oxford University Press).

Lewin, L., Jansson, B. and Sorbom, D. (1972) *The Swedish Electorate 1887–1968* (Stockholm: Almqvist and Wicksell).

Lipset, S.M. and Rokkan, S. (1967) 'Cleavage structures, party systems, and voter alignments: An introduction', pp. 1–64 in Lipset, S.M and Rokkan, S. (eds) *Party Systems and Voter Alignments: Cross-National Perspectives* (New York: The Free Press).

Lloyd, T. (1965) 'Uncontested seats in British general elections 1852–1910', *The Historical Journal,* vol. VIII, 260–65.

Manai, M.A. (1993) 'Influence, corruption and electoral behaviour in the mid-nineteenth century: A case study of Lancaster, 1847–1865', *Northern History,* XXIX, 154–64.

Mathew, H.G.C, McKibbin, R.I. and Kay, J.A. (1976) 'The franchise factor in the rise of the Labour Party' *English Historical Review,* 91, 723–51.

Mayer, A.C. (1962) 'System and network: An approach to the study of political process in Dewas', pp. 266–78 in Madan, T.N. and Sarana, G. (eds), *Indian Anthropology Essays in Honour of D.N. Majumdar* (Mumbai).

Mayer, A.C. (1963) 'Municipal elections: A central Indian case study', pp. 115–132 in Philips, C.H. (ed.) *Politics and Society in India* (London: Allen and Unwin).

Mayer, A.C. (1966) 'The significance of quasi-groups in the study of complex societies', pp. 97–122 in Banton, M. (ed.), *The Social Anthropology of Complex Societies* (London: Tavistock).

McKenzie, R.T. (1954) *British Political Parties* (London: Heinemann).

McKenzie, R T. and Silver, A.(1968) *Angels in Marble* (London: Heinemann).

McLean, I. (1992) 'Rational choice and the Victorian voter', *Political Studies,* vol. XL, 496–515.

McLean, I. (2001) *Rational Choice and British Politics: An Analysis of Rhetoric and Manipulation from Peel to Blair* (Oxford: Oxford University Press).

Meadow, R.G. (ed.) (1985) *New Communication Technologies in Politics* (Washington: Annenberg School).

Mills, D.R. (1980) *Lord and Peasant in Nineteenth Century Britain* (London: Croom Helm).

Mitchell, J. Clyde (ed.) (1969a) *Social Networks in Urban Situations* (Manchester: Manchester University Press).

Mitchell, J. Clyde. (1969b) 'The concept and use of social networks', pp. 1–50 in Mitchell (1969a).

Mitchell, J.C. (1976a) Electoral Change and the Party System in England 1832–1868, unpublished PhD thesis, Yale University.

Mitchell, J.C. (1976b) 'Electoral strategy under open voting: Evidence from England 1832–1880', *Public Choice,* vol. XXVIII, Winter 1976, 17–35.

Mitchell, J.C. (1982a) 'The electoral context', Unit 8, pp. 85–109 in *Introduction to Historical Psephology,* D301 Second Series, *Historical Sources and the Social Scientist* (Milton Keynes: Open University Press).

Mitchell, J.C. (1982b) 'Mobilization, participation and electoral stratification in England, 1832–1868', pp. 159–177 in Steinbach, P. (ed.) *Probleme Politischer Partizipation im Modernisierungsprozess* (Stuttgart: Klett Cotta).

Mitchell, J.C. (1992) 'Velgerskaren og den hemmelige valghandlingen' [Secrecy and the electoral community], pp. 207–18 in Hagvet, B. (ed.) *Politikk mellom okonomi og kultur* (Oslo: Gyldendal).

Mitchell, J.C. and Cornford, J.P. (1977) 'The political demography of Cambridge 1832–1868', *Albion,* vol. 9, no. 3, 242–76.

Mitchell, J.C. and Elklit, J. (1980) 'The legacy of open voting: Patron/client relations and the development of mass politics in England and Denmark', Paper given at the ECPR meeting, Florence.

Moore, D.C. (1961) 'The other face of reform', *Victorian Studies,* vol. V, 7–34.

Moore, D.C. (1966) 'Concession or cure: The sociological premises of the First Reform Act', *The Historical Journal,* vol. 9, no. 1, 39–59.

Moore, D.C. (1967) 'Social structure, political structure and public opinion in Mid-Victorian England', pp. 30–57 in Robson.

Moore, D.C. (1969) 'Political morality in mid-nineteenth century England: Concepts, norms, violations', *Victorian Studies,* vol. XIII, no. 1, 5–36.

Moore, D.C. (1971) 'Reply to E.P.Hennock's "The sociological premises of the first reform act: A critical note"' *Victorian Studies,* vol. XIV, no. 3, 328–37.

Moore, D.C. (1974) 'The matter of the missing contests: Towards a theory of the mid-nineteenth century British political system', *Albion,* vol. 6, no. 2, 93–119.

Moore, D.C. (1975) *The Politics of Deference: A Study of the Mid-Nineteenth Century English Political System* (Hassocks: Harvester Press).

Neale, R.S. (1972) *Class and Ideology in Nineteenth Century England* (London: Routledge and Kegan Paul).

Neale, R.S. (1981) *Class in English History 1680–1850* (Oxford: Blackwell).

Newby, H. (1975) 'The deferential dialectic', *Comparative Studies in Society and History,* vol. 17, no. 2, 139–64.

Nicholas (ed.) (1966) *To the Hustings: Election Scenes in English Fiction* (London: Cassell).

Nordlinger, E.A. (1967) *The Working Class Tories: Authority, Deference and Stable Democracy* (London: MacGibbon and Kee).

Norris, P. (1995) *Electoral Change since 1945* (Oxford: Blackwell).

Nossiter, T.J. (1970a) 'Aspects of electoral behavior in English constituencies 1832–1868', pp. 160–89 in Allardt and Rokkan.

Nossiter, T.J. (1970b) 'Voting behaviour 1832–1872', *Political Studies,* vol. XVIII, no. 3, 380–89.

Nossiter, T.J. (1975) *Influence, Opinion and Political Idioms in Reformed England: Case Studies from the North East 1832–1874* (Brighton: Harvester).

O'Gorman, F. (1989) *Voters, Patrons and Parties: The Unreformed Electorate of Hanoverian England, 1734–1832* (Oxford: Clarendon Press).

O'Gorman, F. (1993) 'The electorate before and after 1832: A reply', *Parliamentary History*, xii, 171–83.

O'Gorman, F. (1997) *The Long Eighteenth Century. British Politics and Society 1688–1832* (London: Arnold).

O'Gorman, F (2007) 'The secret ballot in nineteenth-century Britain', pp. 16–42 in Bertrand, Briquet and Pels.

O'Leary, C. (1962) *The Elimination of Corrupt Practices in English Elections 1868–1911* (Oxford: Oxford University Press).

Olney, R.J. (1973) *Lincolnshire Politics 1832–1885* (Oxford: Clarendon Press).

Ostrogorski, M. (1902) *Democracy and the Organisation of Political Parties* (London, Macmillan) (New edition 1964) (Garden City: Doubleday).

Panebianco, A. (1988) *Political Parties: Organisation and Power* (Cambridge: Cambridge University Press).

Pelling, H. (1967) *Social Geography of British elections 1885–1910* (London: Macmillan).

Perkin, H (1969) *The Origins of Modern British Society 1780–1880* (London: Routledge and Kegan Paul).

Phillips, J.A. (1982a) *Electoral Behavior in Unreformed England 1761–1802: Plumpers, Splitters and Straights* (Princeton: Princeton University Press).

Phillips, J.A. (1982b) 'The many faces of reform: The Reform Bill and the electorate', *Parliamentary History Yearbook I*, 115–35.

Phillips, J.A. (1984) 'Pollbooks and English electoral behavior', pp. v–xviii in Sims,.

Phillips, J.A. (1987) 'Partisan behaviour in adversity: Voters in Lewes during the Reform Era', *Parliamentary History*, vol. 6, 262–79.

Phillips, J.A. (1992) *The Great Reform Bill in the Boroughs: English Electoral Behaviour, 1818–1841* (Oxford: Oxford University Press).

Phillips, J.A and Wetherell, C. (1991) 'The Great Reform Bill and the rise of partisanship', *Journal of Modern History*, vol. 63 (Dec 1991), 621–46.

Phillips, J.A. and Wetherell, C. (1994) 'Parliamentary parties and municipal politics: 1835 and the Party System', pp. 48–85 in Phillips, J.A. (ed.) (1995), *Computing Parliamentary History George III to Victoria* (Edinburgh, Edinburgh University Press).

Phillips, J.A. and Wetherell, C. (1995) 'The Great Reform Act of 1832 and the political modernization of England', *American Historical Review*, c, 411–36.

Plumb, J.H. (1967) *The Growth of Political Stability in England, 1675–1725* (London: Macmillan).

Pomper, G. (1967) 'Classification of Presidential elections', *The Journal of Politics*, vol. 29, no. 3, 535–66. (Reprinted in Clubb and Allen.)

Porritt, E. and A. (1903) *The Unreformed House of Commons* (Cambridge: Cambridge University Press).

Porter, E. (1975) *Victorian Cambridge: Josiah Chater's Diaries 1844–1884* (Chichester: Phillimore and Co).

Powell, G.B. (1973) 'Incremental democratisation: The British Reform Act of 1832', pp. 103–51 in Almond, G.A., Flanagan, S.C. and Mundt, R.J.

Prest, J. (1977) *Politics in the Age of Cobden and Bright* (London: Macmillan).

Pulzer, P.G.F. (1967) *Political Representation and Elections in Britain* (London: Allen and Unwin).

Rintala, M. (1966) 'A generation in politics: A definition', *Review of Politics*, vol. 25, 509–22.

Rintala, M. (1968) 'Political generation', pp. 92–96 in volume 6 of Sills, D. (ed.) *International Encyclopaedia of the Social Sciences* (New York: Macmillan and Free Press).

Robson, R. (ed.) (1967) *Ideas and Institutions of Victorian Britain* (London: Bell).

Rokkan, S. (1961) 'Mass suffrage, secret voting and political participation', *European Journal of Sociology II*, 132–52.

Rokkan, S. (1970) *Citizens, Elections, Parties* (Oslo: Universitetsforlaget).

Rokkan, S. and Meyriat, J. (eds) (1969) *International Guide to Electoral Statistics*, Volume I (Paris: Mouton)

Rokkan, S. and Valen, H. (1962) 'The mobilisation of the periphery', in Rokkan, S. (ed.) *Approaches to the Study of Political Participation* (Bergen: Chr Michelsen Institute); pp. 181–225 in Rokkan.

Rose, R. (1964) 'Parties, factions and tendencies in Britain', *Political Studies*, vol. XX, no. 1, 35–46.

Rose, R. (1974) 'Britain: Simple abstractions and complex realities', pp. 481–541 in Rose, R. (ed.) *Electoral Behavior: A Comparative Handbook* (New York: The Free Press).

Roth, G. (1963) *The Social Democrats in Imperial Germany* (Totowa: Bedminster Press).

Rude, G. (1964) *The Crowd in History: A Study of Popular Disturbances in France and England 1730–1848* (London: Wiley).

Salmon, P. (2000) ' Local politics and partisanship: The electoral impact of municipal reform, 1835', *Parliamentary History*, xix, 357–76.

Salmon, P. (2002) *Electoral Reform at Work. Local Politics and National Parties, 1832–1841* (Woodbridge: Royal Historical Society Boydell Press).

Scott, J.C. (1972) *Comparative Political Corruption* (Englewood Cliffs: Prentice Hall).

Seymour, C. (1915) *Electoral Reform in England and Wales* [Reprint 1970] (Newton Abbott: David and Charles).

Shea, D. (1996) *Campaign Craft: Strategy, Tactics and the Art of Political Campaign Management* (Westport: Praeger).

Sims, J. (ed.) (1984) *A Handlist of British Parliamentary Pollbooks* (Leicester: University of Leicester).

Smith, F.B. (1966) *The Making of the Second Reform Bill* (Cambridge: Cambridge University Press).

Sorauf, F.J. (1964) *Political Parties in the American System* (Boston: Little Brown).

Sorauf, F.J. (1967) 'Political parties and political analysis', pp. 33–55 in Chambers and Burnham.

Speck, W.A. (1970) *Tory and Whig – The Struggle in the Constituencies 1701–1725* (London: Macmillan).

Steinberg, M.W. (1999) *Fighting Words: Working Class Formation, Collective Action, and Discourse in Early Nineteenth-Century England* (Ithaca: Cornell University Press).

Stewart, R. (1971) *Lord Derby and the Protectionist Party* (Cambridge: Cambridge University Press).

Stewart, R. (1978) *The Foundation of the Conservative Party 1830–1867* (London: Longman).

Stokes, D. (1967) 'Parties and the nationalization of electoral forces', pp. 182–202 in Chambers and Burnham.

Summers, S.M. (2002) *Parliamentary Politics of a County and its Town: General Elections in Suffolk and Ipswich in the Eighteenth Century* (Westport: Praeger).

Swerdlow, J. (ed.) (1988) *Media Technology and the Vote* (Boulder: Westview Press).

Taylor, M. (1997) 'Elections, parties and the state: The urban electorate 1820–60', pp. 50–78 in Lawrence and Taylor.

Tholfsen, T.R. (1959) 'The origins of the Birmingham caucus', *The Historical Journal*, vol. II, no. 2, 161–84.

Thomas, J.A. (1950) 'The system of registration and the development of party organisation 1832–1870', *History*, vol. 35, 81–98.

Thomas, K. (1978) 'The United Kingdom', pp. 41–97 in Grew, R. (ed.) *Crises of Political Development in Europe and the United State* (Princeton: Princeton University Press).

Thompson, E.P. (1963) *The Making of the English Working Class* (London: Gollancz).

Thompson, G., Francis, J., Levacic, R. and Mitchell, J. (eds) (1991) *Markets, Hierarchies and Networks: The Coordination of Social Life* (London: Sage).

Tilly, C. (1995) *Popular Contestation in Great Britain 1758–1834* (Cambridge: Harvard University Press).

Trinder, B.S. (ed.) (1967) *A Victorian MP and His Constituents: The Correspondence of H.W.Tancred 1841–1859* (Banbury: Banbury Historical Society).

Vernon, J. (1993) *Politics and the People* (Cambridge: Cambridge University Press).

Vincent, J.R. (1966) *The Formation of the British Liberal Party 1857–68* (London: Constable) [The page references are to the Penguin edition of 1972].

Vincent, J.R. (1967) *Pollbooks: How Victorians Voted* (Cambridge: Cambridge University Press.).

Wald, K. (1983) *Crosses on the Ballot: Patterns of British Voter Alignment since 1885* (Princeton: Princeton University Press).

Winchester, I. (1971) 'The linkage of historical records by man and computer: Techniques and problems', *Journal of Interdisciplinary History I*, 107–24.

Winchester, I. (1973a) 'On referring to ordinary historical persons', pp. 17–42 in Wrigley (1973).

Winchester, I. (1973b) 'A brief survey of the algorithmic, mathematical and philosophical literature relevant to historical record linkage', pp. 128–150 in Wrigley (1973).

Wrigley, E.A. (ed.) (1966) *An Introduction to English Historical Demography* (London: Weidenfeld and Nicholson).

Wrigley, E.A. (ed.) (1972) *Nineteenth Century Society: Essays in the Use of Quantitative Methods for the Study of Social Data* (Cambridge: Cambridge University Press).

Wrigley, E.A. (ed.) (1973) *Identifying People in the Past* (London: Edward Arnold).

Index